LITERATURE AND DOMINATION

SEX,

KNOWLEDGE,

AND

POWER *L*ITERATURE

IN

MODERN

FICTION

M. KEITH BOOKER

AND $\mathcal{D}$OMINATION

University Press of Florida

Gainesville

Tallahassee

Tampa

Boca Raton

Pensacola

Orlando

Miami

Jacksonville

Library of Congress Cataloging-in-Publication Data
Booker, M. Keith.
Literature and domination: sex, knowledge, and power
in modern fiction / M. Keith Booker.
p.   cm.
Includes bibliographical references and index.
ISBN 0-8130-1195-7
1. Fiction—20th century—History and
criticism.   2. Dominance (Psychology) in
literature.   3. Sex role in literature.   4. Power (Social
sciences) in literature.   I. Title.
PN3503.B62   1993
809.3'04—dc20   92-41442

The University Press of Florida is the
scholarly publishing agency for the State
University System of Florida, comprised
of Florida A & M University, Florida
Atlantic University, Florida International
University, Florida State University,
University of Central Florida, University
of Florida, University of North Florida,
University of South Florida, and
University of West Florida.

University Press of Florida
15 Northwest 15th Street
Gainesville, FL 32611

for ADAM BOOKER

CONTENTS

$\mathscr{A}$CKNOWLEDGMENTS

I would like to thank various individuals who read and commented on parts or all of this manuscript, including Robert Cochran of the University of Arkansas and Brandon Kershner, Alistair Duckworth, and Al Shoaf of the University of Florida. Special thanks are due to John Krafft of the University of Miami (Ohio), Hamilton, who read the entire manuscript closely and made numerous helpful suggestions for revision. I would also like to thank the staff at the University Press of Florida, who have been so helpful to me with this and other projects: Deidre Bryan, Larry Leshan, Walda Metcalf, and especially Lisa Compton, who edited the manuscript in a way that was both highly beneficial and quite painless to me. Finally, I would like to thank Dubravka Juraga, who not only read and commented on the manuscript but (as always) provided support and inspiration in numerous other ways as well.

$\mathcal{I}$NTRODUCTION:

LITERATURE

AND

DOMINATION

In act 1 of Samuel Beckett's *Waiting for Godot* we meet Pozzo, a typical Beckettian tyrant figure who enforces his power over his slave Lucky with violence and brute force. Yet Pozzo reappears in the second act as blind and lame, virtually helpless and certainly unable physically to enforce his domination of Lucky. In this sense Pozzo can be read as a representation of the breakdown in traditional structures of authority that so haunts (and inspires) the modernist literary imagination. Importantly, however, Lucky remains as submissive as ever, so attuned to his enslaved condition that he automatically responds to orders even when he is not compelled to do so. In the modern world, traditional figures of authority (God, priests, monarchs, etc.) no longer serve as effective legitimating anchors for the power they once wielded. And yet, in the absence of new authorities to replace the old, that power itself often remains as fully in force as ever.

Vivian Mercier has noted that the Pozzo–Lucky relation has special resonances for Irish audiences, with Pozzo appearing as a stereotypical Irish landlord and Lucky as the typical serflike Irish peasant who is subjugated to him (53). Indeed, Beckett's depiction of the ongoing power of conventional institutions in an age of disbelief resonates powerfully with that of his countryman James Joyce, for whom morally decrepit structures of power continue to hold Ireland in an iron grip. This Joycean/Beckettian analysis of the modern condition contrasts sharply with the position of T. S. Eliot, for whom the modern loss of authority also implies a loss of structures of power, leading to potential chaos. Eliot's reaction to the breakdown of authority in modern society is to attempt to restore the authority of the past and thereby to reinforce structures of power that he sees as tottering on the brink of total dissolution. But for Joyce and Beckett the problem is not that there is insufficient structure in the way power is wielded in the modern world. On the contrary, the problem is that there is too *much* structure, even without any authority for that structure, so that a conservative shoring of fragments like that recommended by Eliot would only serve to make the situation more oppressive than it already is.

The barren city described with such scrupulous meanness in Joyce's *Dubliners* is clearly a reflection not only of life in turn-of-the-century Ireland but also of a quite general early modernist vision of urban decay. As such, Joyce's Dublin has much in common with the unreal Baudelarian London of Eliot. But whereas Eliot's city seems plagued by a lack of any structure that can give meaning to life, Joyce's Dublin, like the world of Beckett's Vladimir and Estragon, is plagued by a paralyzing overabundance of structure. *Dubliners* can be read as a sort of plural *Bildungsroman* in which the characters in the various stories attempt to explore their own creative self-constitution, only to find that the options open to them have already been strictly determined by the preexisting discourses and institutions that hold Dublin in an inescapable death grip.[1] Self-constitution in *Dubliners* is thus not creative at all, and the various characters find themselves doomed to repeat the past selves that already haunt the city's crowded yet desolate streets. Joyce's depiction of the paralysis of Dublin thus makes the important point that the breakdown in authority in the modern world does not necessarily correspond to a breakdown in traditional structures of power. Rather, those structures simply go on operating under their own momentum, even without the legitimating authority of some transcendent originating center.

Writers like Eliot and Pound react to the modernist crisis in power and authority in ways that seem diametrically opposed to the reactions of writers like Joyce and Beckett. But all of these writers do participate in a general social and cultural phenomenon that helps illustrate the central involvement of literature with issues of power, authority, and domination. And it is no accident that other historical periods of intense literary innovation and production—the golden age of Greece, the Renaissance—correspond to similar crises in power and authority. Moreover, the Eliot/Beckett dichotomy of modernism occurs in earlier periods of crisis as well, with some literary works apparently seeking to stabilize threatened structures of official power and others attempting to finish off those structures once and for all. But one should also keep in mind that the relation between literary works and cultural crises is complex. Works that once were radical have often been appropriated by official culture, and works that sought to support authority often do so by acknowledging a crisis in authority in ways that threaten to trigger unpredictable and even antiauthoritarian reactions.

Conservative critics have argued that the reading of works in ways that might be diametrically opposed to the author's original intention is tantamount to the death of literature. But in point of fact it is this tendency of reading to escape prescribed bounds that gives literature its real subversive power. As Terry Eagleton repeatedly reminds us in his recent historical survey of aesthetic theory, the very notion of the aesthetic as we know it arose in conjunction with the rise of bourgeois society. In particular, many of our conceptions of the nature of the work of art (especially those having to do with organic unity) emerge in close complicity with the rise of the autonomous bourgeois individual as the principal paradigm of human subjectivity. Eagleton suggests that the work of art functions as an object of imaginary identification through which the bourgeois subject develops a fantasy of its own wholeness and autonomy, in a process much like the Lacanian mirror stage (87). However, this process is not an entirely simple one. In his discussion of Kant, for example, Eagleton notes the double movement of the beautiful and the sublime in Kantian aesthetics. The beautiful, he suggests, supports this imaginary identification, shoring up the subject and giving it the confidence it needs to compete in a free market, while the sublime performs a humbling function, reminding the subject that, free or not, there are limits that are not to be crossed. This double movement is, for Eagleton, essential to the ideology of bourgeois society:

"For one problem of all humanist ideology is how its centring and consoling of the subject is to be made compatible with a certain essential reverence and submissiveness on the subject's part" (90).

Indeed, much of the point of Eagleton's survey is to suggest that despite the fact that the aesthetic is a thoroughly bourgeois concept whose very purpose is the perpetuation of bourgeois ideology, there is something inherently uncontrollable in the aesthetic that still gives it a considerable subversive potential: "The aesthetic as custom, sentiment, spontaneous impulse may consort well enough with political domination; but these phenomena border embarrassingly on passion, imagination, sensuality, which are not always so easily incorporable" (28). And if Eagleton himself here sounds more like a liberal than a Marxist, it is worth keeping in mind the important role that art has played in the thought of so many modern Marxist thinkers, including Theodor Adorno, Walter Benjamin, and Fredric Jameson—in addition to Eagleton himself.

That art often functions as the enemy of tyranny for both liberal and Marxist thinkers is surely not insignificant, though phenomena like the characterization by Benjamin of fascism as the aestheticization of politics (along with his call for a response that would involve the politicization of aesthetics) indicate that the relation between art and despotism is by no means a simple polar opposition. That modern literature should be so concerned with the same issues that have been the focus of modern cultural critics suggests a potential role for literature as cultural criticism, though this parallel is not entirely surprising given that literature is an important part of the culture that critics such as Adorno, Foucault, and others are examining. Still, such parallels suggest that by dealing with struggles for domination and control both thematically and through enactment in the process of reading, literary texts can help to expose the workings of power in the world at large. And one would like to think that this exposure can lead to an increased awareness of power that will foster an increased capability for resistance.

Such thinking brings to mind Wolfgang Iser's notion that certain literary works challenge the reader's expectations, thus resulting in an expansion of consciousness:

The efficacy of a literary text is brought about by the apparent evocation and subsequent negation of the familiar. What at first seemed to be an affirmation of our assumptions leads to our own rejection of them, thus tending to prepare us for a re-orientation. And it is only when we have outstripped our preconceptions and left the shelter of the familiar that we are in a position to gather new experiences. . . . The production of meaning of literary texts . . . does not merely entail the discovery of the unformulated, which can then be taken over by the active imagination of the reader; it also entails the possibility that we may formulate ourselves and so discover what had previously seemed to elude our consciousness. (290, 294)

On the other hand, this model of enlightenment-induced transformation, especially if it is taken as an encouragement to political resistance, seems to be based on an equation between knowledge and power that is itself central to the structure of domination that this transformation is intended to resist.

Literary critiques of domination thus tend reflexively to become caught up in the very dynamics of domination that they criticize. Art by its very nature involves its own kind of domination through the use of specific forms and techniques that give the art work a certain coherence and unity, no matter how provisional, fragmented, or nontraditional that unity might be. And the more the work of art opposes external principles of determination, the more reliant it becomes on its own alternative principles in order to achieve any effect at all. But this may be largely the point. Indeed, what is distinctive about many modern texts is the reflexive way literary meditations on power, authority, and domination turn inward to involve examinations of textuality and reading as images of the kinds of struggles for mastery that inform society at large. And perhaps this reflexivity suggests that literary knowledge is of a different order than the traditional theoretical knowledge that is equated with power in the West. Literature has the potential to explore and illuminate objects of inquiry in a mode of dialogue and performance rather than by seeking to dominate them in the traditional mode of science. Especially in the difficult and complex texts of modern literature, successful reading requires that readers and texts work together, pointing toward ways the human drive for mastery can be fulfilled through cooperation rather than through demanding the submission of some Other who is being mastered or dominated.

Unfortunately, this somewhat idealized view of the literary experience, with its echoes of Kant's "purposiveness without purpose," is clearly in danger of degenerating into a view of literature—and of art in general—as a realm divorced from real experience in which potentially revolutionary energies can be safely defused without posing any significant threat to the powers that be. This danger is especially keen for modern reflexive literature, which always already—at least on the surface—turns in on itself. But it seems clear that reflexivity in literature does not necessarily mean that literary texts are concerned only with the autonomous world of literature or that they are sealed off from "reality." After all, reflexivity itself is a common characteristic of almost every realm of modern intellectual endeavor. For example, modern scientific developments such as Heisenberg's uncertainty principle acknowledge that scientists are themselves part of the reality they are attempting to describe and that at least some portion of the data gathered by scientific observation is in fact a reflection of the scientist's own activity in gathering those data. And Nietzsche's declaration of the self-referentiality of all human knowledge in his seminal "On Truth and Lies" essay points the way toward a modern recognition that philosophy does not occupy some Olympian height from which it can oversee the world but instead is very much a part of that world, implicated in its own investigations. Such parallels between the reflexivity of modern science and philosophy and that of modern literature are surely more than mere coincidence, and it is worth noting the way Nietzschean successors like Jacques Derrida have worked to break down the traditional hierarchical privileging of philosophy over literature as modes of perceiving the world.

Even intensely engaged social critics are not immune to this reflexive turn, as the paradoxical self-parody of the highly rational Horkheimer/Adorno critique of rationality indicates.[2] It seems clear, then, that even the most reflexive of modern literary texts is in some sense mimetic of trends outside of literature. Thus, a common argument that has been made in favor of the political engagement of metafictional texts is that the "real" world is constructed according to many of the same linguistic codes and conventions as is fiction, and that a reflexive work of literature, with its self-conscious commentary on the means by which fictional narratives are constructed, is thereby commenting on the "real" world as well.

In one of the most extensive investigations in this mode, Robert Siegle examines works by authors such as Thackeray, Conrad, Robert Penn Warren, and John Fowles, emphasizing not only the inherent reflexivity of the texts but also strategies of reading reflexively. For Siegle, "reflexivity suggests that narrative derives its authority not from the 'reality' it imitates, but from the cultural conventions that define both narrative and the construct we call 'reality'" (125). Arguments like Siegle's that the conventions of literature mirror the conventions of society imply that metafiction is, in a sense, actually mimetic of reality, since fiction and reality are very much the same thing. Siegle acknowledges this similarity between reality and fiction but suggests a difference in emphasis, since metafiction calls attention to its fictionality in ways that reality does not: "I conclude that 'literary' texts do *not* differ in any fundamental way from 'ordinary' texts. Instead, they merely foreground what by means of acculturation we 'naturalize'—that is, they underscore the 'literary' or fictional qualities of what they share with all discursive texts" (225).

Siegle sees a powerful political potential in this exposure of the artificiality of the conventions on which the existing order is founded, much in the way that I have argued that a metafictional work like Nabokov's *Lolita* potentially offers an effective critique of other discourses (such as advertising) that are equally fictional but that attempt to pass themselves off as "true." As such, reflexive literature may participate in the same project as Marxist-oriented examinations of bourgeois systems of signification by theorists such as the early Jean Baudrillard.[3] Indeed, Fredric Jameson, arguing from a Marxist perspective reminiscent of Baudrillard's, sees a certain validity in analogies between the conventions of fiction and the conventions of the world at large:

it is a historical fact that the "structuralist" or textual revolution . . . takes as its model a kind of decipherment of which literary and textual criticism is in many ways the strong form. This revolution . . . drives the wedge of the concept of a "text" into the traditional disciplines by extrapolating the notion of "discourse" or "writing" onto objects previously thought to be "realities" or objects in the real world. . . . When properly used, the concept of "text" does not . . . reduce these realities to small and manageable written documents of one kind or another, but rather liberates us from the empirical object . . . by displacing our attention to its *constitution* as an object and its *relationship* to the other objects thus constituted. (*Political* 296–97)

However, Jameson sees a danger that such analogies will be taken too far and that, in the mode of Flaubert's Emma Bovary (or Nabokov's Humbert Humbert), we will come to expect the world to behave strictly in accordance with the conventions of literary fiction. But if reality is already openly fictional, then there is no hidden fictionality left for metafictional works to expose. Jameson thus has many positive things to say about the self-conscious artifice of modernist art, which was produced in a time when the realist paradigms of the nineteenth century were still functional in most areas of society. On the other hand, he sees the overt artificiality of many postmodernist texts as being in mimetic complicity with the contemporary order of late consumer capitalism, in which alienation is so pronounced that the world seems just as unreal as these texts. To Jameson, this phenomenon "consistently affirms the identity of postmodernism with capitalism in its latest systematic mutation" ("Marxism and Postmodernism" 373).

Jameson's suggestion that postmodernist art has become merely a symptom of late consumer capitalism parallels the arguments of Gerald Graff that "conventions of reflexivity and anti-realism are themselves mimetic of the kind of unreal reality that modern reality has become. But 'unreality' in this sense is not a fiction but the element in which we live" (180). Thus, for Graff, literature that calls attention to its own fictionality and criticism that calls attention to the fictionality of literature are largely in complicity with the kind of blatant fictionalizations of reality that inform so much of modern society. But Graff's target is not really reflexive fiction so much as ways of reading fiction reflexively. He himself admits that "even radically anti-realistic methods are sometimes defensible as legitimate means of representing an unreal reality." But, he suggests, "[t]he critical problem—not always attended to by contemporary critics—is to discriminate between anti-realistic works that provide some true understanding of nonreality and those which are merely symptoms of it" (12).

This "critical problem" is a problem indeed, since it suggests that criticism and complicity may be virtually indistinguishable. Graff's

8

concerns are relevant to the more historically oriented work of Peter Bürger, who suggests that prior to the twentieth century bourgeois society was centrally concerned with circumscribing art within a self-contained autonomous realm in which its potentially subversive energies can be contained and rendered devoid of any genuine social or political force. Bürger goes on to note that the thrust of avant-garde art was to smash this separation between art and society in such a way that would lead to revolutionary change in that society, but then suggests that the failure of the avant-garde consisted in the fact that bourgeois society managed to absorb the destruction of this separation without any such changes occurring: "During the time of the historical avant-garde movements, the attempt to do away with the distance between art and life still had all the pathos of historical progressivism on its side. But in the meantime, the culture industry has brought about the false elimination of the distance between art and life, and this also allows one to recognize the contradictoriness of the avant-garde undertaking" (50). As do Jameson and Graff, Bürger suggests that avant-garde art has lost its critical distance by becoming *too* implicated in contemporary social reality.

Graff himself seems to have a tendency to think of specific art works as either "good" or "bad," but the clear parallel between his suggested dichotomy in "anti-realist" works and Jameson's more culturally situated distinction between modernist and postmodernist works offers a potential direction out of the abyss by suggesting that the distinctions Graff and Jameson draw are a property not so much of the works themselves as of how those works function in a social context—in short, how they are read. But how one reads is itself a complicated result of complex cultural factors that go far beyond the content or technique of the individual work being read. For example, Adorno privileges the technique of montage as a revolutionary procedure that explodes the semblance of a reconciliation between man and nature that is created by the organic work. As a result, the nonorganic work mounts a protest against the role art is forced to play in bourgeois society: "Art wishes to confess its impotence vis-à-vis the late capitalist totality and inaugurate its abolition" (*Aesthetic* 232). Bürger agrees that an opposition to organic unity is a principal feature of avant-garde art, but he questions Adorno's conclusions concerning the political force of montage by pointing out that artists of a wide variety of political orientations have employed the technique. As

Bürger rightly points out, "It is fundamentally problematical to assign a fixed meaning to a procedure" (78).

Attributing the insight to Walter Benjamin's discussions of the ways modern art acts to destroy the "aura" traditionally associated with the work of art, Bürger goes on to suggest that "periodization in the development of art must be looked for in the sphere of art as institution, not in the sphere of the transformation of the content of individual works" (31). Bürger's observation seems accurate, though it is good to remember that the functioning of art as an institution—however complex a social phenomenon that might be—is surely not entirely independent of developments within specific art works. It seems obvious that the production and reception of works of art always depend on a complex framework of historical circumstances that go far beyond the work itself. But surely this relation is not all one-way. Even if how we read determines the effect of a text more than the characteristics of the text itself do, revolutionary works (Joyce's *Ulysses* would be a central example) can in fact change the way we read.

In short, history affects literature, but literature may affect history as well. Of course, it is certainly true that resistance and change within the world of literature seem to occur more rapidly and more easily than in the world at large. One revolutionary work can dramatically change the face of literature virtually over night. Indeed, it may be, as the Russian Formalists argued, that the very essence of the literary is an opposition to the prevailing norms of literature. But the Russian Formalists did not suggest that this inherent literary resistance would lead to resistance in the world outside of literature. As Bakhtin (among others) has pointed out, this formalist notion of literary evolution tends to divorce itself from events in the world outside of literature, being concerned only with the "intrinsic, immanent laws of the development of forms within a closed, purely literary system" (Bakhtin/Medvedev 159). Bakhtin's point is that no strict separation between literature and the society around it is possible because both are the products of language.

For Bakhtin, *pace* the Russian Formalists, changes in literary practice are in fact intimately related to changes in the society in which that practice arises. Granted, this model has a tendency to imply that societal changes cause literary innovation, rather than the other way around, but Bakhtin's emphasis on specific literary techniques such as parody points toward ways challenges to existing authority can be initiated from within literature. On the other hand, Graff—agreeing that literature should have a genuine oppositional role in society—argues that many trends toward literary innovation in modern literature may be simply another insidious product of bourgeois society. In fact, Graff suggests that any resistance to the existing order is in danger of paradoxically playing into the hands of the powers that be. He argues that "the real 'avant-garde' is advanced capitalism, with its built-in need to destroy all vestiges of tradition, all orthodox ideologies, all continuous and stable forms of reality in order to stimulate higher levels of consumption" (8). In short, "[t]he adversary culture has carried out the will of its adversary" (29).

Here Graff seems to be in danger of losing the distinction between reform, which is the kind of change that is the lifeblood of capitalism, and genuine revolution, which might potentially lead to its death.[4] But these are important points and ones that should be weighed carefully. Graff is particularly concerned about the way deconstructionists like Paul de Man and J. Hillis Miller seem to be able to read any work of literature from any era and come to the same conclusion—that the work demonstrates the inability of language to represent reality. Thus, "this kind of theorist can give us the meaning of literary works before he reads them. Since the self-reflexive, self-consuming, 'problematizing' nature of all language is given in advance by the critic's definition of language, it follows that all texts *must* testify—whether self-consciously or 'blindly'—to the fictive nature of their own structures" (178).

According to Graff, such critics ignore the real content of texts by imperialistically imposing readings on them. This argument depends in a transparent way on a faith that there is a "real" text to be discovered by readers, but it points to the increased importance of methods of reading in dealing with modern reflexive literature. Graff himself notes the way "[m]odern experimental texts" depend greatly on an active recuperation on the part of the reader in order to gain "meaning and coherence" (164–65), always assuming, of course, that "meaning and coherence" are properties to be valued in a work of literature. For Graff, the goal of reading is to attain mastery of the text, even though he paradoxically insists that this mastery must be based in the content of the text itself rather than in the reader.

Siegle, on the other hand, argues that one of the points of reflexive literature is to teach us to eschew critical mastery. If reflexive literature does not gain its authority from the reality it represents, then criticism likewise does not gain its authority from the text. Thus, the reflexive critic in a very real sense constitutes the work of literature that she criticizes, according to her own set of assumptions in approaching the text. But Siegle sees this realization as a statement not of critical imperialism but of humility: "The reflexive critic, then, has no illusions about devising a master code; he is more likely to inquire after the various diffractions of different critical optics" (227).

Of course, Siegle's reflexive critic is always in danger of reinstalling mastery at the next higher level of critical awareness. Indeed, the opposition in the attitudes toward reflexive reading shown by Graff and Siegle (together with Graff's own charge that the adversary culture is in complicity with that which it claims to oppose) indicates the seeming reversibility of all readings in the contemporary world. Baudrillard sees a similar implication in the hyperreality of postmodern society. With no anchor in reality, such society is governed by the paradoxical logic of the Möbius strip. Marxism is indistinguishable from capitalism, and "the work of the Right is done very well, and spontaneously, by the Left on its own. . . . the Right itself also spontaneously does the work of the Left. All the hypotheses of manipulation are reversible in an endless whirligig" (174).

For Baudrillard, this paradoxical reversibility of all positions in postmodernist society leads to a profound pessimism over the possibility of ever mounting an effective challenge to the existing order. After all, even could revolution be achieved in such a society (a whole family of literary texts like George Orwell's *Animal Farm* springs to mind here), what would be the point of a revolution in which the revolutionaries are indistinguishable from those whom they overthrow? But Baudrillard's discussion of the paradoxical logic of postmodern society resonates with more optimistic assessments of the current situation as well. Eagleton, maintaining at least some hope for a Marxist revolution, argues that the contradictions inherent in postmodernism are in fact a reflection of profound contradictions between capitalist economy and bourgeois culture in our contemporary historical moment. Thus, many postmodernist works are both subversive of the existing order (per Siegle) and supportive of it (per Graff and Jameson): "Much postmodernist culture is both radical and conservative, iconoclastic and incorporated, in the same breath" (373).

Though without the theoretical specificity of Eagleton's Marxist perspective, Linda Hutcheon has employed a similar insight into the contradictory nature of postmodernism in recent extensive examinations of the topic. In *A Poetics of Postmodernism*, Hutcheon employs an impressive array of specific examples from postmodernist literature to argue her point that if postmodernism sometimes seems to reinforce existing paradigms, it is only in order to define targets for its transgressive energies. As a result, "postmodernism is fundamentally contradictory, resolutely historical, and inescapably political" (4). Indeed, Hutcheon conducts an ongoing dialogue with Jameson throughout this book in order to argue the historical engagement and political force of postmodernist literature. In *The Politics of Postmodernism*, Hutcheon continues this same thesis, placing more emphasis on theoretical perspectives than on literature itself, but continuing to describe a "paradoxical postmodernism of complicity and critique, of reflexivity and historicity, that at once inscribes and subverts the conventions and ideologies of the dominant cultural and social forces of the twentieth-century western world" (11).

But if Hutcheon is correct (and I think she mostly is), then it is senseless to make sweeping proclamations about the political engagement and effectiveness of postmodernist literature or of modes of criticism that focus on reflexive literary techniques. Some works of metafiction may be more politically engaged than others, but it is not really a question of determining which works are subversive and which are supportive of the existing order, since most will be both. Indeed, attempts to categorize works of literature strictly (as reflexive or historically engaged, as metafictional or representational, as modernist or postmodernist, etc.) may represent precisely the kind of quest for domination and control that it is the special quality of literature finally to elude.

The literary critic thus faces a dilemma. Reading an individual work in isolation, interesting though the experience may be, is in danger of degenerating into an empty formalism that loses touch with the significance of the work and of its functioning within the institution of art as part of a broad cultural context. But contextual reading is in danger of losing touch with the specificity of individual works of art and of imposing prefabricated reductionist interpretations on works in order to make them fit whatever model of art and of culture the critic happens to hold. This dilemma is inescapable, but at the same time it is surely not disabling. These dangers indicate not that literary criticism is impossible but merely that the literary critic should be wary of the potential pitfalls awaiting her.

Granted, such wariness might potentially result in a situation in which the critic adequately accounts neither for the specifics of individual works nor for the contextual functioning of the work. And such dangers will always exist, of course, since no amount of theoretical reflection on the critical enterprise can serve as a remedy for bad criticism. In this study, I try to steer a path between the Scylla of formalism and the Charybdis of reductionism by focusing in a given chapter on an individual work while allowing each chapter to resonate with all of the others through the common concern with issues of domination and power that all of the texts show. I also try to conduct—at least in the margins—a continuing dialogue between these literary texts and the work of cultural critics such as Adorno and Foucault. All of the texts I examine comment on the drive for domination not only in their specific thematic content but in the ways that the texts themselves resist dominative epistemological readings. In these texts, the process of reading becomes a metaphor for interaction with reality, especially with other people. But this reflexive emphasis should not be allowed to obscure the fact that all of the texts I discuss take on a special poignancy from the way their treatment of power and domination resonates with the real suffering of individuals in a twentieth century that has been scarred by monstrous totalitarian governments, vicious ethnic and racial persecutions, and wars of unprecedented scope and destruction. The concern with power and domination shown in the texts that I read in this study and in the theoretical approaches with which I read them is not a matter of abstract philosophy but of historical reality.

I begin with Beckett's early novel *Watt*, which directly addresses Enlightenment epistemology as a mode of domination. This novel specifically defines itself in opposition to discourses of truth such as science, philosophy, and religion that were central to the Enlightenment epistemological drive that Horkheimer and Adorno so criticize. In *Watt* the self-important claims of such discourses to be able to discover truth are parodied both in Watt's own absurd quest for knowledge and in the resistance of the text itself to a mode of reading based on epistemological mastery. This parody takes the form of a mockery of specific kinds of rational scientific language, while suggesting certain possibilities in alternative poetic forms of language use that point directly toward Beckett's later career. *Watt*, then, is a philosophical novel in the best sense, but it also raises issues of concrete human reality; Beckett's concern with power and domination resonates with centuries of political and religious oppression in Ireland, while the illuminating theoretical discourse of Horkheimer and Adorno arises in direct reaction to the horrors of fascism.

15

In the bulk of this study, I look at texts that in one way or another are concerned with gender issues, since the relations between men and women in patriarchal society might be expected to present clear examples of the dynamics of domination in human relations generally. That Beckett's concern with power and domination is relevant to these texts can be seen by the fact that Irish writers frequently figure Ireland as feminine in relation to the dominating masculine presence of England and other oppressive outside forces. Moreover, Beckett's implicit suggestion that dominative reading strategies mirror the ideology of domination that pervades modern society leads to gender issues in a direct way, since so many gender-oriented critics have addressed just such issues in recent years. For example, Stephen-Paul Martin has discussed the way the difficult, experimental texts of modernism and postmodernism undercut efforts at "masculine" interpretive mastery and demand a "feminine" form of reading: "In short, open or innovative works ask us to create and nurture them, to give them shape over time in the parts of our imaginations that make new forms, and to bring them into full being or maturity through our continued attention. This means that we are forced to exercise feminine qualities, to perceive in a way that is not encouraged by mainstream patriarchal society that has brought us to the brink of annihilation" (9).

Martin's overly direct identification of reading strategies with gender roles is in danger of perpetuating certain essentialist stereotypes, such as the picture of the nurturing mother as feminine ideal. But he is far from alone. Caren Greenberg, for example, has described certain totalizing modes of reading (especially psychoanalytic readings based on the Oedipal drama) as a masculine "struggle for power and pleasure." To Greenberg, this mode of reading implies that both readers and writers are male, while "the mediating text is female" (303). As an alternative, she proposes a "female textuality," a mode of reading in which the reader eschews domination of the text and in which "the relationship of the reader to language is recognized as essential, where the reader perceives the stuff of the text as intrinsically important" (304).[5]

I begin my exploration of gender issues in relation to power and domination with a discussion of Virginia Woolf's *The Waves*, a text that addresses the tribulations of modernity in such a way that gender becomes a principal consideration. Woolf's book explores the difficulties of establishing a viable and stable sense of selfhood in a modern world in which traditional authority has lost its stabilizing function. But Woolf's feminist perspective gives the modern sense of crisis in authority a new twist, since traditional authority never offered that much stability to women in the first place, except as strictly circumscribed objects of male domination. As with characters of Joyce or Beckett, the principals in Woolf's book struggle to define themselves in new and productive ways but often find the path blocked by the rigid expectations of a patriarchal society that allows them to occupy only certain predefined positions. Woolf explores the potential of literature (especially narrative) to surmount these traditional expectations, even while suggesting that narrative itself is a principal means through which these expectations are defined and enforced. She also suggests that those (especially women) who would seek to occupy subjective positions other than the ones rigidly defined by conventional society may find it difficult to find any position to occupy at all. The potentially emancipatory breakdown of the bourgeois subject can be terrifying and unsettling in the absence of viable models of subjectivity to take its place. At the same time, *The Waves* points toward possible alternative models, suggesting that a new communal mode of subjectivity in which intersubjective relation is prior to the individual ego might surmount many of the difficulties of the subject in modern patriarchal society.

The Waves is concerned not so much with the specific dynamics of relations between individual men and women as with the limitations placed on individuals by the large, impersonal structures of power that comprise modern society. But Woolf's vivid depiction of the suffering of her characters (perhaps most powerfully in the case of Rhoda, a character driven to suicide by her inability to occupy a comfortable subjective position in the patriarchal society around her) serves as a useful reminder that, like Beckett, Woolf responds not simply to abstract issues but to the real pain of real people in the situations she describes. This trend continues in Vladimir Nabokov's *Lolita*, a text whose clever and brilliant verbal fabric cannot obscure the monstrous reality that lies beneath this surface. For Nabokov's Humbert Humbert the girl Lolita is not real but a mere literary artifact, and the blatant artificiality of the text at first seem to reinforce his position. After all, *Lolita* is a fiction, and so is Lolita. But rape and child abuse are very real, and many young girls in modern society do in fact suffer Lolita's fate or worse. In this light, Nabokov's focus on the dynamics of domination and submission in the relation between Humbert Humbert and Lolita takes on an added power.

Humbert's drive to dominate Lolita participates in a general drive for domination (especially of his own human nature) that characterizes all of his activities in a way that is highly reminiscent of the Horkheimer/Adorno critique of the Enlightenment. And Nabokov's exploration of the way Lolita and her mother are constituted as individuals by American popular culture—while Humbert is at the same time equally constituted by European "high" culture—suggests ways we as individuals are not nearly so free as we would like to believe. Thus, Nabokov's examination of this relation resonates with certain neo-Marxist critiques of modern society in powerful and interesting ways. At the same time, this resonance calls attention to Nabokov's own avowedly anti-Marxist sympathies and suggests a potential dialogue with the Stalinist terror that looms in the margins of so many of Nabokov's texts.

Thomas Pynchon also explores the motif of domination in relations between the sexes in his novel *V.* In particular, Pynchon situates the drive for domination in sexual relations (represented in strong form by the images of rape in his text) within a constellation of power struggles that he relates to the growth of Western imperialism in the nineteenth century and of fascism in the twentieth. The graphic scenes of sexual violence presented in Pynchon's text serve as reminders of the horrors of both imperialism and patriarchy—or of any ideology that allows one social group to deny the humanity of any other group. And Pynchon's exploration of this theme is made particularly effective by the way he suggests that these horrors are not merely things of the past, that the drive for domination that informed imperialism and fascism is still with us. He reinforces this suggestion with a text that lures readers into the pursuit of dominative reading strategies, then undermines those strategies in such a way as to reveal the ideology behind them.

This focus on reading as a quest for domination of the text is even more clearly the focus of Italo Calvino's *If on a winter's night a traveler*. Calvino's book explores different strategies of reading, most of which involve a totalizing desire for mastery of the text being read, and it does so in a way that directly suggests that these strategies closely parallel certain strategies typically pursued in sexual relations. As with the other authors discussed, Calvino suggests that these dominative styles of reading are ultimately counterproductive and lead to an impoverishing encounter with the text. But even Calvino's overtly reflexive text contains scenes of incarceration, political oppression, rape, and murder that emphasize the real human cost of the ideology of domination he so carefully undermines in his text.

I complete my study with a return to Beckett, whose late novel *The Lost Ones* is in many ways exemplary of the issues I address in this study. Here Beckett presents a rigidly carceral society that directly comments on the oppressive conditions informing life in certain—perhaps all—modern societies. Indeed, despite its abstract tone, *The Lost Ones* clearly participates in the genre of dystopian fiction and thus takes part in much of the same dialogue with political oppression that informs the great modern dystopian texts like *We, Brave New World*, and *1984*. But the most effective commentary on domination in this text is enacted in the reading process itself. *The Lost Ones* tantalizes the reader by offering numerous totalizing recuperative strategies that allow one to read it as a fairly straightforward allegory. But it offers so many of these strategies that each undermines the other, and in the end no attempt at totalizing reading can ever succeed. A careful study of *The Lost Ones* thus offers a number of useful lessons for those who would seek to oppose dominative strategies in both the reading and the teaching of literary texts, even as its resonance with the dystopian tradition provides powerful reminders that a great deal is at stake in this opposition.

Together these six texts constitute a convincing argument for the ability of literary texts to engage issues of power and domination in socially relevant ways. Of course, other readings of these or any texts are possible, and if my attempt to use these texts to illustrate certain points of my own turns out itself to look suspiciously like a form of domination, then that possibility merely serves to illustrate the complexity of the dialogue between literature and domination. And if this complexity dictates that my success must be less than complete, then so much the better, since much of my point here is that literature is inimical to complete mastery.

CHAPTER *1* THIS IS NOT A POT:

THE ASSAULT ON

SCIENTIFIC LANGUAGE

IN SAMUEL BECKETT'S

WATT

Issues of power and domination represent a central concern of Samuel Beckett's entire oeuvre. Perhaps the best-known and most obvious example of this concern is the strain of sadomasochism that runs throughout *Waiting for Godot*, most notably in the domination of Lucky by Pozzo, but virtually every Beckett work contains elements of domination, subjugation, and cruelty.[6] For example, in *Malone Dies* the title character is apparently imprisoned by the "powers that be" in the institution in which he writes, and his only direct encounter with another human being in that institution involves the visit of a strange man who for no apparent reason deals him a violent blow on the head (*Three* 269). Soon after this visit, the dominated Malone then fantasizes about becoming the dominator, passing on this dynamic of sadism by fantasizing about capturing a little girl and making her do his bidding (273).[7]

This sequential sadism illustrates the extent to which a dynamic of domination and submission informs the ideology of bourgeois civilization, whose paradigm of intersubjective relation is, after all, not cooperation but competition. Rather than band together to fight oppression, those who are oppressed in bourgeois society turn against their fellows, passing on the chain of domination in sequential fashion. Beckett images this process most clearly in *How It Is*, where love is defined as "two strangers uniting in the interests of torment" (121), and where intersubjective relations in general consist of an endless string of tormentors and their victims, who in turn become tormentors to additional victims, and so on *ad infinitum*.

The narrator of *How It Is* points out that this dynamic of domina- tion and submission implies that all of us share a common experience:

> in reality we are one and all from the unthinkable first to the no less unthinkable last glued together in a vast imbrication of flesh without breach or fissure . . . linked thus bodily together each one of us is at the same time Bom and Pim tormentor and tormented pedant and dunce wooer and wooed speechless and reafflicted with speech. (140)

That this commonality of suffering seems to do nothing to prevent the torment from continuing is, of course, the true tragedy of modern humanity, and Adorno's work locates the cause of this continuing dynamic in the ideology of domination associated with the Enlighten-ment and with the ongoing effects of the bourgeois notion of the autonomous, independent individual.

Beckett's exploration of domination resonates particularly with the work of Horkheimer and Adorno in the way that Beckett explores the implication in this motif of the epistemological drive that informs Enlightenment thought. For example, Beckett's Murphy (like his later reincarnation Malone) is an idealist philosopher in the Cartesian mode who seeks, per the Enlightenment ideal, contemplation in a cosmos of pure reason untainted by the exigencies of life in the real world. This preoccupation proves fatuous and in fact leads ultimately to Murphy's death. Especially important, however, is Murphy's method for pursuing his quest for pure reason: he sits strapped in his rocking chair by seven scarves, unable to move—and unable to escape, even when the chair overturns, leaving him literally off his rocker (*Murphy* 28). Murphy's bondage thus dramatizes the conten-tion of Horkheimer and Adorno that the Enlightenment quest for domination of nature through the application of human reason leads to the enslavement of the reasoners as that quest for domination turns back on itself. Horkheimer and Adorno point to Odysseus, strapped to the mast as he hears the song of the Sirens, as a central illustration of this phenomenon, and Murphy can be seen as a parodic modern

Odysseus with his rocking chair playing the role of mast and the lure of rational philosophy playing the role of enticing temptress.

As Beckett turns from *Murphy* to *Watt* his parody of rationalist philosophy becomes even more focused. In particular, the mock encyclopedism of the latter resonates with the Horkheimer and Adorno critique of modern science as having abandoned the quest for true knowledge in favor of mere facts, which may be technologically exploitable but contain no genuine understanding.[8] Ronald Swigger presents a useful discussion of encyclopedism in modern fiction, noting that encyclopedists like Flaubert, Borges, and Queneau are consistently skeptical of the Enlightenment drive toward completeness in knowledge. Thus, Swigger discusses *Bouvard et Pecuchet* as "a satirical encyclopedic critique of nineteenth-century perversions of the Faustian impulse to know. . . . Flaubert unmasks the pretentious 'authorities' of the age, the exponents and the popularizers of 'official' history, philosophy, theology, art, literature" (357).[9]

Modern encyclopedists tend to introduce great quantities of information from a variety of disciplines only in order to demonstrate the internal inconsistencies and ultimate follies of those disciplines. The proliferation of information in the texts of such writers is a far cry from the late minimalist texts of Beckett, but early Beckett works such as *Murphy* and especially *Watt* employ similar strategies of parodic encyclopedism. *Watt* is characterized by an exuberant overabundance of data throughout. Within the first few pages of *Watt* we meet a diminutive hunchback, an immense Irish policeman, a pair of illicit lovers, a pregnant woman, and a married couple, the Nixons. We are presented with an obscene poem written by an imprisoned solicitor to his girlfriend, the revelation of the injury that apparently made Mr. Hackett a hunchback, and the Rabelaisian story of the birth of Larry Nixon—after which his mother severed the umbilical cord with her own teeth—all of this before Watt himself even makes an appearance. And the profusion of comic information in these pages is typical of the entire book. *Watt* has more in common with the exuberant encyclopedic excess of texts like *Gargantua and Pantagruel*, *A Tale of a Tub*, *Bouvard et Pecuchet*, and *Ulysses* than with the stark minimalism of *The Lost Ones* or *Ping*.

Mikhail Bakhtin's work on Menippean satire provides what is probably the most extensive theoretical exploration of the parodic energies at work in encyclopedic texts.[10] Bakhtin's work does a great

deal to illuminate the way encyclopedic texts employ parodic energies to undermine authoritarian discourses. *Watt* operates in a constant mode of parody, since it is constructed almost exclusively of the
language of precisely the kinds of discourses of authority—"the old
words, the old credentials" (85)—that it seeks to undermine. The
opening scene sets the linguistic tone for the entire book—exact,
detailed language constantly strives to provide a complete and accurate description of the events at hand, but these attempts at scientific
description invariably collapse into absurdity.

In his later project Beckett will turn to a radical linguistic experimentalism in an attempt to explore alternatives to such authoritarian
uses of language. *Watt*, on the other hand, utilizes such language in
order to undermine it. In fact, Hugh Culik has argued that *Watt* is
Beckett's last attempt to employ such language and that its failure
leads to his later experimentalism: "To the extent that the novel relies
on the type of knowledge and the type of language it rejects, it is
unsatisfying; but to the extent *Watt* identifies central issues of Beckett's later work, the novel is important to Beckett's development"
(70). But the failure of rational, scholarly language in *Watt* is largely
the point, and it is a failure that bespeaks the success of the book.
Beckett's linguistic project in *Watt* is at one with the goal of his later
work—it is just that his later work undermines authoritarian discourses through the exploration of altrnatives, while *Watt* attempts
to dismantle these linguistic practices from within, demonstrating
the madness that lies at the heart of the Enlightenment emphasis on
rational language by showing the inadequacy of this language to the
expression of real human experience.

As *Watt* begins, Hunchy Hackett approaches his favorite bench at
a tram stop, only to find that the seat is occupied by a pair of lovers:

> Mr. Hackett decided, after some moments, that if they were
> waiting for a tram they had been doing so for some time. For the
> lady held the gentleman by the ears, and the gentleman's hand
> was on the lady's thigh, and the lady's tongue was in the gentle-
> man's mouth. (8)

This list of anatomical details foreshadows the many comically exhaustive lists to be found in *Watt*, and Mr. Hackett's quest for even
more information (he is especially eager to know where the gen-
tleman's *other* hand might be) presages the drive for epistemological

completeness that informs the activities of nearly all the characters in the book.

This combination of precise, descriptive language and a persistent rage to know makes *Watt* (like many Menippean texts) read somewhat like a scholarly treatise, though this rational, academic style is consistently undercut by the absurdity and indeterminacy of the events being depicted. An excellent example of this effect occurs in the detailed description of Watt's method of walking:

> Watt's way of advancing due east, for example, was to turn his bust as far as possible towards the north and at the same time to fling out his right leg as far as possible towards the south, and then to turn his bust as far as possible towards the south and at the same time to fling out his left leg as far as possible towards the north, and then again to turn his bust as far as possible towards the north and to fling out his right leg as far as possible towards the south, and then again to turn his bust as far as possible towards the north, and so on, over and over again, until he reached his destination, and could sit down. (30)

The pretensions to seriousness of scientific language are obviously undercut by the comic absurdity of such scenes. Moreover, echoing Joyce and anticipating writers like Robbe-Grillet, the excessive details of such descriptions often tend to de-realize the events being described, making them almost impossible to visualize.

Despite the drive for certainty that informs the language of the text, *Watt* is a text in which nothing is in fact certain. For example, we will find out later that the book is apparently being narrated by one "Sam," who has received all of his information from Watt himself while the two of them were inmates in an insane asylum. Thus, the narration in the book is doubly suspect—not only is it filtered through at least two different narrators before it comes down to us, but both of these narrators are apparently mad. Moreover, a look back at the opening scene reveals that it occurs before Watt makes his appearance in the text, descending from a tram nine pages into the narrative. This whole scene is thus put into question by the fact that Watt apparently could not have related to Sam the events depicted. In addition, the scene seems to be presented from the perspective of Mr. Hackett, raising the question of how Sam knows what is going on inside Hackett's mind—a question with broad applicability to fictional narrators in general.

Sam, of course, is perfectly well aware that his text is filled with such moments, and he asks us to believe that

> when the impossibility of my knowing, of Watt's having known, 25
> what I know, what Watt knew, seems absolute, and insurmountable, and undeniable, and uncoercible, it could be shown that I
> know, because Watt told me, and that Watt knew because
> someone told him, or because he found out for himself. For I
> know nothing, in this connexion, but what Watt told me. And
> Watt knew nothing, on this subject, but what was told, or found
> out for himself, in one way or another. (127–28)

Here, even as Sam attempts to defend the authority of his narrative, he again reminds us of the tenuousness of his sources. Further, the difficulties with Sam's narration go far beyond the question of his sources of information. A close look at the opening scene, which is typical of the entire text, shows a number of curious instabilities in the narrative. On the one hand, seemingly unimportant objects and events are described in great detail. Thus, we are "treated" to an exhaustive relation of Hackett's options on seeing his bench occupied, complete with a typically Beckettian idiosyncratic use of commas:[11] "The dilemma was thus of extreme simplicity: to go on, or to turn, and return, round the corner, the way he had come. Was he, in other words, to go home at once, or was he to remain out a little longer?" (7–8). Yet despite such exaggeratedly complete lists of actions and options, other important events are not related in the text at all. After the description of the lovers, the narrative continues with a policeman's declaration that "I see no indecency" (8). Apparently Hackett has complained to this policeman about the behavior of the lovers, yet neither the appearance of the policeman nor Hackett's complaint to him is actually included in the text. Further, the encounter between the policeman and Hackett ends as Hackett takes his place on the bench, "still warm, from the loving" (9)—apparently the lovers have gone, but their departure is not indicated in the narrative. This alternation between information that is given in excessive and redundant detail and information that is not given at all will continue throughout the text, calling attention to the ways narrative always operates in a mode of selection, emphasizing some details at the expense of the suppression of others.

The necessary incompleteness of narrative is a persistent theme in Beckett's work. As Beckett's Mercier elsewhere explains to his companion Camier, reality is far too complex to be contained within the confines of narrative:

> Even side by side, said Mercier, as now, arm to arm, hand in hand, legs in unison, we are fraught with more events than could fit in a fat tome, two fat tomes, your fat tome and my fat tome. Whence no doubt our blessed sense of nothing, nothing to be done, nothing to be said. (*Mercier* 87)

Beckett's later minimalist texts call attention to their incompleteness by progressively eliminating more and more of the elements that one would expect to find in a fictional text, demonstrating that they can still function even without parts that would have been thought to be essential. *Watt* operates in the opposite mode, comically striving for encyclopedic completeness, only to demonstrate the impossibility (and absurdity) of such a drive for comprehensiveness (and comprehension).

Raymond Federman explains the way *Watt* subverts the conventions of realistic narrative: "Basically *Watt* is a narrative experiment which exploits the inadequacy of language, reason, and logic to reveal the failure of fiction as a means of apprehending the reality of the world" (119). But the metafictional shenanigans of *Watt* comment on far more than the effectiveness of fiction as an epistemological system; they comment on epistemological systems in general. After all, the expectations that readers bring to literary texts are never derived strictly from literature but participate in an entire range of ideological predispositions. As J. Hillis Miller points out, "The notions of narrative, of character, and of formal unity in fiction are all congruent with the system of concepts making up the Western idea of history" ("Narrative" 461). In particular, Miller argues that the Hegelian model of rational history infects our view of fiction in a quite inclusive way:

> The assumptions about history which have been transferred to the traditional conception of the form of fiction . . . include the notions of origin and end ("archeology" and "teleology"); of unity

and totality or "totalization"; of underlying "reason" or "ground" of selfhood, consciousness, or "human nature"; of the homogeneity, linearity, and continuity of time; of necessary progress; of "fate," "destiny," or "Providence"; of causality; of gradually emerging "meaning"; of representation and truth. ("Narrative" 459–60)

Texts such as *Watt* that undermine the expectations that readers bring to realistic fiction thus have the potential of challenging their readers to reexamine a whole host of philosophical attitudes. In *Watt* this challenge is particularly effective because Beckett initiates an explicit dialogue in the text with a variety of specific discourses of authority, including religion, philosophy, science, and psychology, all of which can be associated in one way or another with the Enlightenment quest for mastery critiqued by Horkheimer and Adorno.[12] Even more interesting than thematic content, however, is *Watt*'s exploration of language and, in particular, of the way discourses like philosophy and science use language as a tool to establish and maintain their authority.[13]

Watt's most obvious predecessor in this regard is the "Ithaca" chapter of *Ulysses*, which employs many of the same devices (exhaustive lists, excessively literal descriptions, etc.) to undermine the pretensions to authority of rational language. In this chapter Joyce combines the form of the Catholic catechism with the precise, descriptive language of science to undermine the pretensions of both religion and science as discourses of authority. Parodying the claims of such discourses to have all the answers to life's questions, Joyce presents a series of simple, straightforward queries that are then answered in excruciatingly (and hilariously) complete and complex detail. For example, when Bloom turns on the tap to let water flow into the kitchen sink, the text asks, "Did it flow?" Then comes the reply:

Yes. From Roundwood reservoir in county Wicklow of a cubic capacity of 2400 million gallons, percolating through a subterranean aqueduct of filter mains of single and double pipeage constructed at an initial plant cost of £5 per linear yard by way of the Dargle, Rathdown, Glen of the Downs and Callowhill to the 26 acre reservoir at Stillorgan, a distance of 22 statute miles, and thence, through a system of relieving tanks, by a gradient of 250

feet to the boundary at Eustace bridge, upper Leeson street . . .
(548)

In fact, this single-sentence answer goes on for approximately half a page of densely printed text, supplying a vast amount of superfluous (and partially inaccurate) information that provides more confusion than explanation. In "Ithaca," as in the rest of *Ulysses*, mere facts are always insufficient to provide a complete knowledge of reality, and—far from being a quest for such knowledge—the encyclopedism of the text is a parody that reveals the absurdity of such quests.

Scientific, objective language like that parodied in "Ithaca" (and in *Watt*) was one of the principal tools with which Enlightenment thinkers sought to extend their dominion over nature. Moreover, such dialogues with science have particular political connotations for Irish writers such as Joyce and Beckett. Remarking the surprising absence of science in most histories of Irish culture, John Wilson Foster attributes this phenomenon to the fact that scientific modes of thought have traditionally been associated in the Irish mind with British imperialism. He notes, for example, the "calculated exclusion of science, by the architects of the Irish Cultural Revival around the turn of the century" because of this asssociation (95). Science in Ireland has traditionally been associated with the intrusion of foreign powers, and the dialogues with science in works like *Ulysses* and *Watt* participate in a larger critical examination of the political and cultural domination of Ireland by imperial Britain. Of course, England also dominated Ireland with its language, and the importance of language to the project of the Enlightenment can perhaps best be seen in the intense concern with language shown by those who were involved in the seventeenth-century rise of science as the dominant epistemological discourse of Western society. The growing hegemony of the new science resulted in an entire new worldview, but among other things it was associated with an extensive exploration of new conceptions of language, conceptions that moved away from the earlier view of language as a rhetorical tool and toward a view of language as representation, as a transparent conductor of information. The new science, as exemplified by the Royal Society in England, was highly concerned with the question of language, and it waged a fierce and effective campaign against rhetorical flourish and in support of a plainer and more direct style of discourse. Bacon,

Hobbes, and many other illustrious personages contributed to this campaign, but perhaps the clearest statement of the position of the Society can be found in the writings of its historian, Thomas Sprat:

> They have therefore been most rigorous in putting in execution, the only Remedy, that can be found for this *extravagance:* and that has been, a constant Resolution, to reject all the amplifications, digressions, and swellings of style: to return back to the primitive purity, and shortness, when men deliver'd for so many *things*, almost in an equal number of *words*. They have exacted from all their members, a close, naked, natural way of speaking, positive expressions, clear senses, a native easiness: bringing all things as near the Mathematical plainess, as they can . . . (113, Sprat's italics)

29

The concern voiced by Sprat went beyond matters of style, encompassing programs for the development of universal and natural languages like that described in John Wilkins's *An Essay Towards a Real Character and a Philosophical Language* (1668), in which the intent is to develop a language in which a word might not only stand as a symbol for a thing but also inherently indicate the very nature of that thing. Richard Jones emphasizes the importance of language reform to the new science by noting that it "is hard to overemphasize the fact that science in its youth considered the linguistic problem as important as the problem of the true scientific method" ("Science and Language" 157). The scientific facts discovered by the new science could be used for the domination of nature only if they could be accurately communicated to others.[14]

The kind of direct match between signifier and signified envisioned by Sprat is obviously antithetical to poetry, and it is not surprising that contemporary writers like Swift and Pope reacted vehemently to such scientific programs for literary reform. For example, Swift openly mocks these programs in *Gulliver's Travels* in a variety of ways, most memorably in his depiction of the projectors of Lagado who literalize the advice of Sprat and Wilkins and carry around bags of things themselves, avoiding the need for words entirely:

> An Expedient was therefore offered, that since *Words* are only Names for *Things*, it would be more convenient for all Men to

carry about them, such *Things* as were necessary to express the particular Business they are to discourse on . . . many of the most Learned and Wise adhere to the new Scheme of expressing themselves by *Things;* which hath only this Inconvenience attending it; that if a Man's Business be very great, and of various Kinds, he must be obliged to carry a greater Bundle of *Things* upon his Back, unless he can afford one or two strong Servants to attend him. (158, Swift's italics)

30

Roger Lund explains the opposition of the Scriblerians to the linguistic programs of the new science, arguing that to Swift and Pope man's identity is related to his use of language as a special gift of God, so that a mechanical language will disrupt man's role as a special creature of God, leading inevitably to mechanical men (65). But Swift and Pope also seem to be reacting against the arrogance of the new science itself, an arrogance that does away with the need for God by suggesting that humanity is able to understand and master the world in which it lives through the use of its own resources. In any case, the clash between Swift and Sprat amounts to a clash between two mighty discourses of power, with Swift upholding the traditional authority of religion and Sprat serving as advocate for science as an alternative authority.

While the debate between Swift and Sprat helps to identify the issues at stake in *Watt*, one should also keep in mind that Beckett's attitude is far more radical than Swift's, amounting to a rejection not just of science but of authoritarian (and authoritative) discourses in general. Thus, scientific thinking serves as an especially obvious target in *Watt*, but religion comes in for a great deal of mockery as well. Beckett's story of "a priest who, on leaving with a sigh of relief the chapel where he had served mass, with his own hands, to more than a hundred persons, was shat on, from above, by a dove, in the eye" (91) is emblematic of the treatment of religion in *Watt*. Beckett is also careful to avoid positing literature as an alternative discourse of authority, since *Watt* also effectively undermines the claims of literature (especially narrative) to have a privileged access to reality.

All of the information narrated in *Watt* is highly suspect. For one thing, Watt has accumulated his own information in the course of a journey, much of it through a whole series of previous narrators (Arsene, Vincent, Erskine, Walter, etc.) all of whom are less than totally reliable. Arsene explains this series of unreliable narrations to Watt: "Not that I have told you all I know, for I have not . . . just as Vincent did not tell me all, nor Walter Erskine, nor the others the others" (62). And Sam specifically calls attention to the unreliability of Watt as a source. Even as Sam tells us that Watt was his sole source of information, he acknowledges that there is no "proof that Watt did indeed tell all he knew, on these subjects, or that he set out to do so, for how could there be, I knowing nothing on these subjects, except what Watt told me," (125).[15]

Sam specifically calls attention to the fact that, despite his best efforts, his narrative may be incomplete and inaccurate, suggesting that perhaps all narratives are necessarily flawed:

> It is difficult for a man like Watt to tell a long story like Watt's without leaving out some things, and foisting in others. And this does not mean either that I may not have left out some of the things that Watt told me, or foisted in others that Watt never told me, though I was most careful to note down all at the time, in my little notebook. It is so difficult, with a long story like the story that Watt told, even when one is most careful to note down all at the time, in one's little notebook, not to leave out some of the things that were told, and not to foist in other things that were never told, never told at all. (126)

Despite the apparently authoritative language in which Sam presents his narration, then, we are warned that his descriptions of events cannot necessarily be taken at face value.

Sam's narrative undermines itself in more subtle ways throughout the text, and a close look at the text shows it to be full of gaps, inconsistencies, and errors. Some of these textual effects are quite subtle, and a reader seduced by the authoritative language of the text might miss them entirely. But *Watt* is also filled with more obvious devices that call attention to the text's unreliability and incompleteness. Many of the instabilities in the opening narration of Mr. Hackett's reaction to the lovers on the bench could easily be missed by a casual reader, but in the midst of this scene Hackett makes a comment to himself: "Tired of waiting for the tram, said (1) Mr Hackett, they strike up an acquaintance" (8). This sentence refers to the first of the text's several footnotes, which explains the absence of "to himself" in this sentence: "(1) Much valuable space has been

saved, in this work, that would otherwise have been lost, by avoid-
ance of the plethoric reflexive pronoun after *say*" (8). As Mathew
Winston points out, this footnote serves as an early signal to the
reader that the usual expectations one brings to a literary text will be
constantly disrupted in *Watt* (70–71). In particular, the various footnotes call attention to the artificially constructed nature of the text,
impeding readerly efforts to recuperate the text as a realistic narrative.

As Shari Benstock points out, footnotes have been used in a number of fictional texts, ranging from *Tom Jones* to *Finnegans Wake*.
Benstock notes that footnotes are by their nature at the margins of
discourse and call into question what constitutes a text: "To read a
footnote is to be forcibly reminded of the inherent multi-textuality of
all texts" (220 n. 2). In other words, the existence of a footnote
indicates that the main text is incomplete and requires supplementa-
tion in some way.

The last footnote in *Watt* particularly calls attention to the text's
incompleteness. It explains the inclusion of a variety of fragments, or
"addenda," at the end of the text: "(1) The following precious and
illuminating material should be carefully studied. Only fatigue and
disgust prevented its incorporation" (247). Among other things, the
very existence of these supplemental fragments (like the various
physical gaps and "hiatuses" that are scattered throughout the text)
calls attention to the incompleteness of the text, to the fact that there
is information left out despite the comically precise language and
exhaustive lists that make up so much of the narration. The specific
notation of "fatigue and disgust" also points out that the accuracy and
completeness of the text are limited by the reliability of Sam the
narrator, whose human foibles intrude on his ability to convey information through language without loss and distortion. Sam, in short,
suffers from precisely the difficulty that early scientists like Sprat
hoped to avoid.

The footnotes in the text (like those in Swift's *A Tale of a Tub* and
those in the "Nightlessons" section of *Finnegans Wake*) undermine
not only the conventions of fiction but those of footnotes (and, by
extension, of scholarly documentation) in general. For example, the
first footnote is superfluous (and plethoric), even as it purports to
explain a space-saving gesture in the text. The strangely precise,
scientific language of *Watt*, by seeming so inappropriate to the

matter of the text, creates a disjunction that comments both on the expectations normally associated with fiction and on the traditional Enlightenment faith in reason and in the ability of rational language to order and describe reality.

The assault on Enlightenment rationality in *Watt* can be usefully illuminated by comparing Beckett's text directly to the linguistic program proposed by Sprat. For example, when Sprat suggests that one should strive to bring language "near the Mathematical plainess," he explicitly calls attention to the Enlightenment faith in mathematics as a rational and objective means of describing reality. Beckett's characters often display this same faith, turning time and time again to mathematics in an attempt to make sense of their absurd worlds. These attempts generally lead to comically extended computations that ultimately end in total futility. Perhaps the best-known example of this motif in Beckett involves the laborious calculations of Molloy to try to determine the most efficient way to rotate his sixteen sucking stones among his four pockets in order to use all of the stones equally. It would be a simple problem in probability to devise a scheme whereby, on the average, each stone would receive equal use, but this stochastic solution is not good enough for Molloy: "this was only a makeshift that could not long content a man like me" (*Three* 69). Instead, the Newtonian Molloy seeks a strictly deterministic solution that will guarantee that each stone is employed strictly in turn.

However, unable to accept compromises like numbering the stones, Molloy soon finds that his quest, like all such quests in Beckett, is futile. In the end (after five pages of calculations), he simply throws away all of the stones but one, which then promptly comes up missing. Even then Molloy still insists on exploring all possibilities, suggesting that he "lost, or threw away, or gave away, or swallowed" the last stone (74).[16]

Watt is filled with such futile calculations, and the text constantly appeals to mathematics as a privileged mode of epistemology, resulting in an unexpected prominence of numbers and calculations in an ostensibly "artistic" text. This conflation of literature and mathematics can perhaps best be seen in the threne that Watt hears while lying in a roadside ditch. The lyrics to the two verses of this song begin, respectively, with the numbers 52.285714285714 . . . and 52.1428571428571. . . .[17] These mathematical lyrics already trans-

gress the conventional boundary between music and mathematics
(between what Julia Kristeva would call the semiotic and the symbolic), thus calling into question the Enlightenment privileging of
reason over lyricism. But such distinctions are, of course, highly
artificial. After all, as even Leopold Bloom knows, music itself is
highly mathematical.[18] Moreover, it is significant that the two numbers that appear in the lyrics of Watt's threne (the result of calculating
the number of weeks in a leap year and in a normal year respectively)
are irrational—the last series of digits repeats *ad infinitum* and the
number will never converge into an exact solution. Mathematics
does not necessarily supply complete and rational answers even to
the simplest of problems.

Perhaps the most memorable mathematical moment in *Watt* occurs in the story of Mr. Louit and Mr. Nackybal, narrated to Mr.
Knott's gardener, Mr. Graves, by Arthur, his co-worker at Mr.
Knott's house. Arthur tells the story of Louit's research in support of
his dissertation, *The Mathematical Intuitions of the Visicelts*. Louit,
faithful epistemologist that he is, obtains a research grant and then
sets out on an expedition into the countryside in search of mathematical prodigies among the Irish peasantry. After a variety of ludicrous misadventures (among other things he is forced to cook and
eat his dog for food), Louit's quest for knowledge is rewarded with the
discovery of one Mr. Nackybal, an illiterate bumpkin who can barely
even add and subtract. But Mr. Nackybal is apparently a sort of idiot
savant with the astounding ability of computing (though not entirely
accurately) cube roots in his head for numbers up to six digits.[19]

Louit returns with Nackybal to his university to display the discovery to his supervisory committee, which appears to be a cross between Abbott and Costello and academic committees everywhere—
with a suggestion that there is not much difference between the two.
After spending five pages attempting an exhaustive enumeration of
the ways the committee members might all look at one another before the proceedings begin, the narrative continues with Nackybal's
demonstration, but his performance is overshadowed by the comical
antics of the committee members themselves. All told, this extended
parody of academia runs for twenty-seven pages of exhaustive lists
and mathematical shenanigans, but Arthur runs out of steam before
the story can ever reach its end or make its point, which apparently
has to do with Louit's subsequent academic demise and turn to

smuggling Bando, an illegal sexual stimulant that Arthur recommends to Graves as a remedy for his flagging love life.

Watt's own attempts at understanding reality through scientific inquiry are a central motif of the book, and Watt himself is heavily given to mathematical computation as an epistemological technique. But Watt's excessively careful computations are invariably flawed, often leading to highly comic results. Attempting to ascertain some mathematical relation among the series of dogs, men, and pictures that pass through Mr. Knott's house, Watt remembers a former occasion when (lying in a ditch, as is his wont) he listened to three frogs croaking. We are then treated to a page and a half of "kraks," "kreks," and "kriks" as Watt contemplates the periodic relation among the three, simultaneously evoking literary remembrances of Aristophanes' *The Frogs* and *Finnegans Wake*[20] but also forgetting that the entire effort is futile since there is no reason to suspect that frogs croak with any kind of mathematical regularity in the first place.

Watt's most extended calculation occurs when he is ordered to feed Mr. Knott's leftover food to the dog but must face the problem that Mr. Knott *has* no dog. The obvious solution is to give the food to a dog from the neighborhood, but Watt (like Molloy) is unable to live with any sort of contingency. So he manages to turn this simple and practical solution into an extended problem in logistics, spending several pages (91–100) attempting to compute all possible eventualities to make certain that the food is always eaten. Such assurance, he concludes, can be obtained only by hiring a local man and dog to come by each evening to check for leftover food. But accidents can happen, and Watt (like Molloy) cannot accept uncertainty. So Watt realizes that it will be necessary to have a backup man and dog, just in case. In fact, to cover all possibilities, there must be backups for the backups, and so on, *ad infinitum.*

And *ad absurdum.* Watt's quest for mathematical certainty leads to ludicrous results, and this infinite series of men and dogs is brought to an end only by the expedient of the inimitable Lynch clan. This fecund family can breed their own dogs, generating a constant supply, and meanwhile they will be able to generate their own backups through a massive propensity for incest. In fact, this tendency toward inbreeding among the members of the Lynch clan has already led to a variety of grotesque (and sometimes impossible) congenital ailments, a detailed description of which we are treated to in the text. On an obvious level, the Lynches appear to function as a parody of the Irish nationalist mythology of the purity of the Irish race.[21] But this absurd family also provides the end point of Watt's detailed mathematical solution to the leftover food problem, effectively undermining his pretensions to rationality through their own absurdity.

Amidst Watt's attempts at complete documentation and description of the Lynch clan we learn that among these poor souls is one Kate, "a fine girl but a bleeder." A footnote then explains: "(1) Haemophilia is, like enlargement of the prostate, an exclusively male disorder. But not in this work" (102). This footnote is particularly effective in the way that it undermines Watt's apparently conscientious and careful calculations, reminding us that *Watt* is entirely fictional and need not conform to the laws of verisimilitude or to the scientific project of accurately reflecting nature—with a suggestion that science itself might also not be quite so accurate and reliable as it would like to believe. This notion is further emphasized two pages later in a footnote to the calculation of the cumulative life span of the Lynch clan: "(1) The figures given here are incorrect. The consequent calculations are therefore doubly erroneous" (104). In *Watt* such detailed calculations provide not knowledge but confusion, and the authority of mathematics in general is strongly called into question.

If Watt's misadventures with mathematics act as an ironic counter to Sprat's dream of a mathematical language, his difficulty with language itself provides an even more powerful commentary on the scientific quest for a transparent language with a direct connection between signifier and signified. Watt is at least as eager as Sprat to discover such a well-behaved and dependable medium of communication, and "Watt's need of semantic succour was at times so great that he would set to trying names on things, and on himself, almost as a woman hats" (83). Watt indeed is a sucker for semantics, and his view of language as naming participates in a philosophical tradition that runs from Genesis to Saul Kripke. But Watt is no Adam, and his names tend to come unstuck from the objects they indicate, leading to an unbridgeable gap between signifier and signified that ends his dream of linguistic security once and for all.

Watt contemplates a pot in Mr. Knott's house but is unable to make the name adhere to the object:

For it was not a pot, the more he looked, the more he reflected, the more he felt sure of that, that it was not a pot at all. It resembled a pot, it was almost a pot, but it was not a pot of which one could say, Pot, pot, and be comforted. It was in vain that it answered, with unexceptionable adequacy, all the purposes, and performed all the offices, of a pot, it was not a pot. And it was just this hairbreadth departure from the nature of a true pot that so excruciated Watt. (81)

Here Watt reveals the metaphysical idealism that lies at the heart of all conceptions of language as naming—by labeling the object in Mr. Knott's house as a "pot," one is implying a comparison between this object and some ideal "true pot."

Watt's encounter with the pot recalls the famous parable of the leaf in Nietzsche's "On Truth and Lies" essay. Nietzsche argues that, by applying the name "leaf" to so many different individual leaves, one effaces the differences among those leaves: "This awakens the idea that, in addition to the leaves, there exists in nature the 'leaf': the original model according to which all the leaves were perhaps woven, sketched, measured, colored, curled, and painted—but by incompetent hands, so that no specimen has turned out to be a correct, trustworthy, and faithful likeness of the original model" (83). Nietzsche's critique of this idealistic conception of naming leads him to the conclusion that all language (and all human knowledge) is inherently metaphorical—in short, that the kind of concrete and direct link between signifier and signified envisioned by the early scientists is an impossibility.

The rationalist Watt, unable to accept the vertiginous implications of this radical gap between signifier and signified, apparently descends into madness and enters the asylum, where he meets Sam. In the asylum Watt begins to experiment with more and more radical modifications of traditional language use. Sam meanwhile struggles mightily to recuperate Watt's fractured discourse, converting it back into conventional narrative. Many critics, noticing the similarity in names, have in fact argued that Sam plays the same role as Beckett, attempting to express in language material that ultimately eludes rational linguistic expression. For example, Culik relates Watt's bizarre language to the aphasic speech of brain-damaged patients and notes Sam's efforts to make sense of it: "The problem of Watt (and the problem of *Watt*) is revealed to be Sam's task of interpreting, reporting, and remaining true to Watt's aphasic speech. . . . by his name we understand his task to be similar to Samuel Beckett's artistic task" (68).

But a closer look at Sam's attempts to make sense of Watt's mad speech indicates that Sam may represent the efforts not of Beckett but of rationalists like Sprat who demand that everything make sense no matter what. Watt's language becomes more and more irrational as his narrative to Sam proceeds, yet at every point Sam is able to develop a rational strategy of recuperation that allows him to translate Watt's speech back into "normal" syntax, though acknowledging that there is a significant loss of information in the process.

First Watt begins to alter the order of the words in his sentences, narrating his adventures in a highly unusual syntax. He explains to Sam:

> *Day of most, night of part, Knott with now. Now till up, little seen so oh, little heard so oh. Night till morning from. Heard I this, saw I this then what. Thing quiet, dim. Ears, eyes, failing now also. Hush in, mist in, moved I so.* (164, Beckett's italics)

Sam then responds in typical scientific fashion, performing a detailed analysis of Watt's new mode of discourse and concluding

> that the inversion affected, not the order of the sentences, but that of the words only;
> that the inversion was imperfect;
> that ellipse was frequent;
> that euphony was a preoccupation;
> that spontaneity was perhaps not absent;
> that there was perhaps more than a reversal of discourse;
> that the thought was perhaps inverted. (164)

Culik accurately points out that this list of characteristics provides a good description of the speech patterns of aphasics, especially as described in studies of the 1930s.[22] But the nonstandard word order and preoccupation with euphony in Watt's sentences also parallel certain modernist linguistic experiments, recalling particularly the work of Joyce through *Ulysses*.[23] Sam's analysis allows him to make sense of Watt's peculiar sentences, ignoring the fact that Watt's speech (like Joyce's writing) may be making a comment on the folly of such demands that all language must make sense. Moreover, Sam's scientific approach fails to comprehend the strangely lyric evocativeness of much of Watt's speech, a quality that strongly foreshadows the peculiar poetry of Beckett's later, more radical texts, indicating that language achieves its effects in ways far more subtle than as a mere conduit for intentional meaning. Sam thus recuperates Watt's untraditional language in a traditionally rational manner:

> But soon I grew used to these sounds, and then I understood as well as before, that is to say a great part of what I heard.
> So all went well until Watt began to invert, no longer the order of the words in the sentence, but that of the letters in the word. (165)

Watt's change of strategies here closely parallels Joyce's movement from the nonstandard word orders of *Ulysses* to the fractured portmanteau words of *Finnegans Wake*. As Sam continually reminds us after each of Watt's changes in strategy, "But soon I grew used to these sounds, and then I undertood as well as before." But Sam's efforts to contain and subdue Watt's irrational discourse are not entirely successful, and at each step he admits that "I missed much I presume of great interest." Despite its best efforts, rationality cannot in fact account for all that goes on in language (or in the world), and this point is made clear in the many reminders of the incompleteness and unreliability of Sam's narration, despite his heavy reliance on rational modes of explanation. Sam's own need for semantic succor is so powerful, however, that he continues to attempt to make sense of Watt's speech, even as it becomes more and more bizarre.

To complicate matters, Sam also begins to go deaf, though he assures us that his "mental faculties . . . were if possible more vigorous than ever" (169). This suggestion that Sam may not have even been able to *hear* Watt offers the possibility that the narrator's "mental faculties" may in fact be responsible for much, if not all, of the narrative. In short, Sam may simply have invented much of the story on his own, and it is possible that he has even created Watt from the resources of his own delusional imagination. There is a great deal in the text to suggest that Watt is simply a projection of Sam. As Sam stands in his garden at the asylum, staring across at Watt in *his* garden, Sam admits that "suddenly I felt as though I were standing before a great mirror, in which my garden was reflected, and my fence, and I" (159). [24]

But nothing is certain in *Watt,* and the resulting epistemological instability places the reader of *Watt* in very much the same position as Watt himself—both constantly encounter incidents of "great formal brilliance and indeterminable purport" (73). A recognition of the fact that much of *Watt* may be the invention (or hallucination) of either Watt or Sam (or both) helps to explain the indeterminacy of the text and to reinforce the point that the excessively rational epistemological yearning that informs the narrative is itself a form of insanity. But a recuperation of *Watt* as the ramblings of Watt and/or Sam does not "solve" the text, which is constructed specifically to defeat such attempts at rational solution. Ultimately it is pointless to speculate on whether Sam is "real" and Watt imaginary (or vice versa), since in point of fact neither exists—both were created by Beckett and both are purely fictional characters.

In the final analysis, *Watt'*s most effective attack on epistemology thus occurs not in Watt's absurd quest for knowledge or in Sam's futile attempts to express absurdity within the confines of rational discourse, but in the text's own resistance to epistemological interpretation. Both Watt and Sam constantly attempt to impose rational interpretations on the events they encounter in the text, and readers who do the same are likely to meet with similarly absurd results. Beckett himself notes in his essay on the van Velde brothers that all one can really know about a painting is whether or not one likes it, and perhaps why (*Disjecta* 123). The same might be said for *Watt.* The task of the reader is not to master or to "know" *Watt* (or any other text) but simply to experience it.

Sam's drive to recuperate Watt's discourse in rational form is an obvious commentary on the efforts of readers who would insist on making sense of *Watt* as a whole. That this commentary still has any relevance at all suggests the enduring power of Enlightenment reading strategies even after a century of radical literary experimentation. Indeed, Sam's recuperation of Watt's language can be read as a sort of allegory of modern literary history, of the way criticism has been able to absorb and assimilate the radical linguistic experiments of the literary avant-garde, stripping them of their subversive power. Joyce's installation as the Great Man of modern literary history is probably the most spectacular example of this kind of cultural appropriation, and it may be no accident that the "deterioration" in Watt's language mirrors the progressive radicalism of Joyce's writing in recognizable ways. But what is even more interesting is the way Watt's linguistic experiments foreshadow the later ones of Beckett himself, which can thus be seen as part of a never-ceasing effort to escape rational recuperation within the bounds of respectable bour-

geois art. That the Nobel laureate Beckett was nevertheless accorded such affirmation and respect from the powers that be serves as a telling reminder of just how difficult it is for any artist to escape inscription within prevailing cultural paradigms. Potentially, however, *Watt* can function as a voice from the past that parodies the cultural appropriation of Beckett's later work and reenergizes the radicalism of that work by demonstrating in the ludicrous epistemological endeavors of Watt and Sam the folly of an uncompromising demand for rational understanding.

CHAPTER *2* TRADITION, AUTHORITY,

AND SUBJECTIVITY:

NARRATIVE CONSTITU-

TION OF THE SELF IN

THE WAVES

In *A Room of One's Own* Virginia Woolf makes clear her antagonism toward the domineering pomposity that she associates with traditional masculine egotism. Male figures in the book tend to be pretentious clods, as in the case of the various "professors" who have presumed to write denigrating histories of women in order to make themselves feel superior by comparison. But Woolf is more concerned with universities than with professors—her targets are not so much specific individuals as the general patriarchal attitudes and institutions that contribute to making those individuals who they are. She notes the way in which men are as much the victims as the promulgators of patriarchal tradition:

> They too, the patriarchs, the professors, had endless difficulties, terrible drawbacks to contend with. Their education had been in some ways as faulty as my own. It had bred in them defects as great. True, they had money and power, but only at the cost of harbouring in their breasts an eagle, a vulture, for ever tearing the liver out and plucking at the lungs—the instinct for possession, the rage for acquisition which drives them to desire other people's fields and goods perpetually; to make frontiers and

flags; battleships and poison gas; to offer up their lives and their children's lives. (38–39)

As Woolf's emphasis on images of acquisition and conquest suggests, she sees patriarchal society as leading to a situation in which individual subjects relate to one another primarily through a mode of conflict, with the dominant victors aggrandizing their own egos at the expense of the subjugated losers.[25] Though Woolf showed an intense engagement with social and political issues, her imagination was highly literary, so it comes as no surprise that one of her principal tropes for this patriarchal mode of subjectivity was the role played by the traditional author. For example, she criticized both James Joyce and Dorothy Richardson for centering their writing on their personal preoccupations, on "the damned egotistical self" (Writer's Diary).[22]

Again, however, Woolf's primary target is not individual authors so much as the institution of authorship as it has developed in patriarchal society. She writes against this conception of authorship everywhere in her work, as when she calls on writers to "practise anonymity" (Writer's Diary 119) or when she praises Shakespeare for having transcended his personal passions in his writing:

All desire to protest, to preach, to proclaim an injury, to pay off a score, to make the world the witness of some hardship or grievance was fired out of him and consumed. Therefore his poetry flows from him free and unimpeded. (Room 58–59)[26]

Woolf herself works against authorial egotism in a variety of ways. In Mrs. Dalloway, for example, she writes almost entirely in a mode of indirect speech, so that most of the narration cannot be attributed simply to an omniscient narrator but is also influenced by various characters in the book. In A Room of One's Own Woolf decenters her own voice more explicitly, employing an "I" with a fluid deixis that points first to one subject, then another, never settling into a representation of a fixed, stable speaker: "'I' is only a convenient term for somebody who has no real being . . . call me Mary Beton, Mary Seton, Mary Carmichael or by any name you please—it is not a matter of any importance" (Room 4–5). And in The Waves Woolf employs six different constantly alternating first-person narrators, so that the continual switching from one speaker to another acts to problematize the association of the "I" of the text with any specific speaking subject.

Woolf's rethinking of traditional notions of subjectivity, and especially of the interplay between subjectivity and gender, has justifiably made her a major figure in feminist literary criticism of the past two decades. Anne Herrmann, reading Woolf as a modernist, looks at her highly critical treatment of the masculine literary tradition and concludes that the resulting dialogue is one of the ways in which "Woolf deconstructs the centered, unified subject as such" (1).[27] Patricia Waugh, on the other hand, argues that the issues of concern to mainline modernists and postmodernists were never really central in the writing of many women, who work to establish their own alternative literary tradition. Importantly, this project also involves the establishment of alternative models of subjectivity, since for women and other marginal groups traditional conceptions of the transcendental self were never relevant anyway: "for those marginalized by the dominant culture, a sense of identity as constructed through impersonal and social relations of power (rather than a sense of identity as the reflection of an inner 'essence') has been a major aspect of their self-concept long before post-structuralists and postmodernists began to assemble their cultural manifestos" (3). The new feminine modes of subjectivity cited by Waugh tend to be collective in nature, emphasizing intersubjective relation rather than subjective autonomy: "Much of women's writing can, in fact, be seen not as an attempt to define an isolated individual ego but to discover a collective concept of subjectivity which foregrounds the construction of identity *in relationship*" (10).[28]

Herrmann and Waugh are both right to a point—Woolf seeks both to deconstruct traditional models of subjectivity and to suggest new ones with an increased emphasis on relationality. This dual movement mirrors the duality of subjectivity in bourgeois society, where the myth of the independent individual contributes to the suppression of any true individuality, an effect especially emphasized by Frankfurt school neo-Marxists such as Adorno and Horkheimer. In both cases Woolf shows a clear understanding of the social construction of the self and of the ways in which that ongoing process of construction involves a complex series of relationships, not only with other subjects, but with various traditions, institutions, social practices, and structures of power that would seek to define and restrict

LITERATURE AND DOMINATION

the kinds of subjectivity that are available in any given case. Importantly, Woolf does not see the "damned egotistical self" that she rails against as a reality but as a cultural myth. The problem is not that we have too many strong, stable individuals roaming around dominating society. On the contrary, the individuals are themselves dominated by this myth of selfhood, and the inability to live up to this myth only exacerbates the already tenuous sense of self so often displayed by characters in Woolf's work—and by people in the modern world.

In her fiction Woolf consistently depicts the efforts of individual characters to construct themselves in relation to others within the matrix of constraints and opportunities that comprise modern civilization, anticipating recent projects such as Foucault's exploration of "technologies of the self" and Greenblatt's work on "self-fashioning" in the Renaissance.[29] It is perhaps in *The Waves* that Woolf's thoughts on this phenomenon are enacted most vividly. This most experimental (and most poetic) of Woolf's "novels" (she herself referred to it as a "play-poem") consists of a series of nine chapters in which six "speakers" perform a series of soliloquies in a highly lyrical poetic style. The speakers—Bernard, Jinny, Louis, Neville, Rhoda, and Susan—are clearly differentiated in terms of their personalities and characteristics, though all of the soliloquies are spoken in the same style regardless of the identity or age of the speaker.[30] While there are instances where one soliloquy seems to answer another, or where the thoughts of one speaker seem to spill over into those of another, in general the speeches resemble internal monologues, as the speakers move through various stages of life from early childhood to old age and death, attempting to narrate identities for themselves in language. There is a poignant seeking and yearning in these speeches as the speakers carefully and tentatively investigate the subjective positions that are available to them in the midst of large cultural forces that tend to define and restrict those positions. Meanwhile, the nine chapters in which these soliloquies occur are each preceded by an "interlude" narrated in an extremely impersonal third-person voice that marks the passage of time during a day (and, analogically, through the lives of the characters). As in the "Time Passes" section of *To the Lighthouse*, there is a certain wistful intimation of mortality in these impersonal interludes, a reminder of the inexorable passing of time and of the inevitability of death.[31] In a warning against egocentrism (and androcentrism) the sun rises, moves across the sky, and sets, while waves break on the shore, totally oblivious to the strivings of the six speakers of the chapters. At the same time, the forces of nature in these interludes can also be read as metaphors for the large cultural and political forces at work in society, forces that often seem similarly unconcerned with the efforts of individual humans.

Perhaps the most effective weapon employed by Woolf against individual egoism in *The Waves* is the style of the book itself. The stylistic sameness of the "speeches" of the various characters has provoked considerable negative reaction among critics, as when David Daiches complains of the book's "rigid" prose (107) or when James Naremore suggests that the inflexible form of the book is "rather stifling" (189). Indeed, as Naremore points out, the style of *The Waves* is not only invariant from character to character but also remains constant over time, even though the characters move from early childhood to old age in the course of the book. By way of contrast, Naremore approvingly notes Joyce's *A Portrait of the Artist as a Young Man*, in which the narrative style gains complexity and sophistication as Stephen Dedalus grows and matures (157).

Joyce's method does seem to provide a more vivid and distinct picture of the individual minds of his characters than does Woolf's, but that may largely be the point.[32] The commonality of style among the speakers in *The Waves* tends to undermine any focus on the "egotistical self" of individual consciousnesses and to support a sense of community among the speakers. At the same time, the consistency of style and tone offers the reader a stable subjective anchor in the text, pointing toward the way in which Woolf is concerned not only with a negative deconstruction of traditional myths of selfhood but also with a positive reconstruction of the self along alternative, communal lines.[33] Importantly, however, this stability resides not in the meaning of the text (which is often highly indeterminate), but in the sheer lyric intensity of the book's language.[34]

The characters in *The Waves* pursue a number of strategies in their efforts to construct themselves, though the central mode of subjective constitution in the book is a narrative one. However, Woolf warns us that narrative self-constitution is often a form of entrapment. She herself radically subverts the conventions of narrative in the construction of *The Waves*, while the various characters in the book discover that the routes available to them are already predetermined by various inherited cultural narratives over which they have no control. It is only Bernard, the novelist, who seems genuinely able to construct new narratives of his own (and to appropriate existing narratives for his own use), and consequently it is Bernard who is most successful at constructing himself in ways that go beyond the mere enactment of stereotypes. Similarly, the successful reader of *The Waves* must go beyond conventional and stereotypical modes of reading in attempting to negotiate Woolf's highly unusual book.

The ways in which the various characters in *The Waves* are often caught within the stereotypical expectations engendered by preexisting narratives are most clearly illustrated in the treatment of Percival, a seventh major character in the book. True to his name, the dashing Percival is a stock figure of masculine heroism who takes on almost mythical dimensions. But despite his considerable talents, Percival is the least free and most predetermined of all the book's characters. Other characters may use Percival as a model against which they define themselves in their own efforts to envision themselves creatively, but Percival himself is already so thoroughly defined by the traditional expectations of his role as hero that he is not free to envision himself. To emphasize Percival's lack of freedom, Woolf gives him no speeches in the book—all we know of Percival comes from others' thoughts about him, and he quite literally has no say in his own constitution as a subject.

At the school attended by Bernard, Louis, and Neville as boys, Percival is admired and worshiped by his schoolmates, particularly for his exploits on the cricket field. Sports such as cricket serve as central vehicles for the establishment of a sense of personal mastery in children. But in the British context, cricket is a game charged with very specific cultural coding, and Percival's athletic accomplishments serve not to open creative avenues for self-constitution but to lock him more firmly into the traditional role of hero. After all, it is on the playing fields of boyhood games that British boys learn the codes of conduct that will later serve them on the battlefields of the British Empire, an association that Joyce's Stephen Dedalus makes clear as he describes his students playing hockey in the "Nestor" chapter of *Ulysses*: "Jousts. Time shocked rebounds, shock by shock. Jousts, slush and uproar of battles, the frozen deathspew of the slain, a shout of spearspikes baited with men's bloodied guts" (27).

In *The Waves*, Louis likewise employs military terms to describe

Percival's heroics on the playing field, though mixing them with religious imagery that indicates the depth of his worship for Percival:

> "His magnificence is that of some mediaeval commander. A wake of light seems to lie on the grass behind him. Look at us trooping after him, his faithful servants, to be shot like sheep, for he will certainly attempt some forlorn enterprise and die in battle." (37)

Indeed, Louis, who respects order and authority more than any of the other speakers, is especially drawn to Percival's boyhood heroics, but as a perennial outsider he is relegated to the outer fringe of Percival's circle of admirers:

> "The boasting boys," said Louis, "have gone now in a vast team to play cricket. They have driven off in their great brake, singing in chorus. . . . How majestic is their order, how beautiful is their obedience! If I could follow, if I could be with them I would sacrifice all I know." (47)

Louis finds the discipline of these boys "marching in troops with badges in their caps" reassuring, yet even as a child desperate for some sense of tradition and stability, he recognizes a dark side to these young proto-Nazis. Their discipline and their love of authority and conformity are, as is often the case with these qualities, accompanied by an intense and sadistic cruelty:

> "But they also leave butterflies trembling with their wings pinched off; they throw dirty pocket-handkerchiefs clotted with blood screwed up into corners. They make little boys sob in dark passages. . . . Yet it is what we wish to be, Neville and I." (47)

Neville, who *despises* authority more than any of the other characters do, is the one who forms the most intense attachment to Percival, partially because Percival is for Neville the object of a homosexual fascination, but also because of the close complicity between a total reliance on authority and a total rejection of it. Neville is fiercely anti-Christian and becomes furious even at the sight of a crucifix, yet his love of Percival also takes on many of the aspects of religious worship, as Neville himself explains: "He takes my devotion; he accepts my tremulous, no doubt abject offering" (48).

But despite such religious imagery, Neville manages to see Percival as a figure of resistance to Christianity, as a sort of pagan god. He describes Percival in the school chapel: "His blue, and oddly inexpressive eyes, are fixed with pagan indifference upon the pillar opposite" (36). But Neville, like Louis, recognizes a certain sinister element in the kind of authority represented by Percival. In the next sentences, Neville goes on to suggest: "He would make an admirable churchwarden. He should have a birch and beat little boys for misdemeanors." The implication is that churchwardens (like Joyce's Baldyhead Dolan) are not sincere in their religious beliefs but are simply involved in a quest for power and domination, desiring a position from which they can sadistically exert their authority over others.

Louis, who has great respect and reverence for traditional religion, clearly sees Percival as a strongly Christian figure, perhaps even as a representation of Christ himself.[35] The language he uses to describe Percival is filled with Christian overtones, as when Percival's disciples are referred to as sheep or as a singing chorus. Indeed, the very different uses to which Louis and Neville put their images of Percival—one to reinforce Christianity, the other to undercut it—illustrate the way in which Percival is so thoroughly constituted by the expectations of others. Moreover, his position is determined not merely by the other characters but also by centuries of patriarchal tradition. Bernard summarizes him perfectly: "He is conventional; he is a hero" (123).

Percival goes away to India to serve in the occupying military forces of the British Empire, not so much because he chooses to do so, but simply because that is what British society expects of a dashing young hero. In India he is to serve as a paradigm of British power, authority, and efficiency. Thus, Bernard visualizes him coming upon an overturned cart that the poor native Indians are of course helpless to right:

"But now, behold, Percival advances; Percival rides a flea-bitten mare, and wears a sun-helmet. By applying the standards of the West, by using the violent language that is natural to him, the bullock-cart is righted in less than five minutes. The Oriental problem is solved. He rides on; the multitude cluster round him, regarding him as if he were—what indeed he is—a God." (136)

Percival is, in fact, very much the same sort of figure as Joseph Conrad's Kurtz, who recommends that imperial forces should approach subjugated peoples by demonstrating "the might of a deity" (*Heart* 123).[36] The suggestion that Percival rides a "flea-bitten mare" indicates a certain irony in Bernard's depiction of him as a godlike hero figure to the Indians, though this irony is complicated by the way in which the English characters (especially Louis and Neville) also view Percival as godlike. But however ambiguous this irony, Woolf makes clear her attitude toward the male bravado underlying the ideology of imperialism. Louis turns out to be correct in his childhood premonition of Percival's death, but that death does not occur in a moment of heroic accomplishment. Like Kurtz, Percival experiences a downfall, but in his case it is more literal—his saddle girth has been insufficiently tightened, causing him to tumble off his horse in a fatal fall. The ideology of military imperialism in which Percival is entrapped leads not to the glorious recovery of the Holy Grail but to abject and meaningless death.

Percival is the most obvious representative of the masculine egotistical self in *The Waves*. Yet even as he functions as a powerful image of patriarchal tradition, he also serves as a victim of that tradition and as an illustration of its folly. The most rigidly defined of all the characters, he is also the least whole, because that definition has been provided strictly by others, and the stultifying effects of the stereotypical expectations of the male role lead to his death and to the waste of his considerable talents. His story thus simultaneously undercuts any number of male cultural myths associated with chivalry, military heroism, imperialism, religion, and the general quest for transcendence. But it also shows Woolf's awareness that the problem is not individual males but the conventions of society that force males into invidious roles. On the other hand, it is also clear in *The Waves* that the same patriarchal attitudes that so limit Percival's freedom also provide opportunities to some of the male characters that are not open to the females. Early in the book, it becomes clear that society expects different things from boys than from girls—the six children are separated according to gender and sent to different schools. Louis, Neville, and Bernard all eventually participate in professions (especially professions related to the symbolic order of language) in productive ways, while Jinny and Susan occupy roles that are largely defined in relation to males, and Rhoda is unable to find any role at all to occupy comfortably. Most importantly, in a situation that resonates with Woolf's discussion in works such as *A Room of One's Own* of male dominance in the literary tradition, none of the women write or are engaged with the literary tradition in the way that all three of the male speakers are.[37] Thus, the women are denied an important arena for self-envisionment that is available to the men, and at least the men have an opportunity to contribute to the making of the narratives that define them in ways that the women do not.

Susan, a sort of earth mother, functions very much as the embodiment of the traditional male fantasy of the eternal feminine. Thus, as Bernard sums up his friends in the book's last chapter, he notes that "[i]t was Susan who first became wholly woman, purely feminine" (247–48). A farm girl, she is highly attuned to nature; she is at home walking in the fields, especially in the early morning before human civilization has gotten into gear: "At this hour, this still early hour, I think I am the field, I am the barn, I am the trees; mine are the flocks of birds, and this young hare who leaps, at the last moment when I step almost on him" (97). Moreover, Susan is the only one of the women in the book who will have children, and she is consistently associated with images of fertility, as when she goes for a walk by the river: "All the world is breeding. The flies are going from grass to grass. The flowers are thick with pollen" (100).

Susan marries a farmer, serves as a dependable helpmate on his farm, bears him sons. In short, she acts out her role as feminine stereotype and performs the duties that are expected of her. But she seems to recognize that she is playing a highly artificial part. Unlike Percival, she does not accept without reflection the role defined for her. Her feelings are often highly ambivalent, and she often both loves and hates the nature images with which she is so identified. And she sees through the stereotypical glorifications of her role as mother:

> "I shall be debased and hide-bound by the bestial and beautiful passion of maternity. I shall push the fortunes of my children unscrupulously. I shall hate those who see their faults. I shall lie basely to help them." (132)

Indeed, Susan (at least internally) often rebels against the role into which she has been cast as traditional wife and mother, recognizing that "I am fenced in, planted here like one of my own trees" (190).

Like her mother before her, she has been domesticated, harnessed like a farm animal, her wild spirit placed beneath the yoke of the quotidian. The earth-goddess image may function as a central cultural myth of motherhood, but real motherhood confines her to household chores that separate her from the nature she loves, leading not to life but to death:

> "I pad about the house all day long in apron and slippers, like my mother who died of cancer. Whether it is summer, whether it is winter, I no longer know by the moor grass, and the heath flower; only by the steam on the window-pane, or the frost on the window-pane. When the lark peels high his ring of sound and it falls through the air like an apple paring, I stoop; I feed my baby. I, who used to walk through beech woods noting the jay's feather turning blue as it falls, past the shepherd and the tramp, who stared as it falls, past the shepherd and the tramp, who stared at the woman squatted beside a tilted cart in a ditch, go from room to room with a duster." (172)

Feeling so trapped in her life, Susan is intensely envious of Jinny, whose life as an unmarried society girl in the city is so different from her own: "I am torn with jealousy. I hate Jinny because she shows me that my hands are red, my nails bitten" (132). Jinny's nails, of course, are perfectly manicured. And whereas Jinny's body is like some delicate musical instrument, Susan's—after yeoman service in the role of wife and mother—is like a dependable farm implement: "My body has been used daily, rightly, like a tool by a good workman, all over" (215). Jinny and Susan are in many ways direct opposites, and the young Jinny feels just as much at home in the city as Susan does in the country: "I am native here. I tread naturally on thick carpets. I slide easily on smooth-polished floors, I now begin to unfurl, in this scent, in this radiance, as a fern when its leaves unfurl" (102). But despite her sophistication, social grace, and apparently greater freedom when compared to Susan, Jinny is equally envious of Susan and equally circumscribed within stereotypical male fantasies.

Although she never marries, Jinny perpetually remains the object, and indeed the creature of the male gaze. She cannot pass a mirror without examining herself carefully, attempting to envision how she would appear to a male viewer. A stranger on a train glances approvingly at her reflection in the window, and she feels herself blossom into existence: "My body instantly of its own accord puts forth a frill under his gaze. My body lives a life of its own" (63). As she walks into a social gathering filled with strangers, she is again constituted as an object for the perusal of the men there. Sensing their reaction to her beauty, she experiences a reassuring feeling of mastery:

"The black-and-white figures of unknown men look at me as I lean forward; as I turn aside to look at a picture, they turn too. Their hands are fluttering to their ties. . . . They are anxious to make a good impression. I feel a thousand capacities spring up in me. I am arch, gay, languid, melancholy by turns." (102)

Whenever Jinny meets a man she wishes to attract, she feels confident that she can do so with her physical beauty and grace, needing no help from her wit: "It does not matter what I say" (104). But of course there is a downside to this situation—the fact that it does not matter what she says indicates both the power and the weakness of her physical attractiveness. Men do not *care* what she says because they regard her as a physical object whose mind need not be taken seriously. They are attracted to her body and only to her body, which they believe is her entire self: "My body goes before me, like a lantern down a dark lane, bringing one thing after another out of darkness into a ring of light. I dazzle you; I make you believe that this is all" (129).

Even as a young girl, the graceful Jinny, athletic and a wonderful dancer, derives her image of herself very much in relation to her own body. At school, she hates small mirrors in which one can see only one's head; for her sense of wholeness, she requires an image of her entire body: "So I skip up the stairs past them, to the next landing, where the long glass hangs, and I see myself entire. I see my body and head in one now; for even in this serge frock they are one, my body and my head" (42). Jinny has a special rapport with her own body and thinks with the "body's imagination" (176), anticipating the commentary on the special relationship that women have with their own bodies in the work of feminists such as Hélène Cixous. But if Susan becomes trapped in the country where she once felt so at home, Jinny eventually becomes a prisoner of her own body, doomed to an existence as a purely physical object, an existence that becomes more and more terrifying as she grows older and begins to lose her beauty. Both she and Susan are trapped in roles in which they can explore only a fraction of the potential selves that they might become.

As the years pass, Jinny becomes less confident in her ability to stand out in a crowd: "I am no longer young. . . . I still live. But who will come if I signal?" (193). So she is forced to rely more and more on makeup and clothing to maintain her physical attractiveness:

> "Therefore I will powder my face and redden my lips. I will make the angle of my eyebrows sharper than usual. I will rise to the surface, standing erect with the others in Piccadilly Circus. I will sign with a sharp gesture to a cab whose driver will signify by some indescribable alacrity his understanding of my signals. For I still excite eagerness. I still feel the bowing of men in the street like the silent stoop of the corn when the light wind blows, ruffling it red." (195)

Looking good to excite male attention is indeed Jinny's profession, which she acknowledges by comparing herself to Louis working in his office: "I have sat before a looking-glass as you sit writing, adding up figures at desks" (221).

Clearly, Jinny is very much a victim, though, like Susan, she does not accept her victimization passively. In her own mind she knows that she is more than a body, and though it is through her body that she excites the response from others that she so desperately needs, she does not succumb to despair as that body loses its charms. And she recognizes that the men whom she manipulates are in turn manipulating her as well, comparing her role as lover to that of the prototypical rape victim Philomela (via T. S. Eliot): "Jug, jug, jug, I sing like the nightingale" (177). But Jinny goes on courageously shoring such fragments as she can against her ruins to the very end, as Bernard explains in his parting summation of her: "When the lock whitened on her forehead she twisted it fearlessly among the rest. So when they come to bury her nothing will be out of order. Bits of ribbon will be found curled up" (275–76).

Such solace in the mastery of small things is not available to Rhoda, who lacks Jinny's feeling of bodily integrity and Susan's feeling of communion with nature. Rhoda avoids being predefined by the traditional narratives of feminine roles in patriarchal society, but, lacking any alternative narratives with which she can identify, she is left with no stable sense of self whatsoever.[38] She suffers greatly from her inability to function in the male symbolic order or to cope with the signs and symbols used in rational discourse. Her difficulties appear specifically as an estrangement from symbols, as in a class-room scene she narrates from her childhood:

> "Now taking her lump of chalk she [the teacher] draws figures, six, seven, eight, and then a cross and then a line on the black-board. The others look; they look with understanding. Louis writes; Susan writes; Neville writes; Jinny writes; even Bernard now has begun to write. But I cannot write. I see only fig-ures. . . . The figures mean nothing now. Meaning has gone." (21)

At this moment of crisis, Rhoda feels her fragile sense of identity beginning to dissolve, an experience that she describes in terms of a loss of temporal (i.e., narrative) continuity: "The world is entire, and I am outside of it, crying, 'Oh, save me, from being blown for ever outside the loop of time!'" (21–22). And later she makes this aspect of her difficulty even more explicit:

> "If I could believe," said Rhoda, "that I should grow old in pursuit and change, I should be rid of my fear: nothing persists. One moment does not lead to another. . . . I cannot make one moment merge into the next. To me they are all violent, all separate. . . . I do not know how to run minute to minute and hour to hour, solving them by some natural force until they make the whole and indivisible mass that you call life." (130)

Rhoda's radical alienation can be described as a general failure of self-envisionment, as an inability to constitute any subjective position that she can comfortably occupy. In an anticipation of Lacan's empha-sis on the importance of the mirror phase in establishing a subjective position, and in contrast to Jinny, Rhoda finds that she is entirely unable to relate to her own reflected image:

> "That is my face," said Rhoda, "in the looking-glass behind Susan's shoulder—that face is my face. But I will duck behind her to hide it, for I am not here. I have no face. Other people have faces; Susan and Jinny have faces; they are here. Their world is the real world. The things they lift are heavy. They say

Yes, they say No; whereas I shift and change and am seen through in a second." (43)

Rhoda is not at home even in her own body, which is "ill-fitting" (105). Her body provides no anchor, and she often feels herself beginning to drift out of it, so that "I have to bang my hand against some hard door to call myself back to the body" (44). She cannot constitute herself even as the object of the gaze, and her sense of being "seen through" goes far beyond the cliché of being unable to hide one's "true" self from the gaze of others. Rhoda, after all, has no "true" self, even provisionally. Her sense of self is so fragmented that she feels her body literally to be too insubstantial to be visible: "even my body now lets the light through; my spine is soft like wax near the flame of the candle" (45).

Rhoda's lack of selfhood is excruciatingly painful to her and often quite debilitating. For example, she has virtually no resources on which to draw to deal with unforeseen situations. At one point she starts to cross a courtyard but is confronted with an unexpected puddle. She is so shaken that even this minor obstacle triggers a major crisis in her life: "I could not cross it. Identity failed me. We are nothing, I said, and fell. I was blown like a feather. I was wafted down tunnels" (64).

This sense of dissolution and insubstantiality, coupled with her loss of temporal connectedness, is a frequently observed symptom of life in the modern world, but Woolf shows in her depiction of Rhoda a particular understanding of the role that gender can play in this modern loss of subjective stability.[39] The special difficulty that Rhoda faces as a woman can be seen especially clearly by comparing her to Louis, with whom she shares so much. Both are outsiders, both display a fundamental inability to feel at home and at ease in their surroundings. But whereas Louis is able to stabilize himself through an identification with authority, no such solution is available to Rhoda. Louis will grow up to exert control over a business empire that involves ships that sail around the globe. The closest Rhoda can come to this accomplishment occurs in the childhood game in which she floats white petals in a basin of water, pretending that they are ships. By tilting the basin or dropping objects into it, Rhoda can control the movement of these "ships," thus gaining some sense of mastery (18–19). But in the presence of others, this provisional sense of security dissolves, and she feels helpless. Lacking skills such as Susan's ability to sew or Jinny's ability to dance, she has nothing with which to guarantee her own coherence:

> "Alone, I rock my basins; I am mistress of my fleet of ships. But here, twisting the tassels of this brocaded curtain in my hostess's window, I am broken into separate pieces; I am no longer one." (106)

Among the other speakers, it is Louis to whom Rhoda is closest. As Rhoda undergoes her crisis in the classroom, Louis senses her discomfort and sympathizes: "She has no body as the others have. And I, who speak with an Australian accent, whose father is a banker in Brisbane, do not fear her as I fear the others" (22). Much in the mode of Stephen Dedalus, who because his father is not a magistrate feels a sense of isolation and shame at Clongowes Wood in Joyce's *A Portrait of the Artist as a Young Man,* the young Louis is intensely aware of his foreign accent and of the fact that his father the banker was a failure at his profession. So it is only natural that he and Rhoda should be attracted to one another and perhaps unsurprising that they eventually become lovers.

Indeed, Rhoda and Louis share a special interpersonal communication (in some ways reminiscent of that shared by Peter Walsh and Clarissa Dalloway). The speeches of most of the characters are generally presented as separate soliloquies with no dialogic interaction. But during the two key gatherings of the adult characters (the first to bid farewell to Percival as he departs for India, the second a later reunion dinner at Hampton Court), there are moments when the speeches of Louis and Rhoda are enclosed together within parentheses, indicating a special private communication between the two of them (140–41, 226–27). And after the reunion dinner, when the friends decide to walk out into the garden, Rhoda and Louis linger together behind the others, "[l]ike conspirators who have something to whisper" (227).

Yet both Louis and Rhoda seem ultimately incapable of genuinely relating to others, so it also comes as no surprise that their relationship fails:

> "If we could mount together, if we could perceive from a sufficient height," said Rhoda, "if we could remain untouched with-

out any support—but you, disturbed by faint clapping sounds of praise and laughter, and I, resenting compromise and right and wrong on human lips, trust only in solitude and the violence of death and thus are divided."

"For ever," said Louis, "divided." (231)

However, whereas Rhoda's sense of isolation drives her apart from society and eventually to suicide, Louis's drives him into the very mainstream of society, where he seeks to compensate for his outsider status by showing an inflated respect for tradition and authority and by becoming an overachiever, first as the star pupil in his school days and then in the world of business.

Louis's reliance on figures of authority to provide a stabilizing center to his life can be seen in his admiration for Percival and also in his reaction to Dr. Crane, the headmaster of the school attended by Louis, Bernard, and Neville: "Dr. Crane mounts the pulpit and reads the lesson from a Bible spread on the back of the brass eagle. I rejoice; my heart expands in his bulk, in his authority" (34). This ability to identify with patriarchal tradition and authority gives Louis a narrative in which he can participate and allows him to establish a certain sense of belonging and continuity that is not available to Rhoda:

> "Now all is laid by his authority, his crucifix, and I feel come over me the sense of the earth under me, and my roots going down and down till they wrap themselves round some hardness at the centre. I recover my continuity, as he reads. I become a figure in the procession, a spoke in the huge wheel that turning, at last erects me, here and now." (35)

This notion of being part of a long tradition, of having roots, occupies Louis's thoughts almost continuously—as when he frequently fantasizes having descended from the ancient Egyptians. This same longing for integration also informs Louis's interactions with the present. Even after achieving success, he remains a "strange mixture of assurance and timidity" (119), perpetually uncertain of acceptance, tending to observe and imitate the motions of the people around him in an effort to make them feel that he is one of them. And any symbol of substance and security holds great attractions for him:

> "I love punctually at ten to come into my room; I love the purple glow of the dark mahogany; I love the table and its sharp edge;

and the smooth-running drawers. I love the telephone with its lip stretched to my whisper, and the date on the wall; and the engagement book." (168)

Eventually, Louis becomes a stereotypical image of male success: "I have inherited a desk of solid mahogany in a room hung with maps" (219). His male mastery extends across the globe in the worldwide ventures of his company: "The globe is strung with our lines. I am immensely respectable" (200). Yet Louis pays a price for his success. He is both stabilized and victimized by the authority to which he appeals. It allows him to assume a role that yields him a sense of mastery, but it defines that role for him and limits his ability to go beyond the expectations of that role. He remains cold, aloof, and alone.

Louis, like Jinny and especially like Susan, recognizes the restrictions that have been placed on his freedom. Despite his Eliotic sense of the solidity of tradition, he displays a typically modernist sense of a crisis in that tradition, recognizing something sinister about it. His musings on the importance of tradition are frequently accompanied by the ominous image of a "chained beast stamping," waiting like the rough beast of Yeats to bring down the present order. And Louis also has a private strategy of resistance to authority, retaining even in his success a small, attic room to which he can repair after a day at the office to read poetry and think poetic thoughts.

Louis may read the poems of others with admiration, but in his unwavering acquiescence to authority he is unable to write poetry of his own. Though he retains, like Leopold Bloom, a touch of the artist, he is unable to express himself poetically, is limited to the positing of "unwritten poetry" (66). The female speakers may be unable to write poetry because of their lack of connection to the male symbolic order, but Louis suffers a similar inability because of being overly connected to that order. Indeed, one of the central themes of *The Waves* (emphasized by the lyric intensity of all the soliloquies) seems to be that all of us have poetry within us but patriarchal society often tends to repress those poetic impulses. In *The Waves*, then, Woolf uses her own poetic talents to give expression to the poetic thoughts of the characters (Rhoda, Susan, Jinny, Louis) who are unable to write poetry for themselves.

One character who *is* able to write poetry is Neville, who in fact becomes a successful poet in adulthood. Neville seems the antithesis of Louis in his attitude toward authority and tradition, and it is his staunch refusal to submit to authority that gives him the freedom to write that Louis lacks. Thus, whereas Louis reveres Dr. Crane and the tradition he represents, Neville reacts to the headmaster with revulsion and ridicule:

> "This brute menaces my liberty," said Neville, "when he prays. Unwarmed by imagination, his words fall cold on my head like paving-stones, while the gilt cross heaves on his waistcoat. The words of authority are corrupted by those who speak them." (35)

Yet despite his constant rebellion against authority, Neville remains intensely concerned with order. As his reverence for Percival shows, Neville's rebellion disguises a deep need for the security of some anchoring center, which he will seek throughout life in the series of lovers who come and go, worshiping them like gods and then suffering terribly when they move on.[40] His great need is "to offer my being to one god; and perish, and disappear" (52). He is still defined in relation to authority, even if that relation in his case is exclusionary as opposed to Louis's strategy of identification.

One might compare Neville to Joyce's Stephen Dedalus, who reacts so violently against the Catholic church that church teachings inform his every thought. As Stephen's friend Cranly tells him in *Portrait*, "It is a curious thing . . . how your mind is supersaturated with the religion in which you say you disbelieve" (240).[41] Indeed, for Neville as for Stephen, poetry functions as a substitute for religion. As he begins to learn language in early childhood, Neville marvels at its order and structure: "'Each tense,' said Neville, 'means differently. There is an order in this world; there are distinctions, there are differences in this world'" (21). Unable to accommodate the mess, he, like Robert Frost (and like Stephen Dedalus), constructs his poems as a momentary stay against the confusion of history. Indeed, Neville pays the same sort of tribute to poetic tradition, represented by poets such as Pope, Dryden, Catullus, and Shakespeare, that Louis pays to the traditions of patriarchal society.

In fact, of all the characters in *The Waves*, Louis and Neville are clearly the most alike. Both are neat, punctual, meticulous, and fastidious, and both have difficulty relating to others, even if Louis shows this difficulty by attempting to meet the expectations of others whereas Neville shows it by defiantly refusing to do so. Neville is, in short, almost as thoroughly determined by authority as is Louis, both because of his own search for an alternative to the existing patriarchal order and because, by reacting so directly against that order, he allows it to determine the positions he is able to occupy.

Bernard, like Neville, is a professional writer. However, as a novelist he is less concerned with order than is the poet Neville, and it is in contrast to Neville that Bernard's style of personal constitution begins to become clear. Bernard tries to accommodate the mess, to recognize and accept the flux and impermanence of history. He explains the difference between himself and his friend: "above all he desires order, and detests my Byronic untidiness; and so draws his curtain; and bolts his door. . . . All changes. And youth and love" (90). Whereas Neville seeks in his writing to shut out life, Bernard seeks to encompass and incorporate it. Bernard is more successful in avoiding the determination of his own identity by existing narratives because he does not simply react against them but appropriates them to make them his own. He is characterized by flexibility, sympathy, and compromise, neither accepting authority with the blind acquiescence of Louis nor opposing it with the rigidity of Neville. As a result, his sense of self is fluid, multiple, and complex:

> "I am not one and simple, but complex and many. . . . That is what they do not understand, for they are now undoubtedly discussing me, saying I escape them, am evasive. They do not understand that I have to effect different transitions; have to cover the entrances and exits of several different men who alternately act their parts as Bernard." (76)

Bernard consistently shows this all-the-world's-a-stage attitude in his approach to life.[42] In a moment of special insight, he suggests: "I was like one admitted behind the scenes: like one shown how the effects are produced" (266). Bernard seems quite conscious of his attempts to constitute himself through narrative, viewing himself as a participant in a play or as a literary character. He often sees his life as it might be described by a biographer, and he frequently refers to himself in third person or even addresses himself directly. Moreover, many of his own models are highly literary, though the heroes with whom he identifies turn out to include a dialogic mixture of figures of authority and figures of rebellion:[43] "For I changed and changed; was Hamlet, was Shelley, was the hero, whose name I now forget, of a novel by Dostoevsky; was for a whole term, incredibly, Napoleon; but was Byron chiefly" (249). In short, Bernard constitutes himself very much in the same way that he writes his novels, assimilating bits and pieces of experience, especially other people and other authors, into a heterogeneous whole. As Louis punningly notes of him: "He is composed" (30).

Among other things, Bernard's recognition of the fictionalized nature of identity lends him the flexibility to continue his self-constitution indefinitely without ever becoming fixed in any single role. He thus becomes a paradigm of the creative constitution of the self. At first glance, his view of his own life as a literary work is similar to the attitude of modern authors like Norman Mailer, who announces that "the first art work in an artist is the shaping of his own personality" (284). However, whereas Mailer's advertisements for himself make him the center of his own fictions in an overt effort at the kind of self-aggrandizement that Woolf associates with masculine egotism, the self that Bernard constructs is thoroughly decentered and oriented toward others. He views not just himself but everyone he meets in terms of the narratives in which they might participate as characters. Neville realizes this tendency even in childhood: "Bernard says there is always a story. I am a story. Louis is a story. There is the story of the boot-boy, the story of the man with one eye, the story of the woman who sells winkles" (37–38). In short, "We are all phrases in Bernard's story, things he writes down in his notebook under A or under B" (70). Importantly, though, Bernard's narratives do not cast people in rigid roles, nor does he expect the messiness of reality to be rigidly ordered by his narratives:

> "Life is not susceptible perhaps to the treatment we give it when we try to tell it. Sitting up late at night it seems strange not to have more control. Pigeon-holes are not then very useful." (267)

And though Bernard at times yearns after "one true story" that will explain everything, he knows that it will never be found, because something has always been left out of any story that we can tell:

"Let a man get up and say, 'Behold, this is the truth,' and instantly I perceive a sandy cat filching a piece of fish in the background. Look, you have forgotten the cat, I say." (187)

Although we do not actually see any excerpts from the novels that Bernard writes, his nontotalizing conception of narrative seems to have much in common with Woolf's own in *The Waves*, a book she characterized as having been written "to a rhythm not to a plot" (*The Diary*, Vol. 3, 316).[44] Bernard's stories similarly refuse to be driven inexorably onward by plot, not surprisingly causing discomfort in those, like Neville, who feel that literature is meant to provide order to life: "Bernard's stories amuse me . . . at the start. But when they tail off absurdly and he gapes, twiddling a bit of string, I feel my own solitude. He sees every one with blurred edges." (51)

Because of his occupation as novelist, it is not surprising that Bernard's discourse gradually becomes dominant in the book, finally taking over the narration entirely in the final summing up.[45] In doing so Bernard subsumes the identities of the other five speakers:

"I am not one person; I am many people; I do not altogether know who I am—Jinny, Susan, Neville, Rhoda, or Louis: or how to distinguish my life from theirs. . . . I have been talking of Bernard, Neville, Jinny, Susan, Rhoda and Louis. Am I all of them? Am I one and distinct? I do not know." (276, 288)

Indeed, Bernard's relations with other people involve an intense sense of interrelatedness and identification as opposed to the isolation felt by Neville and Louis, who remain thoroughly enclosed within themselves just as they remain circumscribed within the fields of force exerted by authority and tradition. In the company of others Louis and Neville feel threatened; they retreat defensively within themselves. But Bernard opens up even to strangers, like a flower to the sun, seeking to merge his own identity with theirs:

"Louis and Neville," said Bernard, "both sit silent. Both are absorbed. Both feel the presence of other people as a separating wall. But if I find myself in company with other people, words at once make smoke rings—see how phrases at once begin to wreathe off my lips. An elderly and apparently prosperous man, a traveller, now gets in. And I at once wish to approach him; I instinctively dislike the sense of his presence, cold, assimilated, among us. I do not believe in separation. We are not single." (67)

Bernard seems able to relate to anyone, to horse breeders and plumbers as well as to scholars, poets, aristocrats, and his own friends—and the more the better: "My being only glitters when all its facets are exposed to many people" (186). Indeed, Bernard's own sense of self is defined largely in relation to the various people he meets, whoever they may be: "Thus my character is in part made of the stimulus which other people provide, and is not mine" (133).[46] This dependence on others is in many ways reminiscent of Jinny, as when Bernard himself explains: "I need an audience" (115). However, Bernard is able to take a much more active role in his own strategies of constitution than is Jinny, particularly through the construction of narratives that give meaning to his experience as he observes the world around him: "And striking off these observations spontaneously I elaborate myself" (115). In contrast to Jinny, Bernard is an observer, not an object of observation—when he experiences his escape from the self late in the book, he notes: "I saw but was not seen" (286).

This ability to observe life without dominating the observations with the projections of his own personality makes Bernard in many ways Woolf's ideal of the artist. His intense feeling of relatedness to others prevents him from assuming the traditional role of the ego-tistical male author. Moreover, he shows a powerful negative ca-pability that enables him to assimilate a wide variety of experience, giving him a symphonic richness of perspective that is lacking in the monotonic viewpoints of Louis and Neville:

> "And I am so made, that, while I hear one or two distinct melo-dies, such as Louis sings, or Neville, I am also drawn irresistibly to the sound of the chorus chanting its old, chanting its almost wordless, almost senseless song that comes across courts at night." (246)

The song heard by Bernard here is reminiscent of that of the singing "battered old woman" from *Mrs. Dalloway* (122–23). Sandra Gilbert sees this old woman as one of Woolf's "most striking female artists" (218). However, as I have discussed elsewhere, the old woman's song is filtered through the consciousness of the male Peter Walsh, so that it in fact includes aspects of both sexes (*Techniques* 174). But this combination of perspectives is precisely that privileged by Woolf in her discussions of the ideal artist, in which she emphasizes the necessity of a certain amount of androgyny before creation can take place at all. In *Room* she notes that

> It is fatal to be a man or woman pure and simple; one must be woman-manly or man-womanly. . . . Some collaboration has to take place in the mind between the woman and the man before the act of creation can be accomplished. Some marriage of opposites has to be consummated. (108)

Woolf figures this notion of the androgynous artist most vividly in her picture of the mythical "Anon, who wrote so many poems without signing them" (*Room* 51). Woolf explores the figure of Anon at great length in a late essay by that title, noting particularly the primal qualities of Anon as a nameless, androgynous singer, dating back to the silence of the primeval forest:

> The voice that broke the silence of the forest was the voice of Anon. Some one heard the song and remembered it for it was later written down, beautifully, on parchment. . . . Every body shared in the emotion of Anons [sic] song, and supplied the story. Anon sang because spring has come; or winter is gone; because he loves; because he is hungry, or lustful; or merry; or because he adores some God. Anon is sometimes man; sometimes woman. ("Anon" 382)[47]

Anon's song is reminiscent of that heard by Bernard, who is similarly able to take on the characteristics of both sexes: "For this is not one life; nor do I always know if I am man or woman, Bernard or Neville, Louis, Susan, Jinny or Rhoda—so strange is the contact of one with another" (281). In fact, as an artist he is highly androgynous: "'joined to the sensibility of a woman' (I am here quoting my biographer) 'Bernard possessed the logical sobriety of a man'" (76).[48]

For Woolf, the historical artist who comes closest to matching the mythical Anon is Shakespeare, whom she celebrates for both his selflessness and his androgyny as an artist. Drawing on Coleridge's suggestion that the truly great mind is an androgynous one, she thus notes that "one goes back to Shakespeare's mind as the type of the androgynous, of the man-womanly mind" (*Room* 102). Significantly, Shakespeare is also an important predecessor of Bernard, who often wanders about mumbling quotations from Shakespeare to himself as counters to the demands of everyday life: "'Hark, hark, the dogs do bark,' 'Come away, come away, death,' 'Let me not to the marriage of true minds,' and so on" (259).

Woolf's image of Shakespeare as the androgynous artist who serves as a sort of melting pot for diverse opinions and attitudes represents an understanding of Shakespeare's work that has been common since Coleridge's suggestion of Shakespearean androgyny and Keats's comments on negative capability. It also closely anticipates Greenblatt's more recent discussion of Shakespeare's knack for "empathy," for being able to see things from the positions of others. Indeed, Greenblatt's suggestion that this empathy is related to an ability to submit to "self-fashioning" through narrative makes the parallel between Shakespeare and Bernard here particularly clear.[49]

On the other hand, Greenblatt's realization that this same empathy is also the special genius of Iago—for whom "imagined self-loss conceals its opposite: a ruthless displacement and absorption of the other" (236)—indicates a dark side to this process of narrative self-constitution. Woolf is far too subtle and sophisticated as an artist and as a thinker to believe that Bernard's mode of interactive subjectivity will result in an immediate and magical solution of all the problems facing modern society. Despite the success of many of his strategies, Bernard is far from immune to the same large cultural forces that are so stultifying for the other characters. He often feels oppressed by the mechanical nature of everyday life and by the way in which conventional expectations of behavior "compel us to walk in step like civilised people with the slow and measured tread of policemen" (259). In some ways Bernard does conform to these expectations, and on one level he is a highly conventional solid citizen, a professional success with a small inheritance from his uncle, a loyal husband and father. But there are "many Bernards" (260), and his personality goes far beyond this conventional side, especially in his use of literature as a weapon against the life-sapping banality of the quotidian.[50]

The sense of merger with others that Bernard feels contributes to this multiplicity of self, but it is sometimes so overwhelming that he is in danger of losing himself entirely. Such times can be frightening even for Bernard, but they can be even more frightening for those around him. Bernard's attempts to fuse with others are sometimes perceived as threatening, especially by those such as Neville for whom the idea of merging with the other is seen as a challenge to his own identity, rather than as an opportunity for fulfilling interaction. At one point Neville sees Bernard approach and begins to feel threatened by what he knows will be an attempt at intimacy:

> "Yet how painful . . . to have one's self adulterated, mixed up, become part of another. As he approaches I become not myself but Neville mixed with somebody—with whom?—with Bernard? Yes, it is Bernard, and it is to Bernard that I shall put the question, Who am I?" (83)

The images of merger and fusion in Woolf's depiction of Bernard, related to the experience of Freud's "oral" stage (often referred to as the "oceanic feeling"), are inherently contradictory, involving both a blissful feeling of merger and a threatening feeling of engulfment.[51] Indeed, there are ways in which Bernard's diffuse personality resembles that of Rhoda, who finally dissolves entirely.[52] The highly equivocal nature of Bernard's knack for merger becomes especially clear in the final pages of the book as he at last succeeds for a brief moment in escaping his selfhood entirely. This experience has frightening and disorienting aspects, though it is finally positive. Unlike Rhoda, Bernard has a strong enough sense of self that he is able to return to the world from this moment of vision with a new intuitive knowledge; and even though he knows that he will never be able to express this knowledge in words, he is still filled with the poetry of the moment.[53] At last "[t]his difference we make so much of, this identity we so feverishly cherish, was overcome" (289).

At this moment Bernard's negative capability is at its peak:

> "Here on my brow is the blow I got when Percival fell. Here on the nape of my neck is the kiss Jinny gave Louis. My eyes fill with Susan's tears. I see far away, quivering like a gold thread, the pillar Rhoda saw, and feel the rush of the wind in her flight when she slept." (289)

Not only does he experience this intense sense of sharing, but the world is filled with poetry and beauty. Yet one cannot escape reality merely by thinking poetic thoughts, and suddenly reality returns with a vengeance.[54] With the disgust of his old model Hamlet, Bernard acknowledges this abject return:

> "Lord, how unutterably disgusting life is! What dirty tricks it plays us, one moment free; the next, this. Here we are among the breadcrumbs and the stained napkins again. That knife is already congealing with grease. Disorder, sordidity and corruption surround us. We have been taking into our mouths the bodies of dead birds." (292)

But there is more at stake here than a simple recognition of human physical mortality. Bernard's antivision also includes the everyday forces of society that conspire to limit personal freedom:

> "Always it begins again; always there is the enemy; eyes meeting ours; fingers twitching ours; the effort waiting. Call the waiter. Pay the bill. We must pull ourselves up out of our chairs. We must find our coats. We must go. Must, must, must—detestable word." (293)

Successful creative self-envisionment requires eternal vigilance. It is an activity that must never end, lest we stagnate and succumb to the banality of cliché and the predictability of the expected. But Bernard faces this formidable task bravely. Faced with the ultimate modernist sense of crisis, he responds not with quietism and despair but with determination and bold action. Refusing to suffer passively the slings and arrows of outrageous fortune, Bernard elects to take arms against a sea of troubles, though knowing full well that he cannot finally by opposing end them. Like Gabriel Conroy at the end of "The Dead," Bernard narrates himself into a typical scene of knightly heroism, but unlike Gabriel he eschews the egotistical illusions of the traditional male hero. Moreover, whereas Gabriel turns toward death, Bernard turns toward life, continuing his battle valiantly to the end, riding forth against death with a final brave cry: "Against you I will fling myself, unvanquished and unyielding, O Death!" (297).

And so Bernard, like the dying Hamlet, succumbs to his fate.[55] But the text is not finished. The impersonal narrator of the interludes absents herself from felicity a while longer, lingering in the text to add one final line to Bernard's story: *"The waves broke on the shore"* (297). And so at last the world is literally seen without a self. In her closing statement of the folly of masculine vanity and its associated drive for domination, Woolf reminds us that, despite the heroism of Bernard's dying defiance, life goes on whenever individuals die. We are none of us the indispensable center of the world, regardless of how much we would like to think so. Bernard's final heroism is that he opposes death not in an effort to evade mortality but in open recognition and acceptance of it. Like Beckett's Unnamable, Bernard knows that he can't go on, but he goes on anyway, as long as he can— which is about the best any of us can hope to do.

CHAPTER *3*   ADORNO, ALTHUSSER,

AND HUMBERT HUMBERT:

NABOKOV'S *LOLITA* AS

NEO-MARXIST CRITIQUE

OF BOURGEOIS

SUBJECTIVITY

The fiction of Vladimir Nabokov has been widely discussed and justifiably admired for its linguistic virtuosity and formal brilliance. Few critics, however, have explored the social and political dimensions of Nabokov's work, perhaps largely because of Nabokov's own denials that his work *had* such dimensions. In thinking of Nabokov and politics, one turns immediately to works like *Bend Sinister* and *Invitation to a Beheading,* both of which depict in excruciating detail the horrifying human cost of totalitarian political regimes. Yet we have Nabokov's own disclaimer of political interests in his author's introduction to *Bend Sinister*:

> I have never been interested in what is called the literature of social comment . . . I am neither a didacticist nor an allegorizer. Politics and economics, atomic bombs, primitive and abstract art forms, the entire Orient, symptoms of "thaw" in Soviet Russia, the Future of Mankind, and so on, leave me supremely indifferent. (vi)

Nabokov, apparently sitting atop the Olympus of "pure art," here seems to deny that he has any interest in real-world events at all.

Indeed, he goes on to proclaim that *Bend Sinister* bears no relationship to the political and historical context within which it was written:

> Similarly, the influence of my epoch on my present book is as negligible as the influence of my books, or at least of this book, on my epoch. There can be distinguished, no doubt, certain reflections in the glass directly caused by the idiotic and despicable regimes that we all know and that have brushed against me in the course of my life: worlds of tyranny and torture, of Fascists and Bolshevists, of Philistine thinkers and jack-booted baboons. No doubt, too, without those infamous models before me I could not have larded this fantasy with bits of Lenin's speeches, and a chunk of the Soviet constitution, and gobs of Nazist pseudo-efficiency. (vii)

A curious denial indeed—one that calls specific attention to the "reflections" of specific totalitarian regimes in his book, even signaling the reader to be on the alert for specific allusions to the authoritarian practices of both Soviet Russia and Nazi Germany.

Clearly, Nabokov's work is not so entirely divorced from its historical context as Nabokov would apparently like us to believe. Indeed, one of the positive critical trends of the past decade has been a growing recognition that *no* work is entirely independent of the social, political, and ideological context of its specific historical moment. In the case of works like *Invitation to a Beheading* and *Bend Sinister*, the dialogue with totalitarianism, especially Stalinism, is so direct that the political intonation of the works is quite obvious. But even a work like *Lolita*, a spectacular demonstration of verbal dexterity without obvious references to any particular political programs, can have strong political implications, as critics are coming to see. Dana Brand, for example, notes the way the treatment of popular culture (especially advertising) in *Lolita* provides a powerful commentary on American consumer society. And Elizabeth Deeds Ermarth notes certain parallels between Nabokov's verbal experiments and the work of Julia Kristeva, both of which unsettle traditional notions about language and subjectivity.

Neither Brand nor Ermarth makes reference to neo-Marxist political theory, but both point toward an understanding of the political significance of Nabokov's work that can be greatly enhanced by an appeal to the work of such theorists as Theodor Adorno and Louis

Althusser. Both Adorno and Althusser focus much of their critiques of bourgeois society on the formation and functioning of the human subject within the context of that society, and it is in this same area that a work like *Lolita* functions most powerfully as a social and political statement. Nabokov's own critical attitude toward bourgeois society shows through in his Cornell lecture notes on Flaubert's *Madame Bovary*, itself an important source and model for *Lolita*. Beginning the lecture with a typical Nabokovian proclamation that "literature is of no practical value whatsoever" (*Lectures* 125), Nabokov goes on to explain Flaubert's use of the term *bourgeois* as a synonym for "'philistine,' people preoccupied with the material side of life and believing only in conventional values" (126). From the tone here and from comments elsewhere one can surmise that Nabokov endorses Flaubert's critique of philistinism, though he specifically distances himself from a critique of bourgeois society in a Marxist sense by arguing that by Flaubert's definition Marx himself was a bourgeois thinker, "a philistine in his attitude towards the arts" (127).

Nabokov's assessment of Marx as "bourgeois" is debatable—one might compare Terry Eagleton's contrary notation of "Marx's impressively erudite allusions to world literature" (1).[56] In any case, modern neo-Marxists in the West have consistently treated literature as a privileged discourse and as a potential locus of powerful subversive energies within the framework of bourgeois society.[57] But Nabokov's attempt here to implicate both Marxism and bourgeois thought in a single criticism is not unusual. For example, his attacks on Stalinism often included a suggestion of the philistine vulgarity of Stalin's regime, but this critique tends to extend to the vulgarity of much American culture as well.[58] Indeed, David Rampton suggests that Nabokov's attempts to initiate two-pronged attacks on the tyranny of totalitarianism and the vulgarity of American popular culture ultimately undermine the effectiveness of his criticism of either (42–43). In *Lolita*, however, Nabokov's satire seems directed almost entirely at American culture. Perhaps, then, it is not so terribly surprising that the critique of bourgeois ideology in *Lolita* resonates with such critiques in the work of commentators like Adorno and Althusser in a way far richer than Nabokov himself might like to believe. For example, Humbert Humbert's drive for mastery and domination of everything and everyone that he encounters in *Lolita* (including his own internal nature) resonates quite directly with the comments of Adorno and Max Horkheimer on the ideology of domination that they see as central to Enlightenment (i.e., bourgeois) thought. Humbert is in some ways the paradigmatic bourgeois subject, fiercely individualistic yet ultimately constrained by his own drive for personal dominance, both of the girl Lolita and of life in general. And Nabokov's depiction of the way the various characters in *Lolita* are determined by preexisting cultural forces provides a vivid illustration of Althusser's comments on the constitution of the subject by ideology in bourgeois society.

Early in *Lolita* Humbert sets the tone of sexual domination that will pervade the entire text. In his first sexual encounter with the nymphet Lolita, he secretly masturbates with the girl's legs sprawled across his lap, and his own description of the scene clearly indicates the drive for mastery that motivates him. After some initial uncertainty over the feasibility of this maneuver, Humbert reaches a point where he feels that success (i.e., orgasm) is assured:

> What had begun as a delicious distension of my innermost roots became a glowing tingle which *now* had reached that state of absolute security, confidence, and reliance not found elsewhere in conscious life. With the deep hot sweetness thus established and well on its way to the ultimate convulsion, I felt I could slow down in order to prolong the glow. Lolita had been safely solipsized. (62, Nabokov's italics)

"Security, confidence, and reliance" assured, mastery achieved, Humbert has now safely converted Lolita into an object of his own desires, effectively obliterating her own subjective identity. He himself later acknowledges that in this act, "[w]hat I had possessed was not she, but my own creation, another, fanciful Lolita" (64). Lolita, in short, is entirely commodified, and Humbert, that erstwhile critic of consumerism, consumes the girl with gleeful greed.[59]

In some ways, masturbation (the ultimate sexual expression of bourgeois individualism) provides even more sexual mastery than does sadism, since in this act the Other is indeed "safely solipsized." The element of mastery inherent in this scene is reinforced by the fact that Lolita (munching away on a suggestively symbolic apple) is apparently unaware of what is going on, so that Humbert can pursue his quest for orgasm without any consideration of her possibly conflicting desires—a motif that will recur in his later plan to drug the girl so that he can molest her in her sleep without her knowledge. Thus, according to Humbert, his masturbation had "affected her as little as if she were a photographic image rippling upon a screen and I a humble hunchback abusing myself in the dark" (64). He himself acknowledges his feeling of power and domination in this scene by proclaiming that in delaying his orgasm as long as possible "I was a radiant and robust Turk, deliberately, in the full consciousness of his freedom, postponing the moment of actually enjoying the youngest and frailest of his slaves" (62).

It is clear that a major part of Humbert's fascination with "nymphets" derives from their relative helplessness, from the relative ease with which they can be dominated, allowing him to shore up his sense of self through the exertion of his power over them. Yet this domination is highly paradoxical—the strictures of society dictate that Humbert's quest for nymphets go largely unfulfilled, so (prior to Lolita) his mastery of nymphets is restricted to his own imagination (where he, of course, reigns supreme) and to encounters with prostitutes (where he, as a paying customer purchasing a specific commodity, is again in charge). In addition, nymphets represent for Humbert an anterior lost innocence, and thus function as emblems of the impossibility of mastery in a hopelessly fallen world. It is this tension between Humbert's drive for mastery and his simultaneous realization of the impossibility of achieving that mastery that gives the book much of its energy.

That Humbert's quest for sexual gratification is consistently a drive to achieve a sense of personal mastery is obvious from any number of passages in *Lolita*. Humbert constantly reminds us (and himself) of his overwhelming handsomeness and sexual attractiveness. He thus claims early in the book that he could probably have his pick of the world's beauties, but suggests that he chose "fat Valeria" for his early bride because she was "a soothing presence, a glorified *pot-au-feu*, an animated merkin," and most of all because of "the imitation she gave of a little girl" (27). In short, she was someone he could dominate and treat as an object, without fear that she would rebel.[60] And he reinforces this domination with physical brutality, often forcing Valeria into compliance with his point of view by twisting her "brittle wrist." But he miscalculates: she *is* a person, and the marriage goes awry. Valeria refuses to conform to his stereotypical notions of what she should be. She "acquired a queer restlessness; even showed something like irritation at times, which was quite out of keeping with the stock character she was supposed to impersonate" (29).

Valeria takes a lover and announces her plans to leave, destroying Humbert's illusions of mastery. He is astounded that she could take such decisive action, "because matters of legal and illegal conjunction were for me alone to decide, and here she was, Valeria, the comedy wife, brazenly preparing to dispose in her own way of my comfort and fate" (30). So the marriage ends in divorce, and Humbert decides to restrict himself to nymphets, who will presumably be more pliable, especially since they exist for him primarily as phantoms.

But Humbert's fantasies take a dark turn into reality when he meets Lolita, and especially when the death of Charlotte Haze delivers the little girl into his hands. Humbert clearly derives a great deal of satisfaction from the authority implied by his nominal position as Lolita's father. And her social and economic dependence on him greatly increases this sense of mastery, since, as he explains, "she had absolutely nowhere else to go" (144). But his domination of Lolita is not so firm as one might think. He spends much of his time developing methods to keep the sometimes rebellious child "in submission" (150), including a variety of bribes, threats, and even physical violence. As he himself puts it, "I succeeded in terrorizing Lo" (153). In his drive to master Lolita, to convert her into his possession, Humbert attempts to make her a creature of myth rather than a "typical kid picking her nose while engrossed in the lighter sections of a newspaper." He also longs to exert complete dominion over her body, inside and out:

> My only grudge against nature was that I could not turn my Lolita inside out and apply voracious lips to her young matrix, her unknown heart, her nacreous liver, the sea-grapes of her lungs, her comely twin kidneys. (167)

In short, no matter how much mastery he achieves, the fundamentally insecure Humbert always wants more, just as his sexual appetite for Lolita can never be sated. There is always an inner Lolita that Humbert cannot know. He is thus terrified that Lolita will accumulate enough funds to be able to run away, so he monitors her finances carefully. And for Humbert potential rivals lurk behind every bush, these phantoms finally materializing in the form of Clare Quilty, who takes his Lolita away. This final blow to his mastery is so devastating that Humbert cannot rest until he finds and destroys his nemesis.

Humbert's desperate drive for sexual mastery clearly bespeaks a deep-seated insecurity, indicating the way the dynamic of domination that informs bourgeois subjectivity leads the subject into a position not of power but of helplessness. But Humbert's insecurities concerning Lolita derive from more than his own fears of sexual inadequacy. They also come from the realization that his quest for mastery of the girl is ultimately doomed by the mortal and temporal nature of human life. Once Humbert removes his nympholepsy from the realm of aesthetic contemplation and projects it into the reality of the physical world, he is doomed to failure. He at some point must come to grips with Lolita's existence as a separate individual with her own wants and needs. Moreover, as he is painfully aware, she can remain a nymphet only for a short while; the facts of mortal existence dictate that children grow to adulthood.

Humbert's drive for domination, in the best Enlightenment tradition, is centrally informed by the desire to dominate nature itself. That mortality and physicality are obstacles to Humbert's mastery even more than is Quilty is indicated by the extreme fastidiousness that Humbert, rapist and pervert though he is, shows toward physical matters throughout the course of his narrative. He never fails to notice (and to note) various images like buzzing flies that serve for him (as for Shakespeare, among others) as intimations of human mortality. He is often horrified at what he finds at motels where he and Lolita stop in the course of their travels, and where "flies queued outside at the screenless door and successfully scrambled in, the ashes of our predecessors still lingered in the ashtrays, a woman's hair lay on the pillow" (212).

Humbert, "a very fastidious male" (40), is repelled by reminders of the physical side of human life. Bathrooms, for example, tend to evoke expressions of horror, and Humbert experiences "a spasm of fierce disgust" when he enters the bathroom he shares with Valeria to find that Valeria's Russian lover has urinated in the toilet without flushing afterward (32).[61] Humbert is consistently repelled by such traces of the physicality of his male rivals, which of course serve as reminders of his own physical nature. He is revolted to find the handle of his tennis racket still warm after having been held by Quilty (238), and when he spots Quilty in a bathing suit, he is sickened by "his tight wet black bathing trunks bloated and bursting with vigor where his great fat bullybag was pulled up and back like a padded shield over his reversed beasthood" (239). Indeed, the effect is so strong that Humbert literally vomits, though he describes his disgorgement with suitable artistic circumlocution as "a torrent of browns and greens that I had never remembered eating" (240).

Horkheimer and Adorno argue that the Enlightenment drive to gain dominion over nature inevitably leads to a repressed internal nature, and Humbert's attempts to repress the abject realities of physical existence seem to substantiate the point. For example, Humbert's early hopes of converting Valeria into an object of his fantasy are very quickly interrupted by the intrusion of her physical reality:

> But reality soon asserted itself. The bleached curl revealed its melanic root; the down turned to prickles on a shaved skin; the mobile moist mouth, no matter how I stuffed it with love, disclosed ignominiously its resemblance to the corresponding part in a treasured portrait of her toadlike dead mama. (28)

Humbert is generally disgusted with the physicality of adult women. They are variously described as having pumpkins for breasts (20), having heavy hips and coarse skin (74), being of "noble nipple and massive thigh" (78), being reminiscent of mares (91), and as being ripe and reeking (245). Most telling is Humbert's direct association of women with death and decay. His attempts at sexual intercourse with Charlotte are described as a movement "through the undergrowth of dark decaying forests" (79). Humbert here participates in a broad trend in Western cultural history. Simone de Beauvoir notes the traditional tendency to identify women with the physical aspects of life in Western culture: "The uncleanness of birth is reflected upon the mother. . . . And if the little boy remains in early childhood sensually attached to the maternal flesh, when he grows older, becomes socialized, and takes note of his individual existence, this same flesh frightens him . . . calls him back from those realms of immanence whence he would fly" (136). This association of women with the flesh reflects a disdain for the animality of human corporeality. The male thus opposes himself as "spirit" to the woman as flesh, as "the Other, who limits and denies him" (129).[62]

Humbert is particularly repelled by coeds, with their reminders of what Lolita would soon become:

> there are few physiques I loathe more than the heavy low-slung pelvis, thick calves and deplorable complexion of the average co-ed (in whom I see, maybe, the *coffin of coarse female flesh* within which my nymphets are buried alive. (177, my italics)

This image of the female body as a coffin—echoing Stephen Deda-lus's meditations in *Ulysses* on the phonetic similarity of womb and tomb (40)—is powerful indeed and makes especially clear that women stand as reminders of the inevitability of death in a fallen world. On the other hand, to Humbert nymphets represent a lost innocence, pointing back toward a time of primordial and timeless bliss.

This theme in *Lolita* recalls the Lacanian depiction of human subjectivity as a condition of inevitable and irremediable loss. Within a neo-Marxist framework, this theme of loss—so central to all of Humbert's thinking—also suggests the Althusserian notion that the bourgeois subject always arises within a matrix of preexisting ideologies that already determine its course of development.[63] Al-thusser stresses the inevitability of this determination—or "interpel-lation"—despite our bourgeois illusions of individuality. After all, the process begins even before birth in the expectations that society (especially family members) develops in relation to the unborn infant (176).

Humbert's desire for Lolita clearly involves an attempt to escape such inevitabilities. In particular, he seeks to restore his own lost childhood innocence, but his relationship with the girl cannot re-store his childhood. Instead, it destroys Lolita's childhood as well. The past is irretrievable, beyond mastery. There is, however, one last possibility for mastery in the realm of art. Art, after all, is a traditional locus of mastery in Western culture. Alfred Appel ex-plains: "If the artist does indeed embody in himself and formulate in his work the fears and needs and desires of the race, then a 'story' about his mastery of form, his triumph in art is but a heightened emblem of all of our own efforts to confront, order, and structure the chaos of life, and to endure, if not master, the demons within and around us" (lvii). Perhaps Humbert can find some consolation by evoking the past in literature, a realm in which he can still exert some control through formal manipulation of the materials at hand, plot being much more amenable to human intervention than is history:

> Unless it can be proven to me—to me as I am now, today, with my heart and my beard, and my putrefaction—that in the infinite run it does not matter a jot that a North American girl-child named Dolores Haze had been deprived of her childhood by a maniac, unless this can be proven (and if it can, then life is a joke), I see nothing for the treatment of my misery but the melancholy and very local palliative of articulate art. (285)

Humbert (again like Stephen Dedalus) would seem to conform quite closely to the stereotype of the artist seeking to escape the nightmare of history via an appeal to the timeless and deathless world of art. Humbert notes how unsettling it can be when people we know surprise us, refusing to conform to our expectations, expectations which, for Humbert, are generally derived from literature. People, in short, change with time. Literary works, on the other hand, are forever fixed in print, providing a stay against the confusion of temporality:

> No matter how many times we reopen "King Lear," never shall we find the good king banging his tankard in high revelry, all woes forgotten, at a jolly reunion with all three daughters and their lapdogs. Never will Emma rally, revived by the sympathetic salts in Flaubert's father's timely tear. (267)

This privileging of the permanence of art over the chaos of history is a familiar aestheticist theme, echoing, for example, the meditations of Oscar Wilde in "The Critic as Artist."[64] Wilde's Gilbert argues that "in life one can never repeat the same emotion" but that in art emotional experience is fixed, waiting to be encountered again and again at the reader's pleasure (96).

Gilbert invokes Dante as his central example of the permanence of art, and rightfully so. It is clear that Dante's work, so central to the idealistic tradition in Western culture, is closely related to this view of the world of art as a realm of permanence and freedom from the mess of reality. Humbert links his own sexual obsessions directly with Dante, Petrarch, and the Western idealistic tradition:

After all, Dante fell madly in love with his Beatrice when she was
nine, a sparkling girleen, painted and lovely, and bejeweled, in
a crimson frock . . . And when Petrarch fell madly in love with
his Laureen, she was a fair-haired nymphet of twelve running in
the wind. (21)

Links with such illustrious predecessors are again part of Humbert's
attempts at self-justification. They are also highly appropriate, since
Humbert's aestheticized view of Lolita is largely derived from the
works of such literary predecessors. Humbert's overt demonstration
of the dark core of his idealistic fascination with Lolita results in a
powerful suggestion that a similar darkness underlies the emphasis
on youthful feminine purity and chastity in the Dantean/Petrarchan
tradition.

Like any good Petrarchan sonneteer, Humbert seeks to immor-
talize his love "once for all" in art, a goal that will remain with him
throughout his narrative, which in fact ends with a conventional
Petrarchan conceit of the immortalizing power of poetry. He writes,
he says to an absent Lolita, to "make you live in the minds of later
generations. I am thinking of aurochs and angels, the secret of
durable pigments, prophetic sonnets, the refuge of art. And this is
the only immortality you and I may share, my Lolita" (311). Poetic,
perhaps, but Humbert's aestheticization of Lolita is an objectification
of her that denies her separate subjective reality. Further, his (and
ostensibly Nabokov's) treatment of the aesthetic as an autonomous
realm separate from reality is a paradigmatic bourgeois gesture,
echoing the general movement of bourgeois society, the result of
which is not an elevation of art but a strict divorce between the
aesthetic and the social that deprives art of any genuine political
force.[65]

Despite his efforts to aestheticize his relationship with Lolita,
Humbert seems driven to confess the sexual nature of that relationship, a phenomenon that recalls Michel Foucault's argument that
modern society has been marked by a consistent compulsion to
confess, especially to confess one's sexual activities, and even more
especially if those activities happen to lie outside the accepted norm.
To Foucault, this intense emphasis on expressing the sexual is related
to a persistent belief that sexuality is somehow "harboring a fundamental secret," and that by bringing the sexual out into the open, one

can discover hidden truths about the human condition. Sexuality, then, reveals "the fragment of darkness that we each carry within us" (*History* 69).

This view of sexuality as a privileged form of epistemology particularly shows up in the tradition of confessional literature, a tradition in which *Lolita* is a clear, if parodic, participant. Foucault could almost be speaking directly of *Lolita* when he describes this "literature ordered according to the infinite task of extracting from the depths of oneself, in between the words, a truth which the very form of the confession holds out like a shimmering mirage" (*History* 59). The obsession with sexuality in Western discourse, then, is primarily an epistemological drive, an aspect of that fundamental mechanism of power that Foucault refers to as the "will to knowledge." This will consists of an urge to master reality by understanding, ordering, and circumscribing it within the confines of well-behaved human concepts. Knowledge and sexuality are, for Foucault, intimately related, and the will to knowledge involves highly erotic pleasures: "pleasure in the truth of pleasure, the pleasure of knowing that truth, of discovering and exposing it, the fascination of seeing it and telling it, of captivating and capturing others by it, of confiding it in secret, of luring it out in the open—the specific pleasure of the true discourse on pleasure" (*History* 71).

This will to knowledge is, of course, the central driving force of Enlightenment science and philosophy. Foucault's thesis, borne out so nicely by the sexual pun "to know," provides a useful gloss on the Horkheimer/Adorno critique of the conflation of truth and power in the Enlightenment and is clearly consistent with the highly epistemological nature of Humbert Humbert's preoccupations as well. Humbert is by profession a scholarly researcher, and his obsession with Lolita is very much a search for knowledge—thus his obvious delight when he discovers in a bookstore a volume entitled *Know Your Own Daughter* (176). The very structure of *Lolita*, in which the first part involves Humbert's quest for Lolita and the second part involves the "cryptogrammic paper chase" in which he explicitly serves as a detective deciphering clues, sets up a parallelism between seduction and detection that makes the epistemological nature of Humbert's desire for Lolita quite clear. Not only does he wish to "know" Lolita, but, because of her youth and innocence, he hopes thereby to learn some truth more fundamental and primal than that which would be available directly to acculturated adults. However, this quest is thwarted by the same paradox that inheres in the myth of virginity: Humbert seeks a special knowledge in innocence, but once knowledge is gained, innocence is destroyed. Like that of Adam and Eve (and that of the Enlightenment in general, per Horkheimer and Adorno), his quest for knowledge inevitably results in loss.

Readers who approach Nabokov's text with such epistemological inclinations will suffer a similar loss. *Lolita* acts to thwart such efforts at interpretive mastery in a variety of ways, as imaged perhaps most clearly in Humbert's efforts to sabotage psychoanalytic readings of his predicament, readings that function as examples of impoverishing and domineering styles of interpretation in general. Humbert, in his own encounters with psychoanalysts during a stay in a sanatorium, takes great pleasure in making a mockery of their inflexible procedures:

> I discovered there was an endless enjoyment in trifling with psychiatrists: cunningly leading them on; never letting them see that you know the tricks of the trade; inventing for them elaborate dreams, pure classics in style (which make *them*, the dream-extortionists, dream and wake up shrieking); teasing them with fake "primal scenes"; and never allowing them the slightest glimpse of one's real sexual predicament. (36)

Moreover, aware that psychoanalysts are studying his present case as well, Humbert has liberally sprinkled his narrative with similar hermeneutic booby traps, taunting psychoanalytic readers with a number of overt Freudian symbols, the self-consciousness of which undermines their validity as interpretive clues. Humbert's dialogue with psychoanalysis is in many ways representative of the relationship between Humbert and his readers in general. His text is interlaced with complex patterns of imagery into which even the most unpsychoanalytic reader is tempted to read significance. Yet the interpretation of those patterns is consistently undermined by the fact that Humbert so self-consciously put them there as part of his artistic technique. In addition to his own self-interest in presenting the story as an apologia, Humbert's credibility is undercut by the highly literary nature of his discourse. Though the text is presented as a true confession, it is clear that many of the details are nothing more than literary devices, and the real truth of virtually all of Humbert's statements is highly suspect.

Many of the people and events in Humbert's narrative lend themselves suspiciously well to description through literary allusion, an effect that is enhanced by Humbert's renaming of most of the characters to make them correspond to characters in literature. For example, Lolita deceives Humbert by pretending to go to piano lessons with "Miss Emperor," lessons that she does not attend, instead using the time to get out of his smothering presence for a brief while. Humbert openly admits that the teacher's name is an allusion, noting that it is what "we French scholars may conveniently call her" (204). The reference is to Flaubert's Emma Bovary, who pretended to attend piano lessons with a Mlle. Lempereur in order to get away from her husband to meet her lover. And the allusion to *Madame Bovary* is doubly significant, since so much of *Lolita* is informed by the kind of *bovarysme* of which Emma is the paradigm. In particular, most of the ordinary Americans Humbert meets seem to have had their consciousnesses almost entirely formed by advertising, magazine articles, movies, and other elements of popular culture. But *Lolita* is far from an attack on the mind-numbing effects of popular culture relative to the mind-expanding potential of "high" culture. One should not forget that Humbert's own mind is itself constructed largely from an amalgam of literary references, a fact that helps make him able to commit the most heinous of crimes in the name of art. Indeed, Humbert and the other characters in *Lolita* approach reality with a system of prefabricated interpretations that seem suspiciously similar to those employed by the psychoanalysts whom he so derides.

Althusser's comments on the interpellation of the subject suggest that these interpretations originate not with the characters themselves but with the various forces that constitute those characters as subjects. In Althusser's view, we do not form our attitudes so much as they form us, and "the category of the subject is only constitutive of all ideology insofar as all ideology has the function (which defines it) of 'constituting' concrete individuals as subjects" (171). We are all always already interpellated by specific ideologies, and no amount of sophistication will allow us to escape that process. Thus, Humbert's view of the world is determined just as much by literary discourse as Charlotte and Dolly Haze's views are determined by the discourse of American popular culture.

In its attempts to constitute the populace as a collection of potential consumers, advertising would seem to be a classic example of the process of interpellation, and it is significant that advertising plays such a prominent role in *Lolita*. When Humbert first arrives in America, he takes a job with a New York ad agency. This job "consisted mainly of thinking up and editing perfume ads. I welcomed its desultory character and pseudoliterary aspects" (34). America, then, is immediately associated with advertising, and with an especially appropriate form of advertising at that: as a veil over reality, advertising acts as a sort of rhetorical perfume, so perfume advertising acts as a double imposition between the subject and reality. Humbert here indicates a certain complicity between these ads and literature, but he makes it clear that he himself has no use for the material of his job, immediately noting his disgust with the "deodorized career girls" he meets in New York. He is so unhappy, in fact, that he suffers a mental breakdown and is forced to spend more than a year in a sanatorium.

When Humbert later meets Lolita he is taken by her "twofold nature," consisting of a "dreamy childishness . . . stemming from the snub-nosed cuteness of ads and magazine pictures" and an "eerie vulgarity" like that of "very young harlots disguised as children in provincial brothels" (46). Already, then, advertising has been linked with artificiality (perfume), with insanity, and with prostitution, and these themes will continue to echo throughout the book. And when Lolita indicates (at least to the narcissistic Humbert) her infatuation with him by posting on the wall above her "chaste bed" pictures of models in magazine ads that roughly resemble Humbert, we are reminded of the stark contrast between the appearance of the glossy ads and the reality of the depraved Humbert (71).

The sophisticated Humbert, a former insider in the advertising business, presumably sees through the false veneer offered by advertising, but the Americans he meets (most notably Charlotte and Lolita) seem to have their visions of reality constituted almost totally by advertising and related commercial genres. Indeed, Humbert uses his superior insight to manipulate Charlotte's advertising-induced expectations, creating for her consumption a narrative of his past that involves a series of past mistresses "all nicely differentiated, according to the rules of those American ads where schoolchildren are pictured in a subtle ratio of races, with one—only one, but as cute as they make them—chocolate-colored round-eyed little lad, almost in the very middle of the front row" (82).[66] In this way, the invidious effects of advertising are linked not only with the exploitation of women but also with the ideology of racism, and in similar fashion the contents of the ads mentioned by Humbert throughout the book are worth considering carefully. Advertising interposes itself between individuals and reality; racism and sexism do the same, resulting in the treatment of persons of other races or genders not as real individuals but as representatives of the kind of stereotypical formulations associated with advertising—just as Humbert treats Lolita not as a real little girl but as a member of the mythical species of nymphets.

The most vivid evocations of advertising in *Lolita* occur as Humbert and Lolita travel across the country, encountering not America but an ad agency depiction of America. Humbert, of course, continues to enjoy his position of lofty superiority, not only regarding the ads as misleading and mendacious but also taking considerable delight in subjecting them to the kinds of close readings that one might associate with literature. Thus, his own penchant for *double entendre* leads him to derive "a not exclusively economic kick from such roadside signs as TIMBER HOTEL, *Children under 14 Free*"(149). But Lolita religiously believes the ads that she reads, lobbying to stay at various hotels and motels or to visit various restaurants on the basis of their descriptions in travel ads:

> If a roadside sign said: VISIT OUR GIFT SHOP—we *had* to visit it, *had* to buy its Indian curios, dolls, copper jewelry, cactus candy. The words "novelties and souvenirs" simply entranced her by their trochaic lilt. If some café sign proclaimed Icecold Drinks, she was automatically stirred, although all drinks everywhere were ice-cold. She it was to whom the ads were dedicated: the ideal consumer, the subject and object of every foul poster. (150)

Humbert's mention of the "trochaic lilt" of ad slogans again suggests a certain complicity between literature and advertising. But most importantly, his depiction of Lolita as the "ideal consumer" indicates that she has been constituted as a subject by the culture in which she lives, created by American consumer society specifically as a buyer of goods.

Numerous other elements of American culture contribute to

Lolita's and Charlotte's constitution as ideal consumers. Charlotte's view of the world, for example, is derived from "soap operas, psychoanalysis and cheap novelettes." Lolita is particularly susceptible to ads appearing in movie magazines, and movies figure prominently in the formation of the stereotypical expectations of the characters in the book. Humbert, however, again sees through all this nonsense, attempting to use it to his advantage. When he first sees Lolita, he attempts to impress her with his "movieland manhood" (41). Later, he muses that Lolita might be responsive to his advances because of the romantic expectations common to "[a] modern child, an avid reader of movie magazines, an expert in dream-slow close-ups" (51). And he comments on the inaccurate depiction of reality in movies when he compares his scuffle with Quilty late in the book to "the obligatory scene in the Westerns," except that this real fight lacks many of the special effects that have come to be associated with movie fisticuffs. At the end of the inconclusive tussle, "both of us were panting as the cowman and the sheepman never do after battle" (301).

Clearly, much of *Lolita* can be read as a scathing condemnation of the misleading view of reality derived from advertising, film, magazines, and other elements of popular culture in America. But Nabokov does not hold up "high" art as a privileged alternative to popular culture. Though Humbert appears to see through the way the Americans he encounters are being duped by their culture, his view of reality (derived mainly from French "high" literature) is at least as distorted as theirs, and this distortion leads in his case to even more horrific results. As Ellen Pifer notes, "If Lolita is the victim of American pop culture, she is even more cruelly the victim of Humbert's aesthetic proclivities" (170). Indeed, there is a close correlation between Humbert's belief that he can possess in reality what his imagination has envisioned as the ideal nymphet and Lolita's belief that she can possess the idealized consumer goods presented in advertising. As Brand notes, "Belief in the possibility of the actual possession of an image is . . . the means by which advertisements reduce people to thralldom" (19).

Nabokov, however, is not suggesting that we somehow put aside all representations of reality in exchange for the thing itself. On the contrary, everywhere in his fiction Nabokov makes clear his belief that there is no unmediated access to reality. As he writes in his postscript to *Lolita*, "reality" is "one of the few words which mean nothing without quotes" (314). Our access to reality is always belated, always filtered through our own expectations of reality. Pifer has discussed in some detail this aspect of Nabokov's work as part of her strong argument for Nabokov's ethical and moral commitment. She notes that it is not mediation to which Nabokov objects, but rather mediation that attempts to pass itself off as a direct access to reality. This attitude explains Nabokov's antipathy toward realistic fiction and the highly artificial quality of his own work. As Pifer puts it, "Nabokov, who found that even recorded history may be a kind of romance, or fiction, was understandably averse to *any* literary method that aspires to the authenticity of ultimate and objective reality" (129).

Indeed, Nabokov stated that "I do not believe that 'history' exists apart from the historian" (*Strong* 138). Pifer's assessment of Nabokov's ethical and moral dimension is probably accurate, but this dimension has a specifically political aspect as well. As Brand suggests, Nabokov's treatment of the consumerist *bovarysme* of American society in *Lolita* suggests that "the society which claims to have freed itself from traditional forms of coercive authority has evolved new and more covert forms to replace the old" (14). The stereotypes promulgated by advertising, pop culture, and various other forces (particularly psychoanalysis) exert a control over human lives that is potentially as invidious as that which is exerted in more overt ways by totalitarian governments. Thus, Nabokov suggests that we not rest too comfortably on the democratic reputation of bourgeois society, since that reputation is itself a product of advertising and propaganda.[67]

Lolita's critique of advertising clearly participates in the same movement by which its self-consciously literary language exposes the fictionality of society's conventions. But are such critiques really effective? Eagleton points out the postmodernist tendency to identify truth with authority and thus to assume that any attack on truth is thereby subversive: "But it is considerably too convenient to imagine that all dominant social ideologies necessarily operate in accordance with absolute, self-identical concepts of truth, which a touch of textuality, deconstruction or self-reflexive irony is then capable of undoing" (378). Eagleton goes on to point out that, given that contemporary governments base so much of their operations on outright lies, it may be that "true facts" themselves can be explosive weapons of subversion (379).

Eagleton does not explain just how one determines what a "true fact" is, but his point is well taken.[68] One might point, for example, to Jean Baudrillard's argument that the blatant fictionality of Disneyland works in clear support of the existing capitalist order by making that order appear genuine in comparison (171–72). It may then be that an exposure of the fictionality of advertising does not necessarily lead to resistance against the coercion to consume embodied in advertising discourse. In point of fact, advertisers quite often make no effort to present their discourse as true, relying on a complex system of codes and signals to induce heavily conditioned consumers to purchase their products in an almost Pavlovian reflex action. As the recent Isuzu "liar" commercials exemplify, advertising has never relied primarily on the perception that its claims are literally true. Instead, advertising interpellates prospective consumers, offering them a well-defined space that they can occupy with a sense of comfort and mastery.[69]

But then, *Lolita*'s critique of advertising does not necessarily rely on an exposure of the fictionality of advertising. It relies, in fact, on an exposure of this process of interpellation, of the way consumers are conditioned to respond to the signals contained in ads and are in a large measure constituted by those signals. Further, it reinforces this critique of the interpellation carried out by advertising with its depiction of Humbert Humbert's interpellation by literature. Humbert and his predecessor Emma Bovary do not literally believe the literature they later confuse with reality—that is not the point. The point is that both allow literature to define and determine the subjective positions that they themselves then occupy.[70]

Nabokov's text works to undermine this process of interpellation. By centering so exclusively on the consciousness of Humbert, it offers only Humbert's position as one with which readers can identify. And it seductively invites such identification by making Humbert charming, erudite, and articulate. But this identification (a process on which realistic fiction depends so heavily) is then undercut with graphic reminders that Humbert is a criminal and a pervert, capable of being cruel and excessively violent toward the helpless child Lolita. In addition, the hermeneutic instability of Nabokov's language unsettles any attempt to interpret the text in a univocal way.

Lolita thus suggests no subjective position that the reader can comfortably occupy and indeed warns against other texts/discourses that might suggest such positions. The complex rhetorical functioning of the book thus works against the dynamic of domination and submission that Horkheimer and Adorno associate with the Enlightenment heritage of bourgeois society *and* against the interpellation of the subject by preexisting bourgeois ideologies described by Althusser. Nabokov's own anti-Marxist sympathies notwithstanding, his best-known and most widely read book thus provides substantial literary support for the neo-Marxist critique of bourgeois society.

CHAPTER *4* MASTERY AND

SEXUAL DOMINATION:

IMPERIALISM AS RAPE

IN PYNCHON'S *V.*

Severin, the protagonist of Leopold von Sacher-Masoch's *Venus in Furs,* presents us with a model of relations between the sexes based strictly on a process of domination and submission. To Severin, a man "has only one choice: to be the *tyrant* over or the *slave* of woman. As soon as he gives in, his neck is under the yoke, and the lash will soon fall upon him" (62). Actually, as it turns out, Severin rather likes being under the lash, as apparently did Sacher-Masoch himself. In the end, however, Severin sees the error of his ways (perhaps having had some sense beaten into him), as well as diagnosing the system of patriarchal domination that leads to such problematic relationships. If woman is man's enemy, it is because man has made her that way: "She can only be his slave or his despot, but never his *companion.* This she can become only when she has the same rights as he and is his equal in education and work" (210).

Sacher-Masoch has since been immortalized by Krafft-Ebing, and his book has been immortalized as, among other things, a favorite of Joyce's Leopold Bloom. Further, his study provides an especially direct commentary on more recent theoretical explorations (such as those by Theodor Adorno) of the drive for domination of others that seems to inform bourgeois society in a central way. Sacher-Masoch's picture of human relationships also foreshadows similar pictures in a number of more contemporary literary works. In Thomas Pynchon's *V.*, for example, the diminutive Rachel Owlglass sets the tone of the book when she muses on the exploitation of her roommate Esther Harvitz by the sinister plastic surgeon Shale Schoenmaker, wondering if there is in that relationship an emblem of the domination and submission that inform human relations in general:

> What is it, she thought, is this the way Nueva York is set up, then, freeloaders and victims? Schoenmaker freeloads off my roommate, she freeloads off me. Is there this long daisy chain of victimizers and victims, screwers and screwees? (49)

Rachel's question turns out to be central to the events depicted in *V.*, which has a number of affinities with *Venus in Furs*. For example, most of the action of Sacher-Masoch's book takes place in and around Florence, which figures as an important site in *V.* as well. Moreover, Severin's fantasies are spurred by a painting of the goddess Venus (Titian's *Goddess with the Mirror*), just as another painting of Venus (Botticelli's *Birth of Venus*) will furnish one of the central images of *V.* in Pynchon's book. And both *Venus in Furs* and *V.* employ Puccini's *Manon Lescaut* as an important intertext.

But the principal parallel between the books is the shared vision of serial victimization in human relationships. *V.* is centrally informed by various apocalyptic notions of the collapse of modern civilization, particularly the notion of entropy, part of what Pynchon himself has referred to as his onetime "somber glee at any idea of mass destruction or decline" (*Slow* xxiii). Allon White has warned that ostensibly transgressive works that rely on erotic violence for their effects may in fact serve only to shore up existing structures of domination (66). Yet, as Sacher-Masoch's feminist conclusion indicates, there is a great deal of positive emancipatory potential in the way both he and Pynchon interrogate the dynamics of power in human relationships. There is much in both authors to suggest that the negative images of life they portray result not so much from universal facts of the human condition as from particular characteristics of specific political structures. In particular, both expose the kind of drive for mastery and domination that lies at the heart of all totalitarian/patriarchal ideologies.

The political orientation of *V.* can be seen in its dialogue with a number of specific twentieth-century historical developments. Prominent among these is the rise of fascism. The specters of Hitler and Mussolini haunt the entire book—just as they haunt the projects of thinkers like Adorno and Walter Benjamin. And if it is possible to read *V.* as a suggestion that fascism was an inevitable symptom of a more fundamental disease of the human spirit, it is also just as possible to read it the other way around, as a suggestion that the degraded conditions of modern life are in fact the results of which totalitarian systems like fascism are the cause. That being the case, then, of course, the next obvious question would be, what caused fascism? *V.* is very much an attempt to answer that question, as well as a warning that this cause was not unique to fascism. It was, Pynchon suggests through his structure of historical parallelism, that same cause that underlay the imperial expansion of the nineteenth century, a cause that still lurks amidst the heated rhetoric of the Cold War in which the contemporary sections of *V.* take place.

This cause, *V.* suggests, is a drive for mastery and domination, and the implication is that we will always have oppressive political systems until we can learn to eschew such mastery, treating the Other (whether that Otherness be a matter of race, gender, religion, or whatever) as a fellow subject rather than as an object for potential domination. In *V.* Pynchon conducts a thoroughgoing investigation into the dynamics of mastery in a variety of human relationships. Most obvious among these is his depiction of the brutal treatment of African natives by their European colonizers, a depiction that pays special attention to relations between the genders and to the ideological complicity between patriarchy and imperialism. But Pynchon pushes this mutual implication further, suggesting at least a partially sexual motivation behind all quests for power, political or otherwise.

The Southwest Africa scenes of *V.* echo Conrad's *Heart of Darkness* in obvious ways, but what is distinctive about Pynchon's treatment of European imperialist practices in Africa is his highly explicit indication of the sexual motivation behind such practices, a motivation at which Conrad only hints. Particularly powerful is Pynchon's depiction of the rich German farmer Herr Foppl as a sadistic beast who derives a powerful erotic charge from the torture of the African natives. As Foppl himself explains concerning the atrocities committed during his youthful service under General von Trotha, "Till we've done it, we're taught that it's evil. Having done it, then's the struggle: to admit to yourself that it's not really evil at all. That like forbidden sex it's enjoyable" (253).

The erotic nature of the domination imposed on the Africans by the Europeans in *V.* is emphasized in a number of passages. For example, as Foppl whips his servant Andreas, he attempts to project a sexual gratification onto his victim: "He doesn't want anything but the sjambok. . . . You like the sjambok, don't you, Andreas" (240). And when another enslaved African revolts against such whipping by Fleische, Foppl's comrade under von Trotha, retribution is swift, brutal, and clearly tinged with a desire for sexual domination: "After Fleische, with the tip of his sjambok, had had the obligatory sport with the black's genitals, they clubbed him to death with the butts of their rifles and tossed what was left behind a rock for the vultures and flies" (263).

In Foppl's reminiscences of the "good old days" under von Trotha, he directly links the imperial domination and brutalization of the African natives by the German military to sexual potency, suggesting that under von Trotha one had to learn "simply not to be ashamed. Before you disemboweled or whatever you did with her to be able to take a Herero girl before the eyes of your superior officer, and stay potent" (257). Such scenes of literal rape add dramatically to the horror of Pynchon's text, and to his suggestions of the relationship between imperialism and a sadistic drive for sexual domination. Thus, during the days of von Trotha, the African natives are pressed into service not only as workers but as sexual slaves:

> Some of the military had brought with them curious ideas. One sergeant, too far down the chain of command to rate a young boy (young boys being rare), did the best he could with pre-adolescent, breastless girls whose heads he shaved and whom he kept naked except for shrunken army leggings. Another made his partners lie still, like corpses; any sexual responses, sudden breaths or involuntary jerks were reprimanded with an elegant jeweled sjambok he'd had designed for him in Berlin. (270)

This insistence on total passivity on the part of the native sexual victims demonstrates that the gratification sought in these relationships derives from mastery and domination. Significantly, Pynchon suggests that this sexually linked drive for imperial mastery is not an isolated sickness unique to the German colonizers of Africa in the early twentieth century. Indeed, there is a suggestion in V. that all great movements of history are sexually oriented. We are thus told about Benny Profane that

> [i]f he'd been the type who evolves theories of history for his own amusement, he might have said all political events: wars, governments and uprisings, have the desire to get laid as their roots; because history unfolds according to economic forces and the only reason anybody wants to get rich is so he can get laid steadily, with whomever he chooses. (214)

The parodic intonation of this passage aside, such suggestions of direct links among sexuality, violence, and politics are a consistent element of Pynchon's fiction. In *Gravity's Rainbow*, Tyrone Slothrop's erections are mysteriously correlated with the falling of German V-2 rockets on London, a correlation that itself seems somehow linked to veiled hints that Slothrop's penis may have been subjected to certain sinister scientific experiments in his infancy. Thus, the violence perpetrated on Slothrop's penis is linked to the violence of warfare and (ultimately) to the threat of nuclear holocaust. That such violence may be linked to a redirection of sexual energies is also specifically indicated in Pynchon's text:

> We must also never forget famous Missouri Mason Harry Truman: sitting by virtue of death in office, this very August 1945, with his control-finger poised right on Miss Enola Gay's atomic clit, making ready to tickle 100,000 little yellow folks into what will come down as a fine vapor-deposit of fat-cracklings wrinkled into the fused rubble of their city on the Inland Sea . . . (*Gravity's* 588)

Elsewhere in this text, the suggestively named Miklos Thanatz gives us his theory of "Sado-anarchism," which sees political power as a sublimation of sadomasochistic behavior:

> Why will the Structure allow every other kind of sexual behavior but *that* one? Because submission and dominance are resources it needs for its very survival. They cannot be wasted in private sex. In *any* kind of sex. It needs our submission so that it may remain in power. . . . I tell you, if S and M could be established

universally, at the family level, the State would wither away. (737)

In typical Pynchon fashion, the gravity of this theory is immediately undermined by the facetious announcement that "a little S and M never hurt anybody" (737). But there is a serious point here, and the fact that the theory is espoused by a character named Thanatz emphasizes the interrelationship that Pynchon frequently depicts among the triad of sex, death, and power.

The sadomasochistic element of political power is linked to the forces behind World War II in *Gravity's Rainbow*, just as it is linked most explicitly to the forces behind colonialism in *V*. In both books, though, Pynchon makes it clear that the insidious drive for mastery that informs war and imperialism is still alive and well in present-day America. One of the most horrific scenes of sexual brutalization in the Southwest Africa sections of *V*. occurs in the story of Sarah, the native girl whose proud defiance only drives Foppl into a greater desire to dominate her. When she continues to refuse his sexual advances, he takes her by force, employing two other native women to hold her down while he whips her, then rapes her (272). Thus Foppl is able to exert mastery over three native women at once, and his victory is so complete that Sarah's will is broken. She comes to him that night and agrees to be his sexual and domestic slave.

But Foppl is not the only European attempting to exert his sexual mastery over the Africans. Foppl's pederast neighbor is also interested in Sarah:

> The neighbor visited his house during the day, found her manacled and helpless, took her his own way and then decided, like a thoughtful sergeant, to share this good fortune with his platoon. Between noon and suppertime, as the fog's glare shifted in the sky, they took out an abnormal distribution of sexual preferences on her.

When Foppl comes home, he finds her "drooling, her eyes drained for good of all weather" (272). He unlocks her shackles, and she runs away to drown herself in the sea.

This graphic episode presents a striking depiction of imperialism as rape. But it is made even more powerful by Pynchon's suggestion that similar scenes can occur anytime, anywhere, even in contempo-

95

rary America. Sarah's story resonates quite strongly with the story of Fina, the Puerto Rican girl who befriends Benny Profane in 1956 New York. Fina associates with members of a New York street gang, serving as a sort of ministering angel, though Profane questions her motives: "The mother to the troops bit, he guessed—not knowing anything about women—was a harmless way to be what maybe every girl wants to be, a camp follower" (137). Indeed, Profane is concerned that "Fina could find herself on the receiving end of a gang bang, having in a way asked for it" (145). And Profane's fears turn out to be well founded. After an eruption of gang street violence, Profane and Fina's brother Angel discover Fina still in shock after the predicted gang rape, "lying on an old army cot, naked, hair in disarray, smiling. Her eyes had become hollowed" (151).[71]

The parallel between Sarah and Fina is quite clear, as is the suggestion that the drive for dominance that motivated the German colonizers of Africa is in many ways similar to the one that motivates American teenagers to join violent street gangs. But Pynchon suggests that this drive goes far deeper, extending not only to such explicitly violent groups but to more "normal" citizens as well. Profane is anything but violent and dominating, but his suggestion that Fina "in a way asked for it," though a common cliché, is still a telling one, showing very much the same kind of thinking that allows Foppl to convince himself that his African servant enjoys being whipped. And Angel, feeling that his own macho mastery has been violated through the violation of his sister, takes it out on the girl, beating her for having "allowed" herself to be raped.

These links between colonial oppressors and ordinary citizens of the contemporary world are further reinforced by Pynchon's treatment of tourism. Throughout V., Europeans are depicted as tourists in Third World countries, seeing not the realities of life in those countries but a mediated and sanitized version as presented in their Baedeker guidebooks. This distancing prevents the tourists from respecting the genuine Otherness of the inhabitants of these countries, or even from regarding those inhabitants as anything more than stage props: "There's no organized effort about it but there remains a grand joke on all visitors to Baedeker's world: the permanent residents are actually humans in disguise" (78). Pynchon drives this point home, especially in the Alexandria chapter, by presenting events from the perspectives of various native inhabitants, perspectives that often make the situation appear drastically different from that seen by Europeans. For example, the first of this chapter's eight sections (each told from the point of view of a different observer)[72] features the perspective of "one P. Aïeul," the owner of an Alexandrian café with many European clients. The native Aïeul knows that these Europeans see neither the real Alexandria nor the real Alexandrians. Instead, he muses, they see a "false and bastard city; inert—for 'them'—as Aïeul himself" (64).[73] And Aïeul's point is emphasized by the fact that the events narrated in this chapter take place within the context of a clash between British and French imperial forces in northern Africa in 1898.[74]

That this distancing of tourists from the lands they tour is related to the ideology of imperialism seems clear. As Jeremy Hawthorn points out in his discussion of *Heart of Darkness*, "imperialism . . . involves yet more extended, complex and concealed chains of mediation through signs than even life in the domestic city" (22). For Pynchon, this mediation is epitomized by the Baedeker guidebook and by the packaged Cook's tours, which assure that the tourist will experience a prefabricated reality that involves no real engagement with the native context. "Tourism thus is supranational, like the Catholic Church, and perhaps the most absolute communion we know on earth; their Bible is clearly written and does not admit of private interpretation" (409).

This link between imperialism and the interpretation of texts suggests a parallelism among tourism, colonialism, and Catholicism that strongly reinforces Pynchon's connection of the atrocities of colonialism with the more mainstream activities of polite society. Pynchon often depicts Christianity as a sinister force. Molly Hite notes the centrality of religion to the critique of system-building in *Gravity's Rainbow*, arguing that to Pynchon "any comprehensive system for putting everything together is ultimately a variant on the Judeo-Christian myth because it appeals from a time-bound order to a transcendent perspective" (105). Indeed we are told in *Gravity's Rainbow* that "Christian Europe was always death . . . death and repression" (317), and that "[r]eligion was always about death. It was used not as an opiate so much as a technique—it got people to die for one particular set of beliefs about death" (701).

Pynchon's critique of religion in *Gravity's Rainbow* seems directed primarily at Calvinism, because of the oppressive effects of its deterministic thinking. In *V.*, however, the critique is directed largely at Catholicism as an authoritarian structure built on a desire for mastery. The young Victoria Wren is fascinated by the colorful yarns of her Australian uncle, tales of adventure that she associates with the religious stories she is told in her convent school:

> she was given enough material to evolve between visits [of her uncle] a private back of beyond, a colonial doll's world she could play with and within constantly: developing, exploring, manipulating. Especially during Mass: for here was the stage or dramatic field already prepared, serviceable to a seedtime fancy. So it came about that God wore a wideawake hat and fought skirmishes with an aboriginal Satan out at the antipodes of the firmament, in the name and for the safekeeping of any Victoria. (73)

This picture of God as an imperialist subduing the savages and making the world safe for innocent young girls is extremely telling, as is the association of the aboriginal natives with Satan. This passage also indicates that the drive for mastery that informed British colonialism was not restricted to males and was at least partially inculcated by the educational system, especially by religious education. This complicity between colonialism and the high-minded ideals of Christianity is further indicated in Hugh Godolphin's later explanation to Victoria of the ways colonialism is often rationalized:

> "We can always so easily give the wrong reasons," he cried; "can say: the Chinese campaigns, they were for the Queen, and India for some gorgeous notion of Empire. I know. I have said these things to my men, the public, to myself. There are Englishmen dying in South Africa today and about to die tomorrow who believe these words—I dare say as you believe in God." (169)

Among other things, Godolphin strongly recalls here the suggestion of Conrad's Marlow about colonialism that "[w]hat redeems it is the idea only. An idea at the back of it; not a sentimental pretence but an idea; and an unselfish belief in the idea—something you can set up, and bow down before, and offer a sacrifice to" (70). But both Conrad and Pynchon relentlessly drive home the falseness of this idealization of imperialism. Pynchon makes this point strongly in his story of the Jesuit Father Fairing in V. During the dark depression years of the 1930s, this priest became convinced that human civilization was in its last days and that the world would soon be ruled by rats. "This being the case, Father Fairing thought it best for the rats to be given a head start—which meant conversion to the Roman Church" (118). So the good father descends into the New York sewer system, catechism and breviary in hand, to begin the conversion of the city's rats to Catholicism.

The tale of Father Fairing would seem to be so offbeat that surely Pynchon is here, for once, being entirely original. But not so—this episode carries a full complement of rich intertextual echoes. For example, Father Fairing carries with him on his mission to the rats not only religious materials but also (for unexplained reasons) a copy of a book entitled *Modern Seamanship*. Any such odd bit of information in Pynchon usually indicates an allusion to something outside the text, and this book would appear to be no exception. Given the obvious importance of Conrad as an intertextual source for so much of V., I would suggest that Father Fairing's *Modern Seamanship* is in fact an echo of Towser's (or Towson's) *An Inquiry into some Points of Seamanship*, which Marlow finds so comforting when he discovers it as an emblem of civilized order amidst the wilds of the African jungle in *Heart of Darkness* (107–8). And as usual with Pynchon, the allusion is far from gratuitous. The link to Conrad suggests a powerful ideological complicity between the Christian drive to convert "heathen" peoples and the drive for imperial domination that so informs *Heart of Darkness*. Father Fairing is supposedly working for the salvation of his rodent congregation, but he in fact quite literally feeds off them, killing and eating three of them (a symbolically appropriate number for this parodic inversion of the Eucharist) per day for his own sustenance while in the sewers. Fairing's treatment of the rats thus resonates with the hints in *Heart of Darkness* that Kurtz might have descended into cannibalism, while at the same time suggesting that a fascination with cannibalism (perhaps the ultimate form of domination) lies at the heart of Catholic Communion.[75] Moreover, it suggests that colonizing powers (like their collaborators the Christian missionaries) justify their activities with the high-sounding rhetoric of the "white man's burden," while they in fact feed off the peoples they colonize.

Pynchon's conflation in this episode of the Catholic church with sewer rats also initiates a highly subversive dialogue between the "high" cultural realm of Catholicism, with its spirituality and denials of physical reality, and the "low" realm of the New York sewers, with its ever so explicit reminders of the abject realities of the physical side of human life. The mixture of discourses resulting from Father Fairing's juxtaposition with his rat congregation is extremely subversive of the claims to spiritual authority made by the church, suggesting (among other things) that priests have their minds in the sewer. And the sexual motif of V. comes to the fore once more, in the hints of a possible sexual liaison between Fairing and the rat acolyte Veronica, "described as a kind of voluptuous Magdalen" (121). But both Veronica and Victoria are among the text's many avatars of V., so it is not surprising that they should be linked. Like Veronica, Victoria had considered entering the convent, and like the female rat's, her attraction to religion was highly sexual. Indeed, Pynchon likens nuns to a gigantic harem of Christ, suggesting that Victoria had

> for a time considered the Son of God as a young lady will consider any eligible bachelor. But had realized eventually that of course he was not but maintained instead a great harem clad in black, decked only with rosaries. (72)

All of these links between imperialism and a drive for sexual mastery come to an ugly climax late in the book with the story of the young ballerina Mélanie l'Heuremaudit, a living fetish of the lady V. who stars in a ballet entitled, suggestively enough, L'Enlèvement des Vierges Chinoises—The Rape of the Chinese Virgins. The ballet is a virtual dramatization of Edward Said's concept of Orientalism, and its hints of a forbidden sexuality to be found in the East culminate in the ultimate sacrifice of Mélanie, who is impaled at the crotch on a sharp pole and then raised into the air. The effect depends on Mélanie's wearing of a "protective metal device," but in the actual performance she leaves off the device and the pole is driven into her vagina, causing her death (413–14). Whether Mélanie's death is suicide or sheer accident seems unclear, but what is clear is the dark underbelly of Orientalism that is revealed in this episode. The tendency to regard the Orient as a locus of exotic (especially female) sexuality betrays a hidden desire for dominance of which Mélanie's violent and agonizing death in Chinese costume on the "erect" pole provides a shocking and graphic hypostatization.

Given the consistent suggestion of a sexual motivation behind the drive for mastery that informs imperialism, it is not surprising that of the many relationships in V. that seem based on dominance and submission, perhaps the one interrogated most extensively is that between the genders. Interestingly, the most thorough investigation of gender relations involves the interactions with women of Benny Profane, the self-proclaimed "schlemihl" who seems to epitomize the modern sense of helplessness in the face of a world that has become too complex to understand. Profane, in short, is anything but master-ful. As such, he joins the family of Pynchon characters (including most notably Oedipa Maas and Tyrone Slothrop) who display a typically modern sense of powerlessness in the face of the reality that confronts them. Indeed, he participates in a broad trend toward unheroic "heroes" in modern literature, a trend of which Joyce's Leopold Bloom and HCE are central instances.[76]

Pynchon's treatment of the modern loss of mastery often focuses on the way the technology that was developed to help humanity master the world has now itself become the master of humanity. Thus Profane is particularly inept at dealing with machinery, with the various accoutrements of technology that are so central to modern life and that make up such an important part of what Profane refers to as the "inanimate." Interestingly, Profane's interactions with the inani-mate are closely connected to his relationships with women. Very early in the book we see a youthful Profane working for the summer at a New York resort when he is nearly hit by a car: "He reflected that here was another inanimate object that had nearly killed him. He was not sure whether he meant Rachel or the car" (24). This near-accident results in Profane's first meeting with Rachel Owlglass, with whom he will strike up a long-term if ill-defined relationship.

Profane's conflation of Rachel with her car as inanimate objects is a motif that recurs throughout V. Later, for example, he muses as he talks to Mafia Winsome that "sometimes women remind me of inani-mate objects" (288). And his tendency to think of women this way provides an obvious commentary on the objectification of women in general. However, Pynchon's treatment of this theme in V. is far from simplistic. At times, Profane's ineptitude with machinery seems to translate into a feeling of sexual inadequacy, as when he abandons his early hopes for the seduction of Rachel—seeing her "fondle the gearshift," he doesn't feel that he can compete with the car for her sexual favors (29). At other times, in a sort of reverse fetishism, Profane seems to regard women as substitutes for inanimate objects. Skilless schlemihl that he is, he cannot master the inanimate; but even Profane can dominate women. As he and Fina attempt to get on a subway train, she gets in successfully, but Profane (of course) gets caught when the doors close on him. Fina, though, comes to the rescue:

> With a frightened little cry she took Profane's hand and tugged, and a miracle happened. The doors opened again. She gathered him inside, into her quiet field of force. He knew all at once: here, for the time being Profane the schlemihl can move nimble and sure. (41)

Profane, who seems able to do little else, is highly successful at attracting women. Though Rachel is the only woman in the text with whom he has anything approaching a "relationship," Paola Maijstral, Fina, and Mafia Winsome all attempt to seduce him, and he also has no trouble attracting the Puerto Rican girl Lucille and the American tourist Brenda Wigglesworth.[77] And both Paola and Rachel explicitly attach themselves to him as "dependents," despite his schlemihl-hood.

That even a relatively intelligent and capable woman like Rachel Owlglass is still dependent on even a most unmasterful male like Profane indicates that the acceptable roles for women as defined by society leave them in a position of submissiveness to males. Thus, despite being better educated and coming from a more affluent family, the young Rachel acknowledges that the possibilities open to her are far more limited than those available to Profane. In her upper-middle-class New York Jewish society,

> [d]aughters are constrained to pace demure and darkeyed like so many Rapunzels within the magic frontiers of a country where the elfin architecture of Chinese restaurants, seafood palaces and split-level synagogues is often enchanting as the sea; until they have ripened enough to be sent off to the mountains and colleges of the Northeast. (25)

But the male Profane can escape this circumscribed world—thus Rachel's plea that he write her occasionally and tell her of his travels, to give her an indication of "[w]hat it's like west of Ithaca and south of

Princeton. Places I won't know" (27).[78] Brenda Wigglesworth later echoes a similar theme, citing Profane's superior experience of the world: "You've done so much more. Boys do" (454).

That society's standard definitions act to limit the possibilities available to women is a major theme of V. In the course of the book Pynchon trots out a full array of these definitions, showing how all of them are implicated in a dynamics of power intended to leave men dominant and women submissive. For example, the girl Ruby (Paola Maijstral in disguise) invokes the stereotype of women as nonthinking creatures of emotion, telling McClintic Sphere that "a girl doesn't understand. All she does is feel" (281). And even when a woman (like Mafia Winsome) *is* intellectual, she still cannot escape the cycle of domination and submission. Mafia Winsome herself is presented as a somewhat sinister character, a violent racist and anti-Semite. And her husband, Roony, clearly views her as a threatening, castrating figure, whose heroic appetite for sex can never be satiated by any one man. Indeed, Mafia, intellectual or not, spends most of her time engaged in bizarre sexual games with a variety of male partners, usually several at once. As she attempts to seduce Profane, she explains to him her concept of "Heroic Love," which turns out to be a highly stereotypical depiction of sex as a struggle for power:

> "A woman wants to feel like a woman," breathing hard, "is all. She wants to be taken, penetrated, ravished. But more than that she wants to enclose the man." (288)

Profane is unimpressed by her definition, but his retort turns out to be just as stereotypical, showing a view of gender roles derived from popular genre films:

> "Nothing heroic about a schlemihl," Profane told her. What was a hero? Randolph Scott, who could handle a six-gun, horse's reins, lariat. Master of the inanimate. But a schlemihl, that was hardly a man: somebody who lies back and takes it from objects, like any passive woman. (288)[79]

Profane's schlemihlhood, then, is first and foremost a feeling of helplessness, a feeling of lost mastery—similar to that which Karen Klein has labeled in relation to Conrad's *Nostromo* the "feminine predicament."

This association of powerlessness with the feminine resonates throughout *V.* in the many descriptions of women as objects of domination. Esther's feeling of being totally helpless during her plastic surgery—"never before had she been so passive with any male" (108)—translates into a feeling of sexual excitement, "as if Schoenmaker had located and flipped a secret switch or clitoris somewhere inside her nasal cavity" (109).[80] So she initiates an affair in which Schoenmaker continues his domination. Similarly, Roony Winsome conjectures that Pig Bodine is excited by Paola Maijstral's apparently submissive attitude:

> the girl had the passive look of an object of sadism, something to be attired in various inanimate costumes and fetishes, tortured, subjected to the weird indignities of Pig's catalogue, have her smooth and of course virginal-looking limbs twisted into at- titudes to inflame a decadent taste. (221)

But of course there is a flip side to this model of sex as domination: if men derive their feelings of mastery only from the relative help- lessness of women, then women also pose an implicit threat to virility. Indeed, there are numerous images of feminine threat in *V.*, as in the case of Mafia Winsome noted above. Many of these are just as stereotypical as the depictions of feminine submissiveness—in fact, they derive from an inversion of the same stereotypes. During his stay in Foppl's compound, Kurt Mondaugen encounters a mod- ern-day Siren, Hedwig Vogelsang, a young girl singer who proclaims that "my purpose on earth is to tantalize and send raving the race of man" (239). And late in the book there is that stock figure of feminine threat, the witch. Indeed, the sorceress Mara issues a clear challenge to male mastery when she launches a revolt in the sultan's harem and restores potency to those other figures of submission, the harem's eunuchs (463).

Perhaps the clearest statement of the role women are expected to play in patriarchal society is made by Rachel, out of frustration at the limitations these expectations have placed on her life and on the success of her relationship with Profane. She tells him:

> "Anywhere you go there'll always be a woman for Benny. Let it be a comfort. Always a hole to let yourself come in without fear of losing any of that precious schlemihlhood. . . . All right. We're all hookers. Our price is fixed and single for everything: straight,

104

LITERATURE AND DOMINATION

French, round-the-world. . . . Until that thing doesn't work any more. A whole line of them, some better than me, but all just as stupid. We can all be conned because we've all got one of these," touching her crotch, "and when it talks we listen." (384)[81]

Rachel then passively (but sarcastically) offers herself to Profane, "[g]ood stuff, no charge." Profane understands the sarcasm and also understands that to take advantage of Rachel's offer would be a kind of rape. As he looks at the prostrate Rachel, he remembers a mnemonic guide that navy electronics technicians had used to help them recall resistor color-coding: "Bad boys rape our young girls behind victory garden walls (or 'but Violet gives willingly')" (385).

The association here of rape with electronics is not coincidental. Rape involves a denial of the humanity of the victim through a movement that Pynchon sees as related to the general assault on humanity in our increasingly technological society. If only women *weren't* human, then men would be absolved of any guilt for treating them like things, and Profane in his indecision over what to do about Rachel's offer immediately entertains a fantasy of such a woman: "Someday, please God, there would be an all-electronic woman. . . . Any problems with her, you could look it up in the maintenance manual" (385). But this is no solution. Profane the schlemihl would probably be unable to operate an electronic woman correctly, and in any case he well knows that Rachel is human. Yet, "[h]e climbed on anyway" (385), providing yet another demonstration of sex as domination.

One might compare Rachel's depiction of women as whores to Angela Carter's claim that "in a world organised by contractual obligations, the whore represents the only possible type of honest woman. . . . At least the girl who sells herself with her eyes open is not a hypocrite and, in a world with a cash-sale ideology, that is a positive, even a heroic virtue" (57–58). But Rachel has clearly not transcended the stereotypes she derides, despite the fact that she appears more self-aware than most of the other characters in V. Indeed, much of her frustration with Profane seems to derive from his inability (or refusal) to conform to stereotypical expectations of male behavior, indicating that men are just as trapped within the conventional structure of sexual power as are women. And of course the dehumanizing effects of being forced into such predetermined roles form a major part of Pynchon's theme in the book: the gradual loss of humanity that results from the slow conversion by modern society of people into effectively inanimate objects.

Women especially are often treated as objects in *V.* For example, Pynchon provides a striking parable of the general objectification of the female body in his depiction of the bar in which the beer taps are shaped like women's breasts and from which drunken sailors are allowed to drink directly during "Suck Hour" (13–16). Individual women are treated as objects as well. As Stencil starts to leave a gathering of members of the Whole Sick Crew, he passes an orgiastic grouping of "Raoul, Slab, Melvin and three girls." The girls are, significantly, both nameless and speechless: "The girls stood silent. They were camp followers of a sort and expendable. Or at least could be replaced" (57). This treatment of women as so many interchangeable parts anticipates the later treatment of the native African women by the occupying German military. It is, in fact, a motif that runs throughout *V.* On a visit to Washington, D.C., Profane and the inimitable Pig Bodine pick up two interchangeable "government girls" named (appropriately enough) Flip and Flop, who cause Pig to recall his earlier encounter with the airline stewardesses Hanky and Panky: "They were virtually interchangeable; both unnatural blondes, both between twenty-one and twenty-seven, between 5'2" and 5'7" (weights in proportion), clear complexions, no eyeglasses or contact lenses" (374). In short, both served equally well as sex objects, as indicated by the suggestive nicknames given them by the sailors: Pig "never did find out their real names" (374). Hanky and Panky are in fact so interchangeable that Pig and his friend Groomsman have difficulty telling which is which, Pig at one point accidentally bedding down with Groomsman's girl Hanky, while Groomsman makes the same mistake with Pig's girl Panky. But the two men graciously forgive each other the understandable mistake, in a fine gesture of male camaraderie.

Pig Bodine is, well, a pig, and his attitude toward women cannot necessarily be taken as representative of society in general. On the other hand, *V.* suggests that his dehumanizing treatment of women is in fact a symptom of a much larger cultural trend. Everyone seems to regard women as objects in *V.*, often including the women themselves. For example, the most explicit treatment of a woman as an object occurs in the love affair between V. and the ballerina Mélanie. For V., herself apparently obsessed with the inanimate, Mélanie is pure object. When she first meets the girl, she immediately declares, "You are not real." And when the girl seems puzzled, V. explains: "Do you know what a fetish is? Something of a woman which gives pleasure but is not a woman. A shoe, a locket . . . une jarretiére. You are the same, not real but an object of pleasure" (404).

V. continues to treat the girl like a fetish, a treatment with which the girl is in full complicity, apparently having been taught to regard herself as an object by her father, who seduced her when she was a child at Serre Chaude, their estate in Normandy. That the girl at least subconsciously realizes the implications of the way she regards herself is indicated when she dreams that a man comes to her and winds her up with a key in her back, just before she runs down. Yet to Mélanie this dream is not a nightmare but a dream of erotic pleasure: "She woke up, not screaming, but moaning as if sexually aroused" (402).

Mélanie's principal sexual gratification comes from viewing herself in a mirror, a narcissistic tendency that contributes to her own objectification. And the love-play of V. and Mélanie apparently consists only of V. watching Mélanie watch herself. As Herbert Stencil investigates the relationship in his search for V., the narrative indicates the standard interpretations of Mélanie's narcissism and of her relationship with V. but then problematizes those interpretations:

> Lesbianism, we are prone to think in this Freudian period of history, stems from self-love projected on to some other human object. If a girl gets to feeling narcissist, she will also sooner or later come upon the idea that women, the class she belongs to, are not so bad either. Such may have been the case with Mélanie, though who could say: perhaps the spell of incest at Serre Chaude was an indication that her preferences merely lay outside the usual, exogamous-heterosexual pattern which prevailed in 1913. (407)

The exact implication of this statement (as with the results of all of Stencil's investigations) is rather difficult to determine. We do not know how old Mélanie was at Serre Chaude, but she was certainly younger than fifteen, her age at the time of her involvement with V.

Clearly, then, her incestuous relationship with her father occurred at an age when she was too young to make a mature choice, and Stencil's suggestion that this incest merely showed Mélanie's offbeat sexual proclivities resonates with Profane's suggestion that Fina was asking to be raped.[82] On the other hand, there does seem to be a great deal of emancipatory potential in the suggestion throughout Pynchon's work that sexual relationships can potentially take on many other forms than the standard heterosexual stereotype—the missionary position of relationships.

For one thing, an acceptance of alternative forms of sexual behavior presents a strong challenge to the dynamics of mastery inherent in the Freudian family drama, in which the Law of the Father reigns supreme. Marjorie Kaufman notes that *Gravity's Rainbow* presents virtually "the entire range of human (and inhuman) sexual behavior as noted by Krafft-Ebing or invented by the Marquis de Sade." But she suggests that "the final effect of such variety is to reduce the importance of physical gender and intensify that of sexual energy" (200–201). For my present purposes, it is interesting to note that the most striking scene of sexual domination in *Gravity's Rainbow* (indeed, in all of Pynchon's work) involves the domination of a *man* by a *woman*—in the graphic episode of coprophagia and sexual humiliation between Brigadier Pudding and Katje Borgesius (as the dominatrix Domina Nocturna) (232–36).

V. presents a number of challenges to traditional gender roles as well, as evidenced by the "feminine predicament" of Benny Profane. Herbert Stencil, for example, realizes that he may be seeking his own identity in his search for V., which brings up "an interesting note of sexual ambiguity. What a joke if at the end of this hunt he came face to face with himself afflicted with a kind of soul-transvestism" (226). And of course there is the scene of V.'s death as the Bad Priest, her gender causing considerable confusion to the children who disassemble her (342).

The most overt interrogation of traditional gender roles in *V.* occurs in the story of V. and Mélanie. During that relationship Mélanie begins to dress like a boy whenever she is not performing, leading to considerable speculation on the part of the composer Porcépic and his associates in Paris:

since an affair of this sort generally involves one dominant and one submissive, and it was clear which one was which, the woman should have appeared in the clothing of an aggressive male. Porcépic, to the amusement of all, produced at L'Ouganda one evening a chart of the possible combinations the two could be practicing. It came out to 64 different sets of roles, using the subheadings "dressed as," "social role," "sexual role." . . . Perhaps, Satin suggested, there were also inanimate mechanical aids. This, it was agreed, would confuse the picture. (408)

Porcépic's chart indicates that the possibilities for human sexual interaction are far richer than those encompassed by traditional heterosexual stereotypes, by the kind of thinking that Joyce derides for narrowly defining intercourse as "ejaculation of semen within the natural female organ" (*Ulysses* 605). The relationship between V. and Mélanie doubly transgresses against such stereotypes. Not only does the lesbian relationship already challenge conventional notions of sexual behavior, but the submissive Mélanie is identified as the more "male" partner in the relationship, further confounding conventional expectations concerning gender roles. There is even in Porcépic's retrospective account of the relationship between V. and Mélanie a hint that the two may have found "one solution to a most ancient paradox of love: simultaneous sovereignty yet a fusing-together. Dominance and submissiveness didn't apply; the pattern of three was symbiotic and mutual. V. needed her fetish, Mélanie a mirror, temporary peace, another to watch her have pleasure" (409–10).

One of the difficulties with interpreting anything in *V.* is that so much of the text is filtered through the mediating consciousnesses of various characters, not all of whom we can even identify. All of the Southwest Africa scenes, for example, are narrated by Stencil, supposedly as told to him by Mondaugen, who himself got much of his information secondhand. This results in a highly dialogic mode of narration that undermines the claims to authority of any one narrator, just as it undermines any attempt at an authoritative interpretation of the events narrated. This analysis of the relationship between V. and Mélanie may be the work of Porcépic, or Stencil, or both (together with an additional anonymous narrator), but in any case neither is a very reliable analyst, so one might expect the analysis to be flawed. And it is, of course, since V. is clearly the dominant member of the pair, and the pattern of dominance and submission has not been overcome at all. It has, however, been altered by a certain mutuality. In the conventional pattern the dominant partner operates as a subject and the submissive partner as an object. The counter presumably would be to find a way to allow both partners to be subjects. Unfortunately, here both V. and Mélanie operate as *objects*. And the grisly deaths eventually suffered by both partners (assuming that V. really is the Bad Priest on Malta) emphasize the life-denying threats posed by a dehumanizing objectification of individuals.

The central problem investigated in Pynchon's work concerns possible ways this objectification can be avoided. How, he asks, can we achieve a level of intersubjective relation in which both partners are treated as subjects, transcending the subject–object dichotomy that inevitably leads to an attempted domination of the object by the subject? V. herself stands as the most striking example of objectification in the book. We are told that "she recognized—perhaps aware of her own progression toward inanimateness—the fetish of Mélanie and the fetish of herself to be one. As all inanimate objects, to one victimized by them, are alike" (410). Indeed, V.'s "progression toward inanimateness" is one of the central plot lines of the book. As the century progresses, V.'s body gradually fades into the inanimate; and by the time of her gruesome disassembly on Malta (by a gang of sinister children who might have escaped from *Lord of the Flies*), she sports a wig, a tattoo, a glass eye, two artificial feet, and a sapphire implanted in her navel. The allegorical significance of this gradual intrusion of the inanimate into V.'s animate body as a commentary on life in the twentieth century is almost too obvious to be effective— except that it is only obvious to readers who have been duped into reading *V.* much the way Stencil reads V., building a network of connections that are in fact never verified by the text.

Many readers have, of course, interpreted *V.* as a perfectly straight allegorical representation of twentieth-century life. Thus, David Richter announces that "[w]hat Pynchon was attempting to do in *V.* is nothing less than an explanation of the course of Western civilization in the twentieth century and a prophecy of its fate" (103). Likewise, we have the comment by Raymond Olderman that "understanding . . . *V.* is like understanding the twentieth century" (123). Tony

Tanner is more perceptive of Pynchon's subtleties, but even he emphasizes the fact that Stencil, born in 1901, is the child of the twentieth century and that his search for V., since she may be his mother, parallels the fact that much of twentieth-century literature involves the "loss of a sense of origin" (45). Tanner also notes that "the search for V. may be analogous to—identical with—an attempt to trace out the aetiology of twentieth-century history" (47). All of this is true to a point, but one should not miss the fact that Stencil's being born in 1901 is almost too much of a coincidence (compare the many preposterous coincidences in Nabokov's *Lolita*), or that the correspondence of V.'s demise to that of the twentieth century is suspiciously, even flagrantly, neat. David Cowart suggests that V. is "an emblem of Western civilization; her gradual deterioration . . . parallels the decline of the West" (127), but he believes that the book fails because the myth is brought too clearly "into focus" and because the mystery is basically solved, leaving us with only a "clever detective story" (128).

I agree that the myth is brought too clearly into focus, but I do not agree that this situation demonstrates a failure or lack of subtlety on the part of Pynchon. In fact, it further demonstrates the complexity of his technique. It is no accident that readers like Richter and Cowart have declared *V.* a failure, because by focusing on totalizing epistemological interpretations of the novel they have performed exactly the sort of operation that all of Pynchon's work satirizes and have hereby missed most of the richness and plurality of Pynchon's text.[83] V. does symbolize the decline of twentieth-century civilization. But she also symbolizes the overly simplistic explanations that many people have produced to describe that decline, explanations that are themselves related to a drive for mastery that is not unrelated to the theme of sexual domination that sounds throughout the book.

Most critics have in fact seen the main point of *V.* to be a critique of this kind of pattern-building activity. By offering an exquisitely tantalizing array of clues that just miss ever coming unequivocally together, Pynchon tempts his reader to try to make sense of the text, while at the same time warning against the ideology of mastery that underlies such reading by making it impossible to fit all of the pieces of the puzzle together in a neat solution. The will to epistemological domination is directly enacted in the text by Stencil's search for clues to the identity of V. (and perhaps thereby to his own identity as well). But the unwary reader is seduced into duplicating Stencil's search for clues and quest for ultimate meaning, just as the reader of *Heart of Darkness* is tempted to reenact the quest of Marlow.

In fact, Pynchon involves and implicates the reader in his text even more extensively than does Conrad. Any number of critics have commented on the way Pynchon's fiction demands an extraordinarily active participation on the part of the reader, while at the same time satirizing the activities that the reader thereby performs. As Thomas Schaub suggests, the interactive experience that is involved in the reading of Pynchon is "the result of a conscious narrative strategy on his part to engage readers in the activity and condition of meaning" (104). Whitney Balliett produced one of the more felicitous models for the role of the reader of Pynchon when, in an early review of *V.*, he suggested that the book was like a Music Minus One recording, providing the orchestral accompaniment for a solo performance that the listener (i.e., reader) must himself supply (113).

Such effects occur in all of Pynchon's novels, but Pynchon's commentary on reading goes far beyond an analysis of how we read literary texts. As Hite notes, "[O]ne of Pynchon's central insights is that people tend to 'read' experience the same way that they read books" (17). Therefore, Pynchon's characters "act as exempla for the reader because they exemplify a tendency in Western culture" (24). What Pynchon does well in *Gravity's Rainbow* is to make clear that this quest for meaning on the part of his readers is a quest for mastery and that the resistance of his texts to interpretation becomes a struggle for power. Thus, he often includes direct addresses to the reader, addresses that are often combative or even abusive, frequently suggestive of a sexual motivation on the part of the reader in seeking meaning. At one point he lists a number of cities and suggests that the reader may be starting to see sinister connections among them. Then he announces:

> Well, you're *wrong*, champ—these happen to be towns all located on the borders of *Time Zones*, is all. Ha, Ha! Caught *you* with your hand in your pants! Go on, show us *all* what you were doing or leave the area, we don't need your kind around. There's nothing so loathsome as a sentimental surrealist. (*Gravity's* 695–96)

LITERATURE AND DOMINATION

Such passages, together with the many images of rape and sexual domination in *V.*, suggest that an attempt at a totalizing and impoverishing reading of a text constitutes a sort of hermeneutic rape, an imposition of the reader's will on the text without paying the proper respect to the text's own Otherness. In this same way, Stencil's attempt to circumscribe V. herself within patterns of conventional logic constitutes a similar form of rape. One might compare here Frances Ferguson's observation concerning a more famous literary rape that "[m]uch of the most powerful recent criticism of *Clarissa*—particularly that of Warner, Castle, and Eagleton—suggests an equivalence between the violence enacted by Lovelace in the act of rape and the violence of any interpretative gesture" (107). For example, Terry Castle suggests that Clarissa is "a hermeneutic casualty," since she "remains the subject of his [Lovelace's] interpretation" (16). Similarly, V. is the subject of Stencil's interpretation, and the parallel between the slow, lingering death of Clarissa and the gradual deterioration of V. may suggest more than a superficial similarity in their fates.

Of course, Pynchon's readers sometimes feel that it is they who have been victimized by the text, rather than the other way around. Similarly, Stencil is a victim of certain modes of thought prevalent in Western society. Though Pynchon suggests that relationships in the modern world almost inevitably reenact a pattern of domination and submission, his analysis of this phenomenon is far more complex than a simple separation of humanity into victims and victimizers, "good guys" and "bad guys." For Pynchon, human agents are never ultimately dominant. As in the work of Althusser, the real power in the dynamic of domination and submission that Pynchon describes inheres in large, mysterious, impersonal forces that people neither understand nor control. Sometimes such forces are incarnated in huge, bureaucratic organizations, especially in large multinational corporations like the "Firm" of *Gravity's Rainbow*—a clear descendant of Conrad's "Company." At other times these forces are merely represented by a nameless "Them." Everyone is victimized by "Them," which makes it all the sadder that men in turn victimize women, whites victimize blacks, and so on. To Pynchon, it is as a reaction to the feeling of helplessness that victimized groups lash out against even weaker groups, venting their frustrations with the kind of serial domination often depicted by Beckett.

This perception that we are all victims shows up in Pynchon as a deep and ubiquitous sympathy for virtually all of his characters but as an especially compassionate concern for the outcast and downtrodden, those underdog groups that Pynchon likes to refer to as the preterite.[84] Many critics have been charmed and impressed by this aspect of Pynchon's work; others have charged him with sentimentality and romanticism. Philip Kuberski, for example, sees Pynchon's ideology as centrally informed by a nostalgic humanism that is antithetical to any genuinely radical political statement. In particular, Kuberski argues that Pynchon's displacement of the evils of society onto "Them" perpetuates a dualistic ideology that allows us to ecape responsibility for our own actions by blaming everything on someone else. Thus, "in displacing the 'they' within a conspiracy, Pynchon introduces romantic teleology in the degraded form of paranoia" (146).

Kuberski's point is well taken, but one should remember that Pynchon's treatment of paranoia constitutes not an endorsement but merely a diagnosis. Indeed, the paranoid system-building of characters like Stencil, Oedipa Maas, and Tyrone Slothrop is the object of parody and even outright mockery in his texts. Further, Pynchon's texts seem specifically designed to frustrate and elude "paranoid" readers. It is true that there is a strong romantic element in Pynchon's work and that his vision is ultimately humanist, based on a fundamental respect for the dignity and sovereignty of human individuals. This humanism will no doubt continue to trouble radical critics. However, Pynchon's treatment of the various dehumanizing forces in society constitutes a critique of existing power structures that should not be overlooked.

V. is most commonly read as a sort of epistemological fable, particularly as an instance of the importance of the detective story as a structural model for postmodernist fiction in general.[85] But as the Horkheimer/Adorno critique of the Enlightenment suggests, epistemological inquiry includes an ideological element that is closely related to the drive for domination that Pynchon so consistently attacks in his work. Thus, as Robert Holton points out, "There is an almost Pynchonesque irony in the way many critics have maintained a blind spot in their readings of Pynchon's texts, a blind spot that occludes the explicitly social and political dimensions of the work" (324). Indeed, despite isolated instances—such as Paul Coates's reading of *The Crying of Lot 49* as a novel of "revolution"—the highly political nature of Pynchon's project has been largely ignored by critics, even when they focus on issues like his treatment of imperialism. For example, William Plater perceptively notes the centrality of colonialism as a theme in Pynchon's work, yet reads colonialism in Pynchon as a sort of literary device, stripped of politics. To Plater, "colonialism is only one of Pynchon's several metaphors for the uncertainty relations of reality and illusion" (112).

According to this view, Pynchon is willing to use political material for strategic purposes, but he really has bigger game in mind, more fundamental and important issues like philosophy and metaphysics, the ontological and epistemological relationship between truth and fiction. Yet this attitude of privileging the philosophical over the political (a variant of the Augustinian privileging of eternity over history) would seem to arise more from the ideological predilections of Pynchon's critics than from Pynchon's work itself. In Pynchon's actual texts, there is *nothing* more important than politics. In particular, there is no concern more central to Pynchon's project than a thorough interrogation of the dynamics of power relations among individuals, institutions, and nations.

Pynchon's emphasis on the activities of readers asks them to examine their own complicity with the ideologies of mastery and domination that inform imperialism and that are exposed in their most vivid form in rape. However, his attacks on totalizing and impoverishing reading do not imply that we must cede full authority to the text or that we should never bring our own perspectives into the act of interpretation. On the contrary, this kind of passive reading is equally problematic. In V. Pynchon makes it clear that the acceptance of prefabricated readings of the Bible on the part of Catholics or of foreign lands on the part of readers of Baedeker guidebooks is no solution. Likewise, in *Gravity's Rainbow* it is Pointsman's literal and devoted reading of "The Book" (Pavlov's *Conditioned Reflexes and Psychiatry*) that contributes greatly to his inability to think in any but the most rigid and predetermined pattern. But Pynchon's texts themselves demand instead a flexible and dialogic mode of reading in which the reader interacts with the text to produce a joint interpretation that never becomes univocally finalized. Pynchon is under no illusion that his fiction will magically transform society in such a way that we can escape the "daisy chain" of victimization that informs so much of modern history, but he persists in pointing out the evils of basing relationships on a dynamic of domination and mastery rather than on a genuine respect for the integrity of the Other. As Hite suggests, "it is always possible, if highly unlikely in Pynchon's view, that someone will learn" (65).

Early in *Finnegans Wake* Biddy the hen digs up from a garbage heap the letter that will figure so prominently throughout the rest of the book—functioning as a reflexive figure of the *Wake* itself. Not surprisingly, the letter turns out to be rather difficult to interpret: "It is a puling sample jungle of woods. You most shouts out: Bethicket me for a stump of a beech if I have the poultriest notions of what the farest he all means" (112.4–6). Graciously, however, Joyce provides us with some suggested reading strategies. These strategies include psychoanalytical ones, as might be performed by "grisly old Sykos who have done our unsmiling bit on 'alices, when they were yung and easily freudened" (115.21–23) and Marxist-allegorical ones, which might conclude that "Father Michael about this red time of the white terror equals the old regime and Margaret is the social revolution while cakes mean the party funds and dear thank you signifies national gratitude" (116.7–10).

Joyce's presentation of these strategies is parodic, much like Italo Calvino's depiction of the various reading strategies employed by Lotaria's feminist reading group in *If on a winter's night a traveler*. Whenever this group gets together, literary buzzwords fly through the air in a fashion that is disturbingly (but amusingly) familiar to denizens of graduate seminars in literature everywhere:

"The polymorphic-perverse sexuality . . ."
"The laws of market economy . . ."
"The homologies of the signifying structures . . ."
"Deviations and institutions . . ."
"Castration . . ." (91)

The group, in short, represents a hodgepodge of stereotypical readings of literature, with echoes not only of feminism but also of psychoanalysis (especially of the Brown–Marcuse variety), Marxism, and structuralism.

Despite such parodies, both Calvino and Joyce sometimes offer what seems to be legitimate advice for the reading of their texts. The theories of reading espoused by the seven readers in the library late in *If on a winter's night* seem to be genuine ones, and there are any number of passages in the *Wake* that seem to contain sound advice for the reading of this highly difficult text. For example, soon after the above parodies, Joyce reassures his readers that the letter (i.e., the *Wake*) really *can* be read:

No, so help me Petault, it is not a miseffectual whyacinthinous riot of blots and blurs and bars and balls and hoops and wriggles and juxtaposed jottings linked by spurts of speed: it only looks as like it as damn it; and, sure, we ought really to rest thankful that at this deleteful hour of dungflies dawning we have even a written on with dried ink scrap of paper at all to show for ourselves. (118.28-34)

In fact, readers are inscribed throughout the *Wake,* a text that is "sentenced to be nuzzled over a full trillion times for ever and a night till his noddle sink or swim by that ideal reader suffering from an ideal insomnia" (120.12–14). Thus, the job of reading the *Wake* can never be completed, and the text can never be reduced to any one fixed meaning. In fact, Joyce places a curse on any reader who would try to reduce the violent plurality of his text: "every word will be bound over to carry three score and ten toptypsical readings throughout the book of Doublends Jined (may his forehead be darkened with mud who would sunder!)" (20).

This curse suggests that the elusiveness of the *Wake* is intended to prevent the impoverishment of the text (and of the reader) that would result from premature interpretive closure. Such warnings are particularly important in the *Wake*, which, as David Hayman points out, "belongs to a class (not a genre) of works which invite the reader to perpetuate creation" (177).[86] *If on a winter's night* clearly belongs in this class as well, as do many modern texts. In fact, such texts have been a part of Western literature for centuries. In *Inferno* IX, Dante delivers specific instructions to his readers to look for allegorical meanings in his text:

> O you possessed of sturdy intellects,
> observe the teaching that is hidden here
> beneath the veil of verses so obscure. (ll. 61–3)

But what is one to make of such advice? Gerald Prince suggests that in general such inscribed reading strategies do provide guidance for the reader, so that a text including such passages becomes a self-reading one that "acts frequently like a reader organizing his reading in terms of nonlinguistic codes and answering questions pertaining to the cultural, proairetic, hermeneutic, or symbolic meaning and function of the various events and situations that it recounts" (232). Thus, the text acts as its own reader, "determining to some extent the response of any reader other than itself" (237). On the other hand, Prince goes on to acknowledge that the text may also inhibit the reading process through misdirection (239).

But Dante's advice in the above passage certainly does not seem to involve such misdirection. He alerts the reader to look for special allegorical significance in the following lines, in which Dante and Virgil encounter the Medusa. And this encounter is an allegorical one indeed. On a literal level, Dante must avoid the allure of this mythical female monster in order to avoid being turned to stone. But allegorically, the implication seems to be that Dante must remain ever alert in his interpretation of his experiences in the afterworld, since the premature closure of literal interpretation would lead to a petrification that would render his journey pointless. This suggestion for allegorical reading applies to readers of Dante's text as well. As John Freccero points out, this episode functions as an allegory of reading, a warning against the petrification that comes from overly literal and univocal interpretation of texts.[87] On this level, Dante is warning his audience not to impoverish his text, but he is also warning them against the dangers of the *Commedia* itself, imploring the reader not to be so enthralled by his poem that the reader ceases to participate actively in the generation of meaning. If not read properly, Dante's own work becomes a sort of Medusa, "an expression of desire that turns back to entrap its subject in an immobility which is the very opposite of the dynamism of language and of desire" (Freccero 134).[88]

This canto, then, turns out to be an allegory about the workings of allegory. It is, in short, metafiction. And it leads to the same sort of interpretive *aporia* as do the metafictional texts of Calvino and other modern writers—having been warned not to take Dante's text literally, the reader is caught in a bind in which it is impossible to decide whether to take this warning itself literally. In other words, does the "here" in Dante's inscription refer to the lines following the warning or to the warning itself? Dante's reader is, in fact, in much the same situation as Calvino's. Both texts exert a Medusa-like fascination over the reader that is akin to seduction, yet both warn the reader against allowing himself to be seduced and mastered by the text. Meanwhile, both texts themselves resist mastery, refusing in turn to be seduced by the reader.

This *topos* of the text as seductress was a common one in medieval thought. Carolyn Dinshaw notes that "medieval writers from Macrobius to Richard of Bury" imaged the fictional text as "like a woman, extravagantly and seductively arrayed." These writers recommend the reading of such texts via what Dinshaw calls a "heterosexual hermeneutic," a mode of reading in which the interpreter evades the seductions of the body of the text while at the same time stripping it of the garments of its material language and penetrating to the truth or spirit that lies behind the text (27–28). Postmodernist texts continue this interrogation of the link between sexual desire and the desire involved in the reading of texts, though in ways often much more overt than in medieval texts. For example, in Milorad Pavić's *Landscape Painted with Tea* the principal female character, Vitacha Milut, has an illicit lover who turns out to be none other than the reader himself. And this theme is addressed perhaps most spectacularly in William Gass's *Willie Masters' Lonesome Wife*, where the reader's prurient interests are specifically engaged by devices like nude photos of the alluring wife. But when the reader is "seduced" by the wife into reading a footnote, he is told:

Now that I've got you alone down here, you bastard, don't think
I'm letting you get away easily, no sir, not you brother; anyway,
how do you think you're going to get out, down here where it's
dark and oily like an alley, meaningless as Plato's cave? . . . and
it serves you right, too, mister smart ass, because maybe next
time you'll be more careful where you go. (17–18)[89]

Such passages reverse the dominative style of reading that Dinshaw characterizes as "heterosexual"—though it is interesting that
Pavić and Gass apparently assume that their readers will be male.
Dinshaw points out that certain medieval texts run counter to
"heterosexual" reading as well. In particular, she suggests that in
Chaucer's "Pardoner's Tale" the physical fragmentation of the eunuch Pardoner is dramatized in the very language of his text. Dinshaw then argues that this characteristic of the Pardoner's language
calls for an entirely different mode of reading: "The Pardoner enunci-
ates the only possible strategy of using language in a postlapsarian
world, cut off from primary wholeness and unity: he acts according to
what I call the hermeneutics of the partial, or, for short, eunuch
hermeneutics" (28).

Dinshaw's indication of fragmentation in "The Pardoner's Tale"
recalls the radically fragmented *If on a winter's night a traveler,* and
indeed Calvino's text is centrally concerned with the issue of desire in
reading and the resulting implications for strategies of interpretation.
The principal character of *If on a winter's night* is a reader (he is
literally called "the Reader" in the text) who attempts to read a series
of novels but is each time interrupted in his efforts.[90] So he moves
from one book to another, his desire growing all the while but never
being satisfied. Meanwhile, he becomes interested in a woman
(Ludmilla Vipiteno, also called "the Other Reader") who is attempting to read many of these same novels. Indeed, the Reader's desire
for the texts he is reading and his desire for Ludmilla become
inextricably intertwined, emphasizing the fact that he is indeed—
per Dinshaw's terminology—a heterosexual reader.

The novel fragments in *If on a winter's night* show many characters
in an explicit search for domination of the kind implicated in Dinshaw's concept of heterosexual hermeneutics, even while the overall
structure of the text itself radically undermines such strategies. For
example, "Miss Zwida" in the "Leaning from a steep slope" segment

spends her days collecting and drawing seashells "in her search for formal perfection which the world can and therefore must attain" (57). Meanwhile, the narrator of this same segment is obsessed by a sense that the world is falling into disintegration and chaos; in response, he shores fragments against these ruins by seeking order via the scientific mastery embodied in his meteorological instruments, which enable him to "master the forces of the universe and recognize an order in it" (66). This segment thus effects a conflation of the discourses of art and science, which in their own separate ways constitute two central strategies through which human beings typically seek to dominate nature. But there is a dark side to such quests for mastery, as emphasized by the brooding presence of the prison that so dominates the background of this segment and from which Zwida and the narrator (the latter unwittingly) help a prisoner to escape. Indeed, the presence of this prison results in a very Adornian suggestion of the drive for domination that lies beneath both the drawing of Zwida and the scientific investigations of the narrator.

Similar interrogations of domination occur in the other novel fragments in the book as well, and one of the ways *If on a winter's night* achieves a sort of coherence is through the concern with strategies of domination that runs throughout the various fragments. But in keeping with its overtly metafictional nature, the most important investigations of the dynamics of mastery in Calvino's book are at one remove from these inserted texts, in the actions of the various readers and writers of texts who appear in the chapters between novel fragments. *If on a winter's night* depicts the literary text as a sort of experimental laboratory of mastery, a place in which the drive for domination informing both reading and writing shows itself in explicit form, thereby commenting on a quest that informs other areas of human endeavor as well.

For Calvino, central to these links between literature and the world outside of literature is a readerly desire for knowledge of the text that closely parallels the desire for sex. *If on a winter's night* opens, appropriately enough, with an extensive address to the Reader as he undergoes elaborate preparations to begin reading that very text:

You are about to begin reading Italo Calvino's new novel, *If on a winter's night a traveler*. Relax. Concentrate. Dispel every

other thought. Let the world around you fade. . . . Find the
most comfortable position: seated, stretched out, curled up, or
lying flat. Flat on your back, on your side, on your stomach. (3)

These instructions for maximum physical comfort during reading go
on for some time; the anticipation mounts as the reader lovingly
fondles the crisp new volume, enjoying "the special pleasure from a
just-published book," reading the jacket, gradually working toward
the reading of the text itself in a process of what Carl Malmgren has
referred to as "foreplay" (112). Indeed, Malmgren's reading is already
inscribed in this scene. Calvino produces a virtuoso performance of
double entendre that explicitly calls attention to the highly sexual
nature of the desire of the Reader as he spreads apart the book's
covers and prepares to enter the virgin text:

> Of course, this circling of the book, too, this reading around
> before reading inside it, is a part of the pleasure in a new book,
> but like all preliminary pleasures, it has its optimal duration if
> you want it to serve as a thrust toward the more substantial
> pleasure of the consummation of the act, namely the reading of
> the book. (9)

If on a winter's night is replete with such sexually charged language.
Moreover, as Sterne demonstrated long ago in *Tristram Shandy*, this
kind of language is highly seductive—after a few such passages
readers find it virtually impossible not to find sexual meaning in even
the most "innocent" textual gestures. As a result, *If on a winter's
night* is invested with sexual suggestiveness from beginning to end,
and this coupling of the desire experienced by readers and that
experienced by lovers is driven home time and again.

The Reader's desire for the texts he reads seems related to his
belief that literature represents a haven from the contingency of the
historical world, a place in which mastery can, in fact, be achieved.
He had always "preferred a book, something solid, which lies before
you, easily defined, enjoyed without risks, to a real-life experience,
always elusive, discontinuous, debated" (32). But books are, after all,
physical objects, manufactured goods that are part of the everyday
commerce of the real world, and this fact irrupts within the Reader's
dream of aesthetic escape in dramatic fashion. Having completed his
textual foreplay and plunged into the act of reading itself, the reader

suddenly discovers that, through a binding error, the book he is reading contains multiple copies of pages 17 through 32 and no new pages beyond that. Violently frustrated, the reader returns to the bookstore where he bought the volume in the hope of acquiring a sound copy. It is here that the most explicit link between sexuality and textuality in *If on a winter's night* begins to be drawn. In this bookstore, appropriately, the Reader meets Ludmilla for the first time. It turns out that Ludmilla has had the same experience of frustration in attempting to read the same book and has returned to th store for a similar reason. From this point on, the mutual quest of these two readers to find a satisfying text to read quite directly parallels the courtship through which they seek mutual sexual satisfaction as well.[91] Ludmilla at once stirs the Reader's sexual interest, especially since they already have something in common on the basis of the fact that they are reading the same book. They strike up a conversation (about books, of course), and the Reader (addressed by the text in second person) finds that he, too, has been infected with Calvino's penchant for *double entendre:*

> "Let's hope," you say, "that we've got a perfect copy this time, properly bound, so we won't be interrupted right at the climax, as happens . . ." (As happens when, how? What do you mean?) "I mean, let's hope we get to the end satisfactorily." (31)

Meanwhile, the two readers discover that they have not been reading Calvino at all; the fragment they began was apparently from a novel by the Polish author Tazio Bazakbal. Both readers opt to continue the Bazakbal text, shifting objects of desire and trading in their flawed volumes for what they trust are complete copies of the Polish novel. The two readers also exchange phone numbers, and when the Reader returns home to resume his reading he finds his desire for the text and his desire for Ludmilla to be inextricably intertwined:

> You are bearing with you two different expectations, and both promise days of pleasant hopes; the expectation contained in the book—of a reading experience you are impatient to resume— and the expectation contained in that telephone number. (32)

And later, when the Reader and Ludmilla first make love, the encounter is described explicitly as a mutual adventure in reading:

Ludmilla, now you are being read. Your body is being subjected to a systematic reading, through channels of tactile information, visual, olfactory, and not without some intervention of the taste buds. . . . And you, too, O Reader, are meanwhile an object of reading. (155)

The Reader's entry into the new Bazakbal volume is again couched in sexually suggestive terms. This volume, it turns out, is even more virginal than the first, having uncut pages. So the Reader takes up a phallic instrument and begins to deflower the new book: "Armed with a good paper knife, you prepare to penetrate its secrets. With a determined slash you cut your way between the title page and the beginning of the first chapter" (33).

But again this determination is to no avail. Objects of desire in *If on a winter's night* are constantly shifting phantoms, tantalizing but elusive. Having apparently gained possession of the interrupted Bazakbal at last, the Reader suddenly realizes that the book he has in hand is not the one he was previously reading at all. But textual desire being what it is, the Reader becomes involved in this new text as well, once again transferring his desire from one object to another. And the joys of reading this new text are highly sexual, being very much involved with the physical act of penetrating the uncut pages with the paper knife. However, as with sexuality, there is much more at stake here than the merely physical: cutting the pages will "allow you access to its incorporeal substance. . . . Opening a path for yourself, with a sword's blade, in the barrier of pages becomes linked with the thought of how much the word contains and conceals" (42).

This suggestion that literary texts conceal some things while at the same time they reveal others is a key to the textual mechanics of *If on a winter's night*. Indeed, one of the important themes of *If on a winter's night* involves this double motion of revelation and conceal-ment, especially in its recognition of the way the telling of one story inherently conceals alternative stories that might have been told. This suggestion of the duplicitous nature of language indicates that the Reader will never be able to attain full interpretive mastery of the text, despite his desire to do so. Reading becomes a sort of linguistic striptease, as the masculine Reader seeks to undress the feminine text, peeling away layer after layer of signification in the best tra-dition of Enlightenment epistemology, until finally reaching the

Truth.[92] But the Truth in this text is not so easy to come by. Just as the Reader becomes engrossed in the new story, he finds that it breaks off in midsentence, with two blank pages interposed. In fact, the rest of the text is printed in this same peekaboo fashion, with two pages of print alternating with two blank pages all the way to the end.

And these interruptions make the story impossible to follow. Even with the pages cut, even with penetration achieved, the book still fails to yield satisfaction.

This process of displacement from one object of desire to another will continue to resound throughout *If on a winter's night*. Emblematic of this movement is the "Looks down in the gathering shadow" fragment, in which a woman named Bernadette engrosses a man in the act of sex so that her accomplice can murder him. Unfortunately, the murder occurs at an inopportune moment, and the woman is forced to resume her sexual activity at once with the murderer/ narrator: "And she explains to me that when I burst into the room I interrupted her at a moment when she can't be interrupted; never mind whether with one of us or the other, she had to pick up at the same point and keep on till the end" (111).

This moment of coitus interruptus (one of several in the book) parallels the various interruptions in reading in an obvious way, and Bernadette's switch from one man to another mirrors the way the Reader switches novels—driven not so much by desire for a particular object as by desire in general. The textual/sexual desire that so informs Calvino's text operates in a continual mode of metonymic transfer from one object to another as readers shift from text to text and lovers from partner to partner in a never-ending search for satisfaction. This never-ending dynamic of desire is highly reminiscent of that described by Lacan, for whom the immediate objects of human desire are but metonymic replacements for the always already lost *objet a*. Indeed, certain passages in *If on a winter's night* suggest that the books we read are similarly stand-ins for some ideal long-lost True Book. Uzzi-Tuzii, the professor of Cimmerian literature consulted by Ludmilla and the Reader, provides a highly relevant description of the process of reading that gestures toward a recognition of this dynamic of replacement:

"Reading," he says, "is always this: there is a thing that is there, a thing made of writing, a solid, material object, which cannot be changed, and through this thing we measure ourselves against something else that is not present, something else that belongs to the immaterial, invisible world, because it can only be thought, past, lost, unattainable, in the land of the dead. . . ." (72, Calvino's ellipsis)

Uzzi-Tuzii suggests that desire in reading is driven by the impossible urge to restore the fullness of this lost "something else," just as Lacan suggests that all desire springs from a feeling of primordial loss. Such desires for wholeness clearly inform the totalizing reading style of the Reader, a style which he himself best describes as he encounters several other readers in the library near the end of the book:

> "Gentlemen, first I must say that in books I like to read only what is written, and to connect the details with the whole, and to consider certain readings as definitive; and I like to keep one book distinct from the other, each for what it has that is different and new; and I especially like books to be read from beginning to end." (256–57)

Madeleine Sorapure characterizes the Reader's strategies as a pursuit of unity, noting his "obsessive desire to bring disruptive elements into order and under control." She suggests that this desire shows a "detective consciousness," especially when he investigates Ludmilla's apartment in her absence (706). This consciousness is also that of the Enlightenment epistemologist, of course, and within the framework of the Horkheimer/Adorno critique of the Enlightenment it is telling that the Reader's objects of knowledge are so clearly pursued in an attempt to shore up his own visions of personal mastery.

The strength of the Reader's desire for the mastery of interpretive closure is demonstrated by the violence of his reactions when his readings of various texts are continually interrupted. He is willing to go to any length in his quest to complete his reading, just as he is similarly determined to track down Ludmilla when she eludes his grasp. So he ends up traveling the world seeking both Ludmilla and the continuation of his fragmented texts. To Sorapure, the Reader's attempts at totalization (and the accompanying metaphysical desire for full presence) are an object of critique in the book, with the contrasting reading strategies of Ludmilla being presented as a privileged alternative: "Ludmilla remembers the content of the books she has read and is able to recall specific incidents and characters perfectly. She involves herself in the novel and does not, like her male counterpart, try to remain suspended above them. She is attentive to their content and does not merely wait for the conflicts at work in the texts to be resolved and brought into order. Ludmilla is the epitome of the interested reader" (707).

I agree that the fragmentary nature of Calvino's novel enacts an implicit critique of the male Reader's quest for totalization. And it is clear that Ludmilla is more receptive than he to the contents of the books she reads. Arkadian Porphyrich, the director general of the totalitarian state of Ircania, describes Ludmilla's relatively submissive approach to reading (an approach that is vaguely reminiscent of that of Geneva school phenomenologists such as Poulet):

> "For this woman . . . reading means stripping herself of every purpose, every foregone conclusion, to be ready to catch a voice that makes itself heard when you least expect it, a voice that comes from an unknown source, from somewhere beyond the book, beyond the author, beyond the conventions of writing; from the unsaid, from what the world has not yet said of itself and does not yet have the words to say." (239)

Still, it is not so clear that Ludmilla stands as the exemplar seen by Sorapure. The contrast between the reading styles of the male Reader and Ludmilla clearly raises a number of gender issues, especially since the Reader's style of reading seems so stereotypically masculine, while the ostensibly more passive style of Ludmilla seems stereotypically feminine. Teresa de Lauretis, in her reading of *If on a winter's night*, sees Ludmilla as the stereotype of the "good" woman, who passively submits to male desire and to the sovereignty of the male author. And to de Lauretis, Ludmilla is most stereotypically feminine when she displays the organicism of her approach to literature. Ludmilla thus describes to the Reader a highly Romantic vision of organic unity, suggesting that she would like to read a text that develops naturally, "simply allowing you to observe its own growth, like a tree" (92).

Yet the dichotomy between Ludmilla and the Reader is not nearly so clear-cut as Sorapure and de Lauretis (in their different ways) would have us believe. When Ludmilla presents this Romantic model of the novel, the Reader heartily concurs: "On this point you are in immediate agreement with her; putting behind you pages lacerated by intellectual analysis, you dream of rediscovering a condition of natural reading, innocent, primitive. . ." (92). This longing for an ideal primordial reading experience informs much of the text of *If on a winter's night.* In the opening scene, for example, the Reader is especially attracted to the freshness of the volume he is about to read, an attraction that goes beyond the status of the book as a newly manufactured physical object: "No, you hope always to encounter true newness" (6).

The male publisher Mr. Cavedagna offers a similarly nostalgic view of innocent reading, this time linking it to the past days of his childhood, in a gesture worthy of Wordsworth: "In my village there were few books, but I used to read, yes, in those days I did read. . . . I keep thinking that when I retire I'll go back to my village and take up reading again" (97). And, amidst the technological chaos of the modern publishing company, the Reader is "consoled by the faith Cavedagna continues to cherish in the possibility of innocent reading, even here" (115).

Ludmilla's desire for organic unity and for an access to the text unmediated by theoretical preconceptions is thus mirrored in some ways by the approaches of the male Reader and of Cavedagna. Moreover, it is not at all clear whether Ludmilla is quite so passive as de Lauretis indicates. For most of the book, she (like all of his objects of desire) eludes the Reader's grasp, and in most of her interactions with him it is she who appears to be in charge: "You understand by now that Ludmilla, for all her mild manner, likes to take the situation in hand and decide everything for herself: your only course is to follow her" (47). Indeed, as Nietzsche pointed out so forcefully in his analyses of "morality," submission can be a form of domination. Moreover, as Nietzschean successors like Foucault have demonstrated, the mechanisms of power can be subtle, complex, and often paradoxical. In the case of Ludmilla, it is clear that her "submissive" reading strategy is just as totalizing as is the more overtly domineering strategy of the male Reader. If Ludmilla is willing to subjugate her own interests in the act of reading to some idealized vision of authorial intention, it is so that she may envision the author as a figure of power and autonomy, thereby reinforcing her own fantasies of mastery—though it may be telling that such fantasies seem available principally through the identification with *male* authors, making access to them especially problematic for female readers.[93]

Calvino further complicates the gendering of the reading strategies in *If on a winter's night* through the introduction of a third reader, Ludmilla's sister Lotaria. Lotaria, a militant feminist, is a decidedly aggressive, even violent reader. It is she, far more than the male Reader, who provides the antithesis of Ludmilla's reading strategies. Thus, Ian Rankin agrees with Sorapure that Ludmilla is an "ideal" reader, suggesting that "she is a pure reader, reading avidly for the sheer joy of the experience" (127). But to Rankin, it is not the Reader but Lotaria who is "the villain of the piece," along with the translator Ermes Marana (127). Lotaria subjects novels to computer analysis, compiling automated lists of word frequencies, from which she can then surmise the major themes of the books without having to go to the trouble of actually reading them herself. Thus, unlike her sister, who seeks to obtain some direct notion of authorial intention in her reading, Lotaria's approach effaces the presence of the author entirely, reducing novels to so much vocabulary. Thus, when she explains her approach to the writer Silas Flannery, he is greatly disturbed, finding himself unable to write afterward due to the thought of the kind of analysis his work might undergo (189).

That Lotaria's method of reading does considerable violence to texts is emphasized late in the book when we find her (or a simulacrum thereof) working as a computer operator in the totalitarian regime of Ataguitania. This regime has instituted a program of transferring books to computer memory, presumably to gain greater control over them and to keep pace with McLuhanesque developments in electronic media. However, Lotaria accidentally pushes the wrong button, with catastrophic results for the novel of Calixto Bandera, which she has been computerizing. The computer's circuits become demagnetized, and

> [t]he multicolored wires now grind out the dust of dissolved words: the the the, of of of of, from from from from, that that that that, in columns according to their respective frequency. The book has been crumbled, dissolved, can no longer be recomposed, like a sand dune blown away by the wind. (220)

Significantly, this accident occurs within the context of a sexual encounter between "Lotaria" (also variously called Sheila, Alfonsina,

Gertrude, and Corinna in this chapter) and the Reader (now a prisoner in Ataguitania). This scene thus results in a juxtaposition of the motifs of sexual domination, political oppression, and totalizing reading. In keeping with her method of reading, it is Lotaria who aggressively initiates the encounter: "Sheila-Alfonsina-Gertrude has thrown herself on you, torn off your prisoner's trousers; your naked limbs mingle under the closets of electronic memories" (219). Indeed, Lotaria's aggressiveness here has led de Lauretis to read this scene as a rape of the Reader, a rape that mirrors the general treatment of Lotaria and her feminist cohorts as threatening, castrating figures.

Because of her reading strategies, Lotaria does not seem to be treated sympathetically in the text. Yet she can also be interpreted as an exemplary figure of resistance to patriarchal domination.[94] This reading is supported by the fact that so many conventional objects of domination in *If on a winter's night* (be they texts, women, or whatever) refuse to submit to domination. For example, in the book's numerous sex scenes, it is quite often women who are the aggressive partners, as with Bernadette and Madame Miyagi, in addition to Lotaria. De Lauretis's principal evidence for the containment of feminine resistance in the book is the conventional romance ending, in which the Reader and Ludmilla are married. Yet this ending is so clearly a parody of the tradition of such endings that it could just as well be read as a statement against such containment.

I think that de Lauretis is right to a certain extent in viewing Lotaria's action in her scene with the Reader as rapacious, though I do not agree that the major significance of this depiction of Lotaria is that feminism poses a castrating threat to the sorts of stable oppositions upon which signification (and thus authorship) are based. Lotaria, for me, is not a figure of the castrating feminist so much as a figure of the domineering analytic reader of whatever gender. The real rapes (and castrations) committed by Lotaria are not against the Reader (who, after all, very willingly submits to her sexual advances) but against the texts that she reads through overpowering them by brute force. The object of critique here is not feminism per se but any mode of reading that would seek to impose its own objectives and ideologies on a text without paying the proper respect to the text itself. The Reader, Ludmilla, and Lotaria in their various ways all adopt totalizing and impoverishing approaches to the text; all seek to enclose and dominate the text by forcing it to conform to prefabricated models.

Such readers allow texts no genuine Otherness; instead they read merely to find verification for ideas they have already formulated. Flannery explains Lotaria's interest in reading his novels:

> I see that my work serves her perfectly to demonstrate her theories, and this is certainly a positive fact—for the novels or for the theories, I do not know which. . . . but my books seen through her eyes prove unrecognizable to me. I am sure this Lotaria . . . has read them conscientiously, but I believe she has read them only to find in them what she was already convinced of before reading them. (185)

This is the style of reading excoriated by Nabokov in connection with psychoanalysis. In fact, such imperialistic theoretical reading speaks to a number of important issues in contemporary literary theory, and a growing number of observers are becoming increasingly concerned that theorists seem to be losing sight of literature and reading only their own theoretical expectations. Feminism is certainly one context within which Lotaria's theorizing can be read, but there are others as well. For example, Lotaria's theoretical preconceptions resonate with Nietzsche's critique of the dominance of the theoretical consciousness in Western society since Socrates, with Adorno's critique of the ideology of domination behind the Enlightenment, and with Foucault's project of developing a form of knowledge that is not subjugated to the philosopher's demand for reason and theoretical consistency.

Lotaria is right that Flannery privileges the style of reading represented by Ludmilla, and Flannery's immediate attempt to seduce Ludmilla when he first meets her indicates a sexual parallel—the submissive Ludmilla is not only the conventional author's ideal reader but also the conventional man's ideal woman, a fact recognized by both Lotaria and de Lauretis. However, contrary to de Lauretis, I see no evidence that *If on a winter's night* itself privileges the kind of passive reading associated with Ludmilla. On the contrary, all three of the book's central readers represent strategies that are undercut in the text, because all three seek a mastery that will bring to an end the generation of meaning in the text. The Reader seeks to have everything fit together in neat patterns leading to final closure; Lotaria seeks to impose her own theoretical interests on the text; and Ludmilla seeks a sort of organic unity through fusion with some idealized notion of the author.

De Lauretis, a highly sophisticated feminist theorist, reads Calvino's book in a way that seems to bear out his apparent suspicion of theoretical readings in general. After all, de Lauretis appears to repeat many of Lotaria's own interpretive moves, and indeed de Lauretis admits that she identifies with Lotaria as an analytical reader (76). De Lauretis's theoretical concentration leads her to at least two blatant misreadings of Calvino's book. For example, in order to make a point about Marana as a prototypical male artist figure, she quotes a long passage that she says shows the Reader's jealousy of Marana's contact with Ludmilla through his position as author of the texts she reads (75). But Marana himself is not an author, and this passage (p. 159) in fact depicts *Marana's* jealousy of the authors whom Ludmilla reads. Similarly, to emphasize the importance of the "rape" of the Reader by Lotaria, de Lauretis notes that this is "the one sex scene of the novel" (78). Yet there are at least half a dozen explicit sex scenes in the book, and de Lauretis herself even quotes from one of them (in addition to the "rape" scene).

That de Lauretis's reading is of a kind anticipated (and undermined) by Calvino can also be seen from her emphasis on the importance of castration images in the book. After all, "castration" is one of the many critical clichés depicted in Calvino's description of Lotaria's feminist reading group.[95] This is not to say that de Lauretis's reading of *If on a winter's night* is simpleminded or mechanical. On the contrary, her essay may well be the finest and most theoretically sophisticated critical piece written on Calvino's book to date. It is, in fact, the very sophistication of de Lauretis's reading that adds resonance to Calvino's point that no one perspective can ever encompass the full richness of the literary text. Literary texts cannot, in short, be fully mastered (or mistressed) by any reader, no matter how sophisticated or clever that reader might be.

Lotaria's retort to Flannery's description of her approach to reading bears out the notion that she is the antithesis of Ludmilla: "Would you want me to read in your books only what you're convinced of? . . . What you want would be a passive way of reading, escapist and regressive. . . . That's how my sister reads" (185). In short, she asks whether the denial of readerly mastery is to be achieved at the expense of setting the author up as master. Indeed, Rankin (no admirer of Lotaria) suggests that the critique of readerly mastery in *If on a winter's night* demonstrates "the limitless power of the novelist over his audience" (129). To Rankin, the book clearly shows that it is always the author who is in charge of the reading process: "Although *If on a winter's night a traveler* starts out looking like a homage to the importance of the reader, it ends up substantiating the hold of the author *over* the reader. Reader-response criticism, if it is to travel farther, must account for this factor in the literary relationship: namely, the ability of authors to control the readings and the responses of their readership" (129).

Sorapure, on the other hand, sees the treatment of authorship in *If on a winter's night* very differently. To her, Calvino's book constitutes an assault on images of authority. She sees the book as "a destruction of the all-powerful Author of traditional fiction and as a document that invests renewed power in the activity of reading. Clearly, a demystification of authority is part of Calvino's larger accomplishment: the demystification of any metaphysical ideal located outside of time and impervious to the surrounding disruptions and disorder" (703). One need only compare the various readings of Rankin, Sorapure, and de Lauretis to see just how dramatically different readings of the book can be. Such differences clearly show that Rankin's belief in Calvino's firm control over his readers is ill-founded. I agree with Rankin that readers are not in charge in *If on a winter's night*, but authors are most definitely not in command, either.

A great deal of *If on a winter's night* is concerned with an interrogation of the role of the author, an interrogation that radically denies the Romantic vision of the artist as godlike creator. The very nature of Calvino's metafictional text, which conflates the ontological levels of author and text, tends to undermine the notion of the author as a figure who stands behind and originates the text. And the book itself is a mixture of heterogeneous fragments containing numerous mini-allegories of the intertextual construction of all books, allegories that reflect the decentered notions of authorship put forth by such modern theorists as Barthes and Foucault. Perhaps the most vivid of these stories of authorship is the depiction of Irnerio, a "nonreader" who still makes good use of the book as object, employing books for the construction of his own art works:

"I make things with books. I make objects. Yes, artworks: stat-
ues, pictures, whatever you want to call them. I even had a
show. I fix the books with mastic, and they stay as they were.
Shut, or open, or else I give them forms, I carve them. I make
holes in them. A book is a good material to work with; you can
make all sorts of things with it." (149)

Furthermore, Irnerio's art receives so much critical acclaim that a
publishing firm is in the process of putting together a book consisting
of photographs of his works. When this book is published, Irnerio will
use copies of it for the construction of additional works, photographs
of which will go into the making of an additional published collection,
and so on.

This endless cycle demonstrates in an especially concrete way the
contemporary critical insight that books are always composed from
the material of other books. Calvino utilizes this insight frequently in
his work, as in *The Castle of Crossed Destinies*, in which narratives
are apparently generated at random through the dealing of tarot
cards but turn out to be constructed of bits and pieces of classic
stories, including those of Hamlet, Macbeth, King Lear, Faustus,
Parsifal, and Oedipus.

Irnerio's treatment of books as physical material for his own art
works participates in Calvino's broader interrogation of the status of
the book as a physical object, caught up in the general modes of
production of society at large, mediated by a whole system of editors,
ghostwriters, and the like, who problematize the authorial function.[96] The status of the book as a consumer object is highlighted in *If
on a winter's night* through the specific involvement of the publishing industry in the story. The technology of book production figures
prominently in the action, as various printing and binding errors
repeatedly combine to frustrate the Reader in his attempts to attain a
whole copy of any of the various fragments of books that he begins to
read. At one point the Reader visits the offices of a publishing house
on the premise that surely they, at least, would have a complete copy
of their own product. But instead he is merely handed an incomplete
photocopy of a text, and he soon realizes that a publishing house,
involved as it is in the nuts and bolts of book manufacture, is the one
place where books are *not* treated as whole objects. "Somewhere the
complete volume must exist; you look around, seeking it with your

gaze, but promptly lose heart; in this office books are considered raw material, spare parts, gears to be dismantled and reassembled" (115).

Ludmilla refuses to go with the Reader to visit this publishing company, a gesture that de Lauretis interprets as a submissive feminine acknowledgment that the world of writing and publishing is for men only. But it seems more likely that Ludmilla avoids visiting the publishing company in order to protect her own Romantic fantasies of books as emanating from the mind of an author-god, not from the presses of a physical factory. In the publishing industry books are commodities, objects regarded in terms of their commercial exchange value rather than in terms of literary or artistic merit. This commodification of the book as a consumer object is further emphasized in the authorial practices of Silas Flannery, who (following what has become a standard practice in the film industry) literally sells advertising space in the texts that he writes. To Flannery, authorship is big business, a process of mass production of discourse. He writes, for example, numerous novels at once,

> involving banks and financing on an international level, these novels in which the brands of liquor to be drunk by the characters, the tourist spots to be visited, the haute-couture creations, furnishings, gadgets, have already been determined by contract through specialized advertising agencies. (121)

As Ermes Marana explains about Flannery, "It seems his imagination is stimulated, the more advertising commissions he receives" (126).

Because Flannery's books are so blatantly regarded as economic projects rather than as creative expressions of the soul of the artist in the Romantic tradition, it comes as no surprise that when Flannery hits a slowdown in textual production, there is a team of ghostwriters standing by to finish up the process, though Flannery himself resists that alternative. But the process of automated authorship depicted in *If on a winter's night* goes even further. Marana obtains from Flannery a novel fragment, "assuring him that our computers would be capable of completing it easily, programmed as they are to develop all the elements of a text with perfect fidelity to the stylistic and conceptual models of the author" (118). And finally, Calvino injects a comment on the real-world contemporary economic situation by suggesting that the true masters of automated production of consumer texts are the clever Japanese. We learn that

the great skill of the Japanese in manufacturing perfect fac-
similes of Western products has spread to literature. A firm in
Osaka has managed to get hold of the formula of Silas Flannery's
novels, and it manages to produce absolutely new ones, and
first-class novels at that, so it can invade the world market. (179)

This separation between the author and his work clearly participates in the alienation that Fredric Jameson has described as an
integral part of the separation between workers and the products of
their labor in late consumer capitalism. The schizophrenia resulting
from this growing sense of alienation leads, according to Jameson, to
an inability of the postmodern subject to maintain a sense of continuity in time. *If on a winter's night* explicitly posits a fragmented
sense of temporality of exactly the kind described by Jameson,
suggesting that such fragmentation is generic to the modern novel
and that a sense of time as continuous flow can be found only in the
traditional novel of the progress-oriented nineteenth century:

> the dimension of time has been shattered, we cannot love or
> think except in fragments of time each of which goes off along its
> own trajectory and immediately disappears. We can discover
> the continuity of time only in novels of that period when time no
> longer seemed stopped and did not yet seem to have exploded, a
> period that lasted no more than a hundred years. (8)

Calvino's text thus suggests that the modern fragmentation of time
leads to a fragmentation in the novel, of which Calvino's text is itself
symptomatic. This exploration of the novel's complicity in our schizo-
phrenic modern sense of time, especially when carried out within the
context of Calvino's vivid treatment of the book as manufactured
good, resonates with the meditations of Walter Benjamin in his essay
"The Storyteller" on the printed novel as the successor to the dead
oral tradition of storytelling. Indeed, the various aborted story fragments in the book seem to dramatize the impossibility of storytelling
in the modern world, even as the motif of computer text generation
enacts *in extremis* Benjamin's notion of the importance of information
as a new form of communication.[97]

Calvino's lonely Flannery in some ways represents precisely the
isolated novelist envisioned by Benjamin. However, despite his
venality, Flannery does retain certain nostalgic visions of his au-

thorial role and of possible connections between writer and reader. He shows a strong admiration for a woman reader (possibly Ludmilla) whom he observes through a spyglass as she reads while sitting on the terrace of a chalet in the valley that his own quarters overlook. Flannery imagines that the woman is reading innocently, a knack that he, due to professional interests, has lost: "How many years has it been since I could allow myself some disinterested reading? How many years has it been since I could abandon myself to a book written by another, with no relation to what I must write myself?" (169). Then he fantasizes about what she might be reading, linking her ideal mode of reading to the ideal way he would like to write:

> At times I convince myself that the woman is reading my *true* book, the one I should have written long ago, but will never succeed in writing, that this book is there, word for word, that I can see at the end of my spyglass but cannot read what is written in it, cannot know what was written by that me who I have not succeeded and will never succeed in being. (170)

Flannery's voyeuristic desire for this woman reader clearly participates in the general association of sexual and textual desire in Calvino's text. Indeed, Flannery seems completely unable to distinguish between the desire for sex and the longing for an ideal text. When he meets Ludmilla soon afterward and discovers that her organic mode of reading closely matches his ideal model, he immediately attempts to seduce her. At this point, however, the ideology of Romanticism blows up in his face: Ludmilla finds him attractive enough as a man, but she is interested in him only as an idealized image of the Author, not as a physical person.

The extract from Flannery's diary that forms chapter 8 of Calvino's book includes a number of other meditations on the nature of authorship as well. Among other things, Flannery imagines two different authors who, like him, are voyeuristically viewing a distant woman reader. He then meditates on the effect the inspiration of this reader might have on the two writers, like the possibility that she might cause them separately to write two identical texts (174). This sort of Borgesian Pierre Menard effect then invades Flannery's own writing practice. Stymied in his own writing, he begins to copy Dostoevsky's *Crime and Punishment* as an exercise. But he becomes caught up in the process and is tempted to copy the entire book:

For an instant I seem to understand the meaning and fascination of a now inconceivable vocation: that of the copyist. The copyist lived simultaneously in two temporal dimensions, that of reading and that of writing; he could write without the anguish of having the void open before his pen; read without the anguish of having his own act become concrete in some material object. (178)

Much of *If on a winter's night* suggests that authors are, in fact, largely copyists.[98] And such considerations of the origins of texts lead Marana into a meditation on the writing of the Koran, a text transmitted from Allah to the archangel Gabriel, then transmitted to the prophet Mohammed, who in turn dictated it to his scribe. Flannery then presents a little parable (not necessarily consistent with Islamic theology) that describes the way the scribe, Abdullah, comes to suspect the authority of the text being dictated to him because he is being given too much liberty to modify the dictation. But Flannery suggests that the scribe is wrong to be scandalized by the authority being granted him as an agent of writing:

It is on the page, not before, that the word, even that of the prophetic raptus, becomes definitive, that is to say, becomes writing. It is only through the confining act of writing that the immensity of the nonwritten becomes legible, that is, through the uncertainties of spelling, the occasional lapses, oversights, unchecked leaps of the word and the pen. (182–83)

Calvino, however, undercuts Flannery's meditations on divine inspiration by immediately following them with the story of a strange cult whose members believe that a chosen author somewhere in the world is writing the ultimate book under the inspiration of cosmic communications from extraterrestrials. These "UFO observers" obviously parody the notion that the Koran was divinely inspired. On the other hand, they further unsettle Flannery's own already confused notion of his authorial function: "What if it were as they say? If, while I believe I am writing in fun, what I write were really dictated by the extraterrestrials?" (184).

While Flannery at times seems threatened by the notion that he may not be the ultimate originator of his own discourse, at other times he seems to find this notion liberating. Echoing Virginia

Woolf's commentary on the "damned egotistical I" that interferes with the ideal impersonality of the author, Flannery suggests:

> Style, taste, individual philosophy, subjectivity, cultural background, real experience, psychology, talent, tricks of the trade: all the elements that make what I write recognizable as mine seem to me a cage that restricts my possibilities. If I were only a hand, a severed hand that grasps a pen and writes . . . Who would move this hand? The anonymous throng? The spirit of the times? The collective unconscious? I do not know. (171)

And he continues such meditations with a fantasy of the day when writing will be considered a totally impersonal activity, when we will say "it writes" just as we say "it rains" (176).

Flannery is so ambivalent in his own attitudes toward authorship that he is both outraged and fascinated when Ermes Marana comes to him with his project for producing texts that are totally apocryphal (179–80). It is indeed in the figure of the ultimate faker Marana that Calvino's most significant interrogations of the nature of authorship reside. To Marana, "literature's worth lies in its power of mystification, in mystification it has its truth; therefore a fake, as the mystification of a mystification, is tantamount to a truth squared" (180). Marana is certainly a fascinating figure, and Flannery's difficulty in formulating a final attitude toward Marana is mirrored in the critical commentary on Calvino's book. To Rankin, who reads *If on a winter's night* as a glorification of authorship, Marana is understandably villainous. Sorapure, on the other hand, suggests that Marana is "constructed in Calvino's own image." He is "in effect, a metafictionist" (704).

In either case, Marana is a figure who radically undercuts any notion of authorial control over the reading process. Whether this undercutting is "good" or "bad" depends on one's point of view, of course, but it is consistent with the thrust of Calvino's book as a whole. In *If on a winter's night* authors can never retain full control of their works, because they can never anticipate the various ways those works might be read. As Marana is forced to admit to the dictatorial Porphyrich, "In reading, something happens over which I have no power" (240). And Porphyrich agrees that "this is the limit that even the most omnipotent police force cannot broach" (240). Yet Calvino's book also undermines the efforts of readers to exert imperialistic control over the texts they read, texts that always mean both more and less than can be expressed in any one reading of them. In *If on a winter's night* neither readers nor writers are in command of the texts they encounter, and rightfully so.

For Calvino, literature is that realm in which we must eschew dominance in order to avoid premature closure and to appreciate fully the pleasures offered in the experience of reading—or writing. It is a place in which both readers and writers can experience a certain amount of the pleasure of mastery without any particular object of domination. As such, literature is the antithesis of totalitarianism, which, as Porphyrich points out, requires "something to repress" (236) and for which it is necessary for "power to have an object on which to be exercised" (240).

If on a winter's night does not adumbrate a utopian mode of interaction among author, reader, and text in which power struggles play no part. It is not even clear what such an interaction might be. After all, unless the reader of Calvino's book participates to some extent in the desires of the readers inscribed in the text, *If on a winter's night* loses most of its force. But Calvino shows us that the natural desire for hermeneutic mastery of the text need not lead to a totalizing demand for closure and resolution. As Foucault (among others) has emphasized, power can be productive as well as repressive, and the readerly desire for mastery in *If on a winter's night* can produce a salutary experience in reading—as long as one remains open to the virtually limitless ability of the text to support alternative readings as well.

CHAPTER *6* AGAINST EPISTEMOLOGY

IN READING AND

TEACHING: THE FAILURE

OF INTERPRETIVE

MASTERY IN BECKETT'S

THE LOST ONES

Samuel Beckett's *The Lost Ones* is an ideal text for the exploration of the process of seeking mastery and domination through reading and therefore provides a paradigmatic illustration of the concepts discussed in this study. This enigmatic text seems specifically designed to defeat totalizing epistemological readings, yet it also invites such readings by tantalizing readers with the potential for recuperation according to a variety of schemes. And this phenomenon is valuable not only as a lesson in criticism but as a pedagogical tool as well. I have had particularly interesting experiences teaching this text to undergraduates, to whom *The Lost Ones* offers valuable lessons in reading by activating a desire for interpretive mastery while at the same time refusing to satisfy that desire.

In *The Lost Ones* an unnamed narrator describes, often in very precise scientific language, a strange fictional world of the kind that has come to be associated with the later Beckett. This world is inscribed within a cylinder, populated by approximately two hundred "bodies," each (except for the ones who have abandoned hope at last) striving to find some way out of the current situation, each vainly seeking its own particular "lost one." The only tools available for the effort at escape are a group of somewhat decrepit ladders, which the bodies can use to climb up to a series of openings in the upper part of the cylinder wall, all of which lead only into blind tunnels or (at best) back out to other openings of the same nature. As a result, all efforts at escape seem doomed to failure, as signaled by the pessimistic description of the cylinder in the second and third sentences of the text: "Vast enough for search to be in vain. Narrow enough for flight to be in vain" (7).

It is fairly obvious to a "sophisticated" reader that naive attempts to make neat sense of *The Lost Ones* place the reader in a position of direct reenactment of the motions of the seeking bodies within the text—with similarly little chance of success. Descriptions of such reenactments are by now a commonplace of Beckett criticism, and critically aware readers of Beckett are quite fond of congratulating themselves on being able to recognize the places in his oeuvre at which naive readers are bound to run aground in their quests for meaning. However, the earnestness and fervor with which younger students often attack *The Lost Ones* reveal certain important aspects of the reading of Beckett that it is wise for us older and more jaded readers not to forget. For one thing, such innocent readings may in fact have access to certain elements of Beckett's work that the paraphernalia of critical sophistication might act to obscure. For another, a closer examination of various strategies for reading *The Lost Ones* suggests that the differences between naive and sophisticated readings of this text are not so great as we might like to think.

The Lost Ones would seem to be the ideal text for initiating a dialogue between naive and sophisticated readings of Beckett because it at first seems unusually simple for a late Beckett text.[99] But this very simplicity in some ways merely increases the probability that an unwary reader might bludgeon his way through the text, missing its main points. The most obvious pitfall for naive readers of Beckett is presented by the temptation of totalizing allegorical and symbolic readings, which so nicely appease the rage for order that tends to drive such readers. *The Lost Ones* offers itself to such allegorical interpretation in especially overt ways. From the point of view of a sophisticated reader, this text is in fact all *too* easy to read allegorically; it admits too many allegorical recuperations, resulting in a cacophony of interpretations that leads less to order than to confusion if the allegorical meanings are taken too seriously. As a result, *The Lost Ones* also dramatizes in an especially overt way the inadequacy of all allegorical and symbolic readings of Beckett, who, after all, has warned us in *Watt* against finding "symbols where none intended" (254).[100]

Yet Beckett's writing lends itself to symbolic and allegorical interpretation as irresistibly as does that of a Dante or a Bunyan—both of whom (not coincidentally) inform Beckett's work in important ways.[101] For example, an allegorical reader might find circumscribed within the cylinder of *The Lost Ones* Beckett's picture of life on earth. Here are all the great themes that haunt Beckett's work from *Proust* onward—the numbing effects of habit, the insatiability of desire, the consideration of time as a slow and agonizing movement toward death. As a statement of the universal condition, *The Lost Ones* seems to cry out for psychoanalytic interpretation, since psychoanalysis aspires to similarly universal descriptions. Indeed, it is an easy matter to read *The Lost Ones* as a sort of allegory of psychoanalysis, especially Lacanian psychoanalysis, since Lacan's model of the perpetual displacement of desire seems so entirely congruent with Beckett's. Both Beckett and Lacan project models of human desire in which Tantalus becomes the paradigmatic desiring subject, ever yearning but ever finding the objects of his desire moving, like the carafe of water in *Act without Words I,* just out of reach. The "lost one" sought in vain by each of the bodies in the cylinder thus becomes the Lacanian *objet a,* an irreducibly anterior goal, vainly sought and never retrievable because the inexorable passage of time renders it always already unequal to itself. And the inability of sexuality to provide solace to those engaged in "making unmakable love" (*Lost* 37) becomes a graphic demonstration of Lacan's pessimistic dictum that "there is no sexual relation."

Reading *The Lost Ones* through Lacan in fact works all too well. The match is so close that little is added to Beckett's text by invoking Lacan, and in the meantime one is tempted to declare that Lacan has "explained" Beckett and that the job of interpretation has been successfully completed. But even a cursory look at Beckett's text shows that it is far from being exhausted by a psychoanalytic reading. *The Lost Ones* is not a treatise on human life in the world; it is a fictional description of the movements of hypothetical bodies within an imagined cylinder. Any attempt to close off interpretation of the text as an illustration of psychoanalysis or any other system fails to allow for the specifically literary nature of the text. Moreover, even in such a sparse text, Beckett manages to initiate dialogues with a number of different discourses, assuring that no adequate account of the text can be derived through an appeal to any one system of explication.

One of the most striking aspects of *The Lost Ones* (and of much of Beckett's other work as well) is the preponderance of seemingly precise mathematical and scientific language. We are immediately greeted in the first paragraph with a precise description of the dimensions of the cylinder ("fifty metres round and sixteen high") and a concomitant (and accurate) calculation of the cylinder's total surface area as twelve million square centimeters (7).[102] Similar computational passages, like the calculations of the rate of temperature change inside the cylinder (16–17, 41), are liberally sprinkled throughout the text. Indeed, in keeping with Beckett's general technique of involving the reader in some of the same sorts of activities as his characters and narrators, there are even points where the reader is stimulated to perform calculations of her own. Thus, after presenting us with a taxonomy by which the bodies in the cylinder can be separated into four groups (those who constantly move, those who occasionally stand still, "sedentary" ones, and "vanquished" ones), the narrator notes that "the first are twice as many as the second who are three times as many as the third who are four times as many as the fourth namely five vanquished in all" (35). The reader then must perform a quick calculation to find that there is a total of 205 bodies, a number roughly in accord with the information we have been given that there is "one body per square metre of available surface or two hundred bodies in all round numbers" (30).[103]

The prevalence of scientific and mathematical language in *The Lost Ones* suggests that one might perhaps find fruitful allegorical interpretations in the realm of science and mathematics, and indeed such interpretations are easily found. The various calculations presented in the text are often slightly inaccurate, and the narrator often qualifies his seemingly precise figures, as in the above example, by noting that he is speaking in "round" numbers.[104] But "round" is a pun here—it indicates not only approximation but also circularity. The cylindrical nature of the world of this text dictates that all calculations will be only approximate, because computations involving circles inevitably involve *pi*, an irrational number. Henning explains: "Here, as always, the problem is *pi*. . . . *pi* is itself a means of containing factors that disturb all linear calculation and thwart the desire for the purity of whole numbers. The geometric descriptions of the cylinder turn out to be idealizing fictions (like those of the *Timaeus*) that attempt to provide a sense of security and control by masking systematic disharmony" (166).

Hugh Kenner has discussed the importance of irrational numbers in Beckett, relating it to the Pythagorean perception that the very existence of such numbers overturns "one's settled belief that the rational domain will suffice to contain all conceivable entities and all practical operations" (*Samuel Beckett* 107). The inability to express irrational numbers in closed form suggests a symbolic questioning of closure and completeness in general, and the way the exigencies of calculation with *pi* interfere with the efforts of Beckett's narrator to encompass his world within the comforting limits of exact numerical calculations becomes a sort of allegory of the failure of Enlightenment rationality in general. Such irrational numbers remind us that there are more things in heaven and earth than are dreamt of in our philosophy—or science.

The Lost Ones lends itself to more specific scientific interpretation as well. For example, all motion in the cylinder gradually seems to be coming to an end, a fact which the narrator notes in terms highly reminiscent of scientific observation as he suggests that the sedentary bodies will soon become vanquished and so on:

> An intelligence would be tempted to see in these the next vanquished and continuing in its stride to require of those still perpetually in motion that they all soon or late one after another be as those who sometimes pause and of these that they finally be as the sedentary and of the sedentary that they be in the end as the vanquished. (33)

This situation of gradual winding down toward total stasis clearly evokes the motif of entropic decay that informs so much of Beckett's fiction.[105] Indeed, the narrator predicts a final state of the cylinder characterized by darkness and cold that suggests a minimization of enthalpy and a maximization of entropy, as in visions of the heat death of the universe:

> Then light and climate will be changed in a way impossible to foretell. But the former may be imagined extinguished as purposeless and the latter fixed not far from freezing point. (15)

The second law of thermodynamics strictly applies only within a closed system—which the universe itself may or may not be. But the universe of *The Lost Ones* clearly *is* a closed system, and the interpretation of the book as an allegory of entropic decay (so reminiscent of certain readings of the early works of Thomas Pynchon) is reinforced by the way this hermetically sealed cylinder resembles the kinds of laboratory setups used to perform thermodynamic experiments. In fact, the progression of the world of *The Lost Ones* toward stasis parallels entropic decay in a quite sophisticated way. The seekers do not move monotonically toward a vanquished condition but instead experience periodic resumptions of activity that mirror the kinds of statistical fluctuations found in real thermodynamic systems. Indeed, the bodies in the cylinder behave very much like the molecules in scientific experiments.

But statistical fluctuations are contrary to strict causality, and these periodic local reversals of the global trend toward entropic decay seem quite disturbing to the narrator. Indeed, the narrator's scientific activities of description and classification show a rage for order that recalls Molloy's inability to accept the aleatory in the redistribution of his sucking stones, while at the same time running directly counter to Beckett's suggestion that the task of the modern artist is to find a form that will "accommodate the mess." The way this narrator attempts to evade random distribution by carefully sorting bodies and events in the cylinder into neat categories very directly parallels Molloy's manipulations of his sucking stones, as well as recalling the functioning of the Maxwell's Demon box of John Nefastis in Pynchon's *The Crying of Lot 49*.[106] Indeed, the narrator of *The Lost Ones* can easily be seen as an allegorical representation of Maxwell's Demon, sorting bodies in the cylinder rather than molecules. This activity can be read as an attempt to impose an artificial order on nature and to escape from the "mess" that is in fact reality, the implication being that real-world scientists may be involved in the same project.

As Friedrich Nietzsche was one of the first to realize, the quest for ultimate "truth" so central to science is very much the same drive on which religions are based. Not surprisingly, then, *The Lost Ones* also offers itself to allegorical interpretation within a religious framework. Susan Brienza notes that the book "at first seems to demand an allegorical interpretation: the cylinder is hell; the cylinder is the

Tower of Babel" (139). Religious resonances are particularly strong in the fourth and fifth paragraphs, which deal with the hope that there may be a way out of the cylinder: "From time immemorial rumour has it or better still the notion is abroad that there exists a way out" (17–18). This desire for transcendence clearly echoes that which informs many religions, especially Christianity. Beckett reinforces this connection by noting that escape from the cylinder might lead to a "flue at the end of which the sun and other stars would still be shining," recalling the ending of all three books of Dante's *Commedia*.

Dante constantly lurks in the intertextual shadows of *The Lost Ones*, as he does in so much of Beckett's work. But from the point of view of an allegorical reading, perhaps the most important role played by Dante inheres in the way the *Commedia* serves as a model for allegory in general. That Beckett was heavily influenced by this model (even while being highly suspicious of it) can be seen at several points in his work. For example, in *Watt* we are given a concise explanation for the motivation behind allegorical writing: "For the only way one can speak of nothing is to speak of it as though it were something, just as the only way one can speak of God is to speak of him as though he were a man" (77). But this theory of allegory appears to echo directly that provided to Dante by Beatrice in *Paradiso* IV:

> Such signs are suited to your mind, since from
> the senses only can it apprehend
> what then becomes fit for the intellect.
> And this is why the Bible condescends
> to human powers, assigning feet and hands
> to God, but meaning something else instead. (ll. 40–45)

As detailed in the famous letter to Can Grande (whether actually written by Dante or not), Dante viewed his poem as a full-fledged allegory accessible by means of the fourfold exegesis theretofore reserved for Scripture. As such, the *Commedia* represents a human attempt at imitating God's own way of writing (Singleton 112).[107] Reading *The Lost Ones* through the optic of Dante thus places the narrator (ironically or not) in the role of modernist God-like creator of the cylinder-world, initiating a full-scale interrogation of authorial power and intention.[108]

The link to Dante is strengthened by an explicit allusion early in

The Lost Ones when the narrator tells us that those who do not search in the cylinder can be found "for the most part against the wall in the attitude which wrung from Dante one of his rare wan smiles" (14). The reference here would appear to be to *Purgatorio* IV, in which Dante encounters his old friend Belacqua, consigned to ante-Purgatory for the sin of sloth. Dante tells us: "The slowness of his movements, his brief words / had stirred my lips a little toward a smile" (ll. 121–22). The identification of the nonsearchers with the slothful Belacqua is highly appropriate, of course, but this reference becomes particularly rich because of the way it ripples back through Beckett's entire oeuvre, where Belacqua is a recurrent figure in texts like *More Pricks than Kicks, Molloy,* and *How It Is.* Moreover, Brienza is right that the cylinder immediately suggests hell, and the wandering bodies recall many of Dante's damned sinners, perhaps most directly the inhabitants of the first circle, condemned to an eternity in hell not because they sinned but simply because they were unbaptized. Virgil himself is one of these, explaining their plight in terms highly reminiscent of *The Lost Ones:*

> For these defects and for no other evil,
> we are now lost and punished just for this:
> we have no hope and yet we live in longing. (*Inferno*, ll. 40–42)

The apparent injustice of eternal damnation for what would appear to be an administrative detail suggests that if *The Lost Ones* is a religious allegory, it is one that indicts religion in general as an oppressive system that brings little more to its adherents than increased suffering. And the fact that many of the most illustrious inhabitants of Dante's Limbo are famous poets adds to the text's interrogation of authorship, casting authors now not as God-like nail parers but as helpless sufferers, much like Beckett's own authorial persona.

But the negative connotations of religion in *The Lost Ones* occur principally in the critique of the salvation mentality, a Beckett preoccupation that begins with the doomed and ludicrous efforts of Belacqua Shuah and Murphy to escape the temporal world and perhaps reaches its most obvious crescendo in the vain waitings of Vladimir and Estragon for the mysterious God-ot. Virtually all Beckett protagonists are ironic Christ figures, and their total messianic inadequacy serves to undercut the persistent human belief that someday, somehow, a savior will come. *The Lost Ones*, like most Beckett texts, is haunted by images of Christ and especially of the crucifixion. Cross-images proliferate through the text, as in the image of the vanquished red-haired woman, who sits motionlessly against the wall of the cylinder, marking the "north," with "the left foot . . . crossed on the right" (57). And the tunnel openings, those hoped-for portals to salvation that lead only to dead ends, are significantly arranged in crosslike patterns, "disposed in irregular quincunxes" (11).[109]

The Lost Ones makes the point that hoping for some future salvation contributes to the impoverishment of life in the present moment. The narrator notes that the bodies, rather than mounting a concerted effort to improve their lives, are mostly content simply to sit and wait for a savior to come: "And this owing not so much to want of heart or intelligence as to the ideal preying on one and all. So much for this inviolable zenith where for amateurs of myth lies hidden a way out of earth and sky" (21). The wonderful Stevensian phrase "amateurs of myth" shows considerable contempt for those who depend on religion to bring salvation, and the pun on "preying" indicates that they will receive misery instead—perhaps deservedly so.

The Lost Ones, with its extreme concern with bureaucratic organizational details, also addresses itself specifically to the institutional structure of religion. The bodies divide into two different sects in their hope for salvation and transcendence. One group believes that an exit from the cylinder can be found somewhere among the tunnels. Another group holds that the only exit is a trapdoor hidden in the ceiling (18). Because the tunnels are accessible whereas the ceiling is not, these two parties can be associated with those who believe that salvation can be achieved through deeds and those who believe that it can be achieved by faith alone. But in any case, there is little to choose from between the sects, and the narrator has no use for this desire for salvation in general:

> So much for a first aperçu of this credence so singular in itself and by reason of the loyalty it inspires in the hearts of the so many possessed. Its fatuous little light will be assuredly the last to leave them always assuming they are darkward bound. (20)

Again echoing Nietzsche, such passages suggest that by focusing on the hope for a salvation that will transcend conditions inside the cylinder, the bodies squander energy and resources, making their

lives there all the more miserable. For example, one of the principal
sources of discomfort in the cylinder is the lack of space, which
dictates that the bodies can never lie down. There is room in the
tunnels that could be used for such a purpose, but the rules of the
cylinder society forbid such use, since these are "reserved for the
search alone" (61).

This concern with bureaucratic detail also leads quite naturally
into political allegory, and the highly regimented conditions inside
the cylinder seem to provide a commentary on the dehumanizing
tendency of modern corporate states. But this turn from science and
religion to politics is a natural one, since (as Joyce's work so powerfully shows) politics and religion are inextricably intertwined in the
Irish cultural milieu from which Beckett arose. And Beckett's attack
on the salvation mentality has specifically Irish political resonances.
G. J. Watson points out that the vision of Irish history espoused by
the nationalist movement, as exemplified by Yeats's *Cathleen ni
Houlihan*, involved a central "reliance on an enabling fiction of
sudden metamorphosis, or transfiguration" (52). Watson notes that
Joyce mocks this notion of transfiguration, but Beckett's consistent
suspicion of salvationism provides a powerful assault as well. Both
Joyce and Beckett proclaim that the dreariness of Irish history is not
about to be escaped through the transcendence of sudden magical
salvation.

That *The Lost Ones* can be read as political allegory attacking
oppressive regimes in general and conditions in Ireland in particular
should come as no surprise. Beckett was always a political writer and
he became progressively more so as his career advanced, though we
are only now beginning to realize the political significance of his
work.[110] It takes very little imagination to read the strictly regimented conditions that obtain in the cylinder as a commentary on the
kinds of oppression fostered by totalitarian governments, and again
there are a number of specific passages that lend support to such
political readings.

A reading of *The Lost Ones* as a dystopian critique of the carceral
corporate state (which has much in common with the "administered
state" of Adorno in general and with the Dublin of Joyce's *Dubliners*
in particular) is reinforced by the intensely bureaucratic nature of the
seemingly arbitrary rules that govern every aspect of life in the
cylinder. Especially in paragraph six—the "climber's code" section,

which describes the various rules for the use of the ladders—the narrator's language often descends into a sort of legalese (complete with Latin phrases) that seems divorced from any engagement with real conditions in the cylinder. Rules in the cylinder are not designed to make life more pleasant for the bodies; on the contrary, they are designed simply to impose an artificial order that the bodies can mechanically follow without thinking for themselves. The bodies have been thoroughly indoctrinated into following these rules, as is emphasized by their tendency to punish violently any transgressors. For example, a seeker entering the circle of the ladders is allowed to make up to one full circuit before joining the queue for any given ladder. Any attempt to move through more than one full circuit "is quelled by the queue nearest to the point of full circle and the culprit compelled to join its ranks" (48–49). Similarly, the seekers often examine other bodies carefully in search of some unspecified information, but it is strictly forbidden to so examine anyone who is queued up for a ladder: "Woe the rash searcher who carried away by his passion dare lay a finger on the least among them. Like a single body the whole queue falls on the offender. Of all the scenes of violence the cylinder has to offer none approaches this" (59–60).

This mob violence in support of authoritarian control is a familiar scene in twentieth-century history, recalling perhaps most vividly events in the Nazi Germany against which Beckett worked as a member of the French resistance. Indeed, the "irregular quincunxes" in which the tunnel openings are distributed can be read not just as crosses but as broken ones, i.e., as swastikas.[111] But there is also a specifically Irish resonance to this scene, and the tendency of the queues to turn on any of their fellows who would question them can be read as a suggestion that oppressive conditions in Ireland have traditionally been reinforced by the tendency of the Irish to accept such oppression, particularly in the form of the Catholic church.[112] And the intolerance of dissent in the queue mirrors that shown by the Irish nationalists, who sought to "liberate" Ireland from England while pursuing policies as authoritarian and dogmatic as any the British had produced.

The bodies are so conditioned that they can only cooperate in blind enforcement of the rules. Mass action in opposition to the rules would be unthinkable. For example, there are hints that there may be a possible escape route located in the ceiling of the cylinder, and the narrator notes that the longest ladder would in fact reach the ceiling: "All that is needed is a score of determined volunteers joining forces to keep it upright with the help if necessary of other ladders acting as stay or struts. An instant of fraternity" (20–21). But the denizens of the cylinder are so conditioned against creative cooperative action that this kind of fraternity is impossible. In fact, of the various rules that regulate life in the cylinder, the key rule is that no more than one climber can mount a given ladder at a time, a rule upon which "all rests" (22). This rule is a crucial one, "the repeated violation of which would soon transform the abode into a pandemonium" (26).

If such passages are read as political allegory, the climbing of ladders comes to represent any attempt at progressive political action. The implication of the strict prohibition on plural climbing is clear: the forces ruling the cylinder (the "powers that be," as Malone would say) depend on maintaining their subjects as isolated individuals. Should these subjects band together, seeking to effect change through mass action, the existing order would crumble. Here, then, we would appear to have a fairly orthodox Marxist critique of alienation and bourgeois individualism.[113]

Such allegorical readings can go on almost indefinitely. As the narrator of *The Lost Ones* himself explains, "All has not been told and never shall be" (51). But my purpose here is not to attempt an exhaustive exploration of such readings so much as to indicate the ease with which a number of such readings can be produced, all of which succeed in illuminating certain portions of the text while failing to provide a complete explication. For example, Dante is the only figure mentioned by name in *The Lost Ones,* and the allusion to him is the only explicit reference to any reality outside the cylinder.[114] Thus, if one insists on an allegorical recuperation of the cylinder as representing something other than itself, Dante provides the most obvious framework. But reading the cylinder as a Dantean hell seems to be specifically undercut by the narrator's apparently mocking acknowledgment of this connection: "What first impresses in this gloom is the sensation of yellow it imparts not to say of sulphur in view of the associations" (36).

Of course, one could attempt to construct elaborate multilayered allegorical readings, based on something akin to the traditional four-fold biblical exegesis by which Dante constructed his *Commedia.*

Thus, in addition to the literal level on which *The Lost Ones* is simply the story of the bodies in the cylinder, one might see the political, religious, and scientific allegories that I have described as constituting something akin to the traditional allegorical, moral, and anagogical levels. But such attempts are familiar to the experienced reader of Beckett, who constantly finds herself implicated in Beckett's indictment of "the laughable effects of man's attempts to create a semblance of order" (Finney 63). One of the most striking characteristics of all Beckett's fiction is the constant palinodic movement of statement and retraction that makes it nearly impossible to attribute authority to any of the information found in a Beckett text. In *The Lost Ones* this palinodic mode of narration is less obvious than in, say, *Molloy* or *How It Is*, but the narrator's statements are frequently destabilized by qualifications like the "if this notion is maintained" that appears at several places in the text, most importantly at the text's conclusion.[115] Moreover, the very multiplicity of possible allegorical readings initiates a conflict of discourses that prevents any one interpretation from attaining the status of a monological authority. Thus, Henning compares the discourse of *The Lost Ones* to Bakhtin's concept of "internally persuasive" discourse: "For Bakhtin, internally persuasive discourse becomes 'dialogized' when it engages and incorporates a variety of verbal and ideological points of view, approaches, directions, and values, all striving endlessly for hegemony" (194).

If there is a connecting thread running through all of the allegorical recuperations I have suggested for *The Lost Ones*, it is that all concern discourses that are characterized by a fundamental drive for mastery and authority, by the rage for order that Beckett so consistently mocks. Moreover, conditions in the cylinder demonstrate the impoverishing and dehumanizing results that obtain when human societies succumb to authoritarian domination.[116] We are thus quite naturally led to a further allegorical interpretation, to the conclusion that the text is precisely "about" such drives for mastery and that it enacts an opposition to such quests for mastery in its refusal to grant ultimate authority to any one of the conflicting discourses, as well as in its refusal to succumb to authoritative interpretation by any one allegorical scheme.

This course is in a sense the one adopted by Brienza, who, having noted the temptation to read *The Lost Ones* as a religious allegory,

154

veers away from that course and chooses to read the text as a reflexive commentary on the literary experience. She notes that here the very style of Beckett's writing "suggests fruitless waiting, futile searching, and unsatisfied hoping. . . . If *The Lost Ones* presents a statement about humanity's unfulfilled search for order and meaning in the world, this translates into a comment on the reader's futile search for order and meaning in the piece itself and more generally in literature as a whole. Thus the reader becomes one of the searchers trying to find a (critical) 'way out' of the enclosure" (139). Brienza's comment seems highly relevant to the experience of undergraduate readers, whose innocence often leads them into a precise (though often clever) reenactment of the futile search of the bodies in the cylinder. The innocent reader of *The Lost Ones*, lacking Brienza's awareness of the reflexivity of Beckett's writing, is tempted to seek the comfort of allegorical meaning just as the seekers within the cylinder seek their "lost ones." And of course the resultant parody of the hermeneutic contortions performed by such readers of *The Lost Ones* becomes a commentary on readers of texts in general, as well as a commentary on traditional texts that invite and endorse such totalizing readings.

One thinks here of Umberto Eco's description of the "open work," whose subtleties are available only to sophisticated readers: "The naive reader will be unable to enjoy the story (he will suffer a final uneasiness), but the critical reader will succeed only by enjoying the defeat of the former" (10). But, as Peter Murphy points out, Brienza's solution is really only a "further allegorical reading" (73). Too sophisticated to expect scientific, religious, or political allegorical readings to make perfect sense of the text, Brienza takes a step up into meta-allegory and proclaims that the point of the text is its very ability to elude such allegorical recuperations. To Brienza, naive allegorical readers are walking directly into a textual booby trap, but one is tempted to ask whether she herself is not simply walking into a trap at the next higher level in her own quest for mastery. Narratives of the failure of allegory in Beckett can be just as totalizing and impoverishing (and just as allegorical) as allegorical readings themselves, and reading *The Lost Ones* as a temptation to allegory is in danger of converting the text into an allegory of temptation. To Beckett, literature as a discourse has no more authority than does psychoanalysis, science, religion, or politics, and indeed romantic poetry is specifically mocked in the text as another false means of seeking transcendence.[117] Here we run up against the paradox of metafiction in general. If *The Lost Ones* mocks the pretensions of literature to make authoritative statements about reality, it must itself, being literature, be included as a target of that mockery. Epimenides is alive and well inside Beckett's cylinder.

Perhaps this situation can be usefully illuminated by shifting for a moment from allegory to irony. As Paul de Man has pointed out, irony and allegory have much in common, since in both cases "the relationship between sign and meaning is discontinuous" (209). In both modes, language explicitly declares itself to mean something other than what it says. To de Man, the difference between the two is primarily a matter of temporality, with allegory pointing to the past and irony resolutely confining itself to the present. Thus, Brienza's reading, which focuses on the present moment of Beckett's text, might be considered ironic as opposed to the clearly allegorical character of readings that point to other discourses prior to Beckett's text, be they psychoanalytic, scientific, religious, political, or whatever.

Indeed, Brienza's apparently sophisticated (relative, say, to a naive undergraduate) reading illustrates de Man's description of the temptation "to consider ironists as more enlightened than their assumedly naive counterparts, the allegorists." Yet to de Man, the privileging of either mode over the other is an error, since the "knowledge derived from both modes is essentially the same" (226). This knowledge has to do with language itself—the gap between signifier and signified that is openly advertised in irony and allegory illustrates a gap that inheres in all language, so that temporality renders the signified a "lost one" relative to any attempts to capture it in language. But this claim seems to lead to the horrifying conclusion that the ultimate explanatory value of Brienza's sophisticated reading is no greater than that of a reading produced by a naive undergraduate.

Such comparisons provide a salutary reminder that we have not even come close to "mastering" Beckett's complex texts. No matter how powerful our critical and theoretical formulations, no matter how competent we may be as professional readers, it would seem that Beckett, that self-proclaimed prophet of impotence and incompetence, always remains one step ahead of us. If Brienza can raise herself to an interpretive level above that of the allegorical readers and thereby recognize their folly in reenacting the movements of Beckett's seekers, it is equally easy for someone else to move up still another notch and to demonstrate that Brienza is reenacting the movements of the allegorists. And so on, worlds without end.

This image of layered allegories, infinitely nested like Chinese boxes, has the satisfying property of corresponding to similar depictions of infinite regression that can be found throughout Beckett's own work. It also corresponds to a poststructuralist conception of irony in general, the interpretation of which can never come to rest without leaving itself open to mockery by the next layer of irony. Thus Roland Barthes notes that irony can become "a new stereotype." Further, he asks, "how can stupidity be pinned down without declaring oneself intelligent? How can one code be superior to another without abusively closing off the plurality of codes?" (S/Z 206). Along these lines Jonathan Culler argues that readers can invoke the concept of irony to recuperate difficult texts, but he notes that this procedure raises the possibility of just the problem we are discussing here: "This is indeed a crucial question, for from the description offered so far it might seem as though ironic naturalization makes more grandiose claims than the things which it deflates. . . . Irony, the cynic might say, is the ultimate form of recuperation and naturalization, whereby we ensure that the text says only what we want to hear. We reduce the strange or incongruous, or even attitudes with which we disagree, by calling them ironic and making them confirm rather than abuse our expectations" (157).

Culler goes on to suggest, however, that it is possible to read ironic texts in such a way as to avoid totalizing interpretations by regarding "irony itself as project" of the text (159). But this move, similar to that which Brienza makes in reading *The Lost Ones*, does not solve the problem but merely displaces it. By reifying irony in this way (converting it into allegory, one might say), the resultant appeal to uncertainty is just as impoverishing as the certainty offered by any fixed interpretation. Barthes, recognizing such problems, suggests that the only way of avoiding such invidious totalization is through sheer plurality: "Only writing, by assuming the largest possible plural in its own task, can oppose without appeal to force the imperialism of each language" (S/Z 206).

If Brienza's reading corresponds to Culler's "irony as project," then Henning's Bakhtinian reading of *The Lost Ones*, emphasizing the clash among different languages in the text, corresponds to Barthes's emphasis on plurality. But there is no cause for complacency here, either. Henning's reading is highly useful in its emphasis on the failure of various discourses to attain hegemony in Beckett's text, especially since a striving for dominance fundamentally informs most of the discourses involved. Indeed, within this framework *The Lost Ones* can be read as a massive deconstruction of most of the major metanarratives of Western civilization. But Beckett's text is itself implicated in Western culture and therefore undercuts itself as well, warning against the establishment of plurality or dialogism as merely another stereotypical metanarrative structure.

There is, of course, no way out of this impasse, no point at which one can come to rest with an interpretation that is not revealed to be based on an illusion of mastery. And in *The Lost Ones* the impossibility of interpretive closure is directly enacted within the text itself. After writing the first fourteen paragraphs, Beckett abandoned the work in the mid-sixties because of "intractable complexities."[118] And when he "completed" the piece four years later, it was through the addition of a final paragraph that begins by acknowledging the impossibility of any real conclusion: "So on infinitely until towards the unthinkable end" (60). The narrator, it would seem, is also caught in the infinite regression of the text. Knowing that there is no "real" end, he simply posits one that happens to suit his taste: "if this notion is maintained a last body of all by feeble fits and starts is searching still" (60). He then presents us with the story of a Nietzschean Last Man, still wandering through the cylinder when all other motion has ceased. Then the end comes at last: "He himself after a pause impossible to time finds at last his place and pose whereupon dark descends and at the same instant the temperature comes to rest not far from freezing point" (62).

We have here what Beckett elsewhere calls "a termination but not a conclusion."[119] Murphy calls this ending "a patent falsification of the reality of the work in the interests of a rhetorical closure that will satisfy the narrator's need for order" (74). Yet the narrator emphasizes his own awareness of the arbitrary nature of the closure he has imposed by both beginning and ending this final paragraph with his favorite caveat "if this notion is maintained." The ending is not a falsification of the work (of which it is, after all, a part) but an acknowledgment of its unconcludable nature.

Murphy finally attributes this arbitrary ending to Beckett rather than to the narrator, noting that "faced with a potentially forever open-ended work the author opts for the imposition of his own views" (88). The reader, I would suggest, must do precisely the same. Personally, I usually choose to read *The Lost Ones* as a radically oppositional antiauthoritarian political text. I infer from my own inability to attain mastery of the text that it teaches us valuable lessons, particularly political ones, about quests for mastery and domination in general. This unmasterable text, by tempting us to master it, reveals that we are all implicated in the kinds of authoritarian mentalities upon which totalitarian governmental structures are based. Further, by its radical denial of any given interpretive scheme, the text provides a salutary reminder that any political program is in danger of descending into the triteness of dogma and that any political leaders, followed too blindly, have a tendency to become tyrants.

I choose this reading for several reasons, largely having to do with my own interests and preoccupations and my own critical program. But I also choose it for the good old-fashioned reason that it is consistent with the text, even if it in no way reveals the text's secret truth. The fact that I am forced to *choose* a reading pragmatically rather than somehow magically discover one indicates how thoroughly *The Lost Ones* undercuts all pretensions to mastery, critical or otherwise. Moreover, by forcing us to project our own interests and perspectives into the text in order to read it at all, *The Lost Ones* implies that perhaps reading *any* text involves similar choices and projections, and it emphasizes that such choices are fundamentally ideological. There are no politically neutral readings of texts.

But does this radical denial of mastery in *The Lost Ones* really imply that sophisticated readers are in fact no better off than naive ones? Appropriately enough, yes and no. There is a certain amount of cultural literacy involved in reading Beckett, of course, and one is aided a great deal by being able to recognize allusions that are being made, conventions that are being violated, issues that are being addressed, and so on. Moreover, if one is finally forced simply to choose a reading for pragmatic and ideological purposes, then sophisticated readers would presumably be in a better position to make a judicious choice and to defend it well. But if "sophisticated" readers have an ultimate advantage in reading a text like *The Lost*

Ones, it is only insofar as they are able to recognize how unsophisticated they really are and to realize that no interpretation provides a final explanation of the text. No matter the level of sophistication at which we read, there is always a next higher level that reveals the first to have been relatively naive.

Of course, such self-awareness is no small advantage, since the biggest problem with naive readers is that they generally don't know how naive they are. But in my experience the overtness with which *The Lost Ones* eludes interpretive mastery often helps student readers to recognize their naïveté, calling their attention to certain reading strategies that they may have been employing automatically and unconsciously all their lives. And if sophisticated veteran readers of Beckett are in a sense no better equipped to read *The Lost Ones* than are fresh-faced undergraduates, then this situation is not horrifying but entirely helpful and refreshing, especially for classroom purposes. With this text, students and teachers can for once produce readings that are very much on the same level, opening the possibility of some unusually fruitful classroom dialogues. Any given reading of this text requires that the reader adopt his or her own notion of what the text is about, and any reading is good only insofar as this notion is maintained. But of course that itself is a notion, good only insofar as it is maintained, and so on infinitely until towards the unthinkable end. The literary critic who seeks complete mastery of this text will thus find himself very much in the position of Beckett's Moran as he attempts to gain a complete epistemological understanding of the swarming of his bees in *Molloy*:

> And in spite of all the pains I had lavished on these problems, I was more than ever stupefied by the complexity of this innumerable dance, involving doubtless other determinants of which I had not the slightest idea. And I said, with rapture, Here is something I can study all my life, and never understand. (*Three* 169)

$\mathcal{N}$OTES

Introduction

1. This notion of the creative self-constitution of the subject has been widely explored in contemporary critical discourse. Perhaps the richest investigation has been that performed by Michel Foucault, whose later work was centrally concerned with this topic, which he referred to as "technologies of the self." See especially his *The Use of Pleasure* and the volume on this topic edited by Rux Martin et al.

2. See Jürgen Habermas for a useful discussion of the reflexivity of the Horkheimer/Adorno critique of the Enlightenment.

3. Baudrillard's later work, while still concerned with such subjects as contemporary sign systems, moves away from Marxism due to his perception that the structure of contemporary society is determined more by modes of signification than by modes of production. In this sense, despite specific disagreements, Baudrillard's work parallels that of Foucault. An overview of Baudrillard's work (which changes substantially as his career progresses) can be found in his *Selected Writings*.

4. In literature, this distinction parallels that between works of mere technical innovation within art and radical avant-garde works that attack the institution of art itself.

5. Tania Modleski, on the other hand, is critical of Greenberg's analysis of the Echo myth, suggesting that Greenberg preserves no locus of feminine

power and in fact shows "a typically feminine reluctance to admit to the desire for power" (130). But to Modleski, power should be the central concern of feminists. "For feminism, power is the stake of the critical enterprise, and each and every interpretive act involves an exercise of power over a text, whether we like to admit it or not" (136).

Chapter 1

6. Pozzo is only one of many figures of domination who appear in Beckett's work. John Fletcher notes that in Beckett's fictional universe "the only constant is the tyrant, the mysterious overlord who, from Mr. Knott onwards, haunts, even governs, the destiny of the Beckettian hero" (144).

7. All of Malone's stories are informed by sadomasochistic tendencies, as illustrated by the wife-beating of his creation Lambert (200) and even more spectacularly by the brutal multiple murders perpetrated by his Lemuel near the end of the book (287).

8. The encyclopedism of *Watt* also clearly resonates with Walter Benjamin's commentary on the rise of information as a new mode of communication in the modern world. However, Beckett's exploration of information in *Watt* lacks Benjamin's hope that this new mode of communication will yield positive results.

9. Cheryl Herr perceptively compares Joyce's encyclopedic fictions to *Bouvard et Pecuchet* as showing any attempt at complete encyclopedism to be absurd (9).

10. Bakhtin's most extensive discussions of this topic appear in *Rabelais and His World* and in *Problems of Dostoevsky's Poetics*.

11. See Fletcher for a brief discussion of Beckett's frequent and varied use of commas for stylistic effects (134).

12. On the surface, the Enlightenment appears to be antithetical to religion. But early Enlightenment philosophers such as Descartes (the principal target of Beckett's philosophical parodies in *Watt*) were highly theistic in their beliefs. Moreover, as emphasized by thinkers like Nietzsche (especially in *The Genealogy of Morals*), science and religion are very much alike in their central focus on an epistemological drive for ultimate truths. See Rubin Rabinovitz for a useful discussion of the dialogue with philosophy in *Watt* (124–50).

13. Numerous critics have emphasized the importance of language in *Watt*. See, for example, the article by Jacqueline Hoeffer, one of the first and still one of the best on this subject.

14. See also Jones's essay "Science and English Prose Style," as well as the discussions of A.C. Howell, Donald Davie, and Anne Cline Kelly on the importance of language to the early scientists.

15. That this sentence itself ends in a comma rather than a period may or

may not be a simple printer's error, but in either case it nicely contributes to the motif of unreliability and incompleteness in the text.

16. A similar but simpler example of this same phenomenon occurs in *Murphy* when the title character attempts to compute the various orders in which he might consume five biscuits, each of a different kind. He performs his probabilistic computation flawlessly but fails to encompass the contingency of life in the real world. Despite his laborious calculation of alternatives, Murphy fails to consider the one that actually does occur—the biscuits are eaten by Miss Dew's dog, rendering his computations, like those of Molloy, moot (*Murphy* 100).

17. Actually, the text of the Grove Press edition gives the number in the second verse as 51.142857142857 . . . , but the manuscript gives the number as the more meaningful 52.142857142857. . . . See Rabinovitz (153).

18. In the "Sirens" episode of *Ulysses*, Bloom muses: "Numbers it is. All music when you come to think" (228).

19. We later learn that Nackybal is actually named Tisler and that his talent is bogus, being based simply on memory (198). Mathematics, the story seems to tell us, can be misleading.

20. Joyce alludes to Aristophanes' chorus of ghost frogs in hell early in the *Wake*: "Brékkek Kékkek Kékkek Kékkek! Kóax Kóax Kóax!" (4.2).

21. Compare Joyce's depiction in *A Portrait of the Artist as a Young Man* of the dwarfish captain who was produced by the unfortunate effects of incestuous inbreeding among his noble Irish ancestors (227–28).

22. It also bears certain resemblances to the speech of schizophrenics, and some critics have taken this language as evidence of Watt's schizophrenia. See, for example, Russell Mears.

23. See Hugh Kenner for a discussion of the frequent occurrence of idiosyncratic word order in Joyce's sentences (Stoic 31).

24. The absurd description of Sam and Watt walking together between their gardens reinforces this mirror imagery (163).

Chapter 2

25. This suggestion that professors are involved in the same ideology as militarists and imperialists is reinforced in the first section of *Three Guineas*, where Woolf suggests that England's male-dominated educational system encourages the development of attitudes that lead to support for war.

26. Shakespeare is a figure of extreme importance throughout Woolf's work. See Beverly Schlack for a compilation of many of Woolf's specific allusions to Shakespeare. Also, see Beth Schwartz for an excellent discussion of Woolf's use of Shakespeare throughout her career.

27. See my discussion in *Techniques of Subversion in Modern Literature* of Woolf's dialogue with the male literary tradition, especially in *Orlando*.

28. Jean Wyatt explains why such a conception of subjectivity might be

specifically feminine. Because of the identification between mother and young daughter, Wyatt argues (echoing Nancy Chodorow) that "women are more comfortable vaulting over ego boundaries to fuse with what is outside than are men because what Freud calls the 'oceanic feeling' is built into their primary definition of self" (119). On the other hand, a model of subjectivity in which intersubjectivity is primary also inheres in the work of thinkers such as Vygotsky and Voloshinov, who do not see it as specifically feminine.

29. See Peggy Kamuf for a useful discussion of Woolf's treatment of the constitution of the self through the optic of Foucault.

30. J. W. Graham discusses the fact that Woolf originally intended to employ an omniscient narrator in *The Waves* and suggests that the consistent style of the soliloquies gives the reader the feeling of being inside an omniscient consciousness that "recounts to itself, without comment, the consciousnesses of six speakers, each of whom is talking (or thinking) to himself about his own experiences" (206). To Graham, the individual "characters" are thus to be seen as different aspects of a single narrating consciousness, which is approximated by Bernard in the final summation. Woolf herself indicated in a diary entry that the different speakers are not separate characters in any traditional sense. Reacting to a positive review of the book, she wrote: "Odd, that they (*The Times*) should praise my characters when I meant to have none" (*Writer's Diary* 170).

31. Both this theme and the imagery with which Woolf presents it are highly reminiscent of Shakespeare's sonnets, an important intertext for the book as a whole. See Darlene Beamon for a discussion of parallels between *The Waves* and Shakespeare's Sonnet 60. However, though this sonnet, with its opening waves making toward the pebbled shore, is the most obviously relevant, others (particularly Sonnet 73) seem equally important, and it is probably most valuable to read Woolf's text in the light of the sequence as a whole.

32. On the other hand, a close reading shows that the intensely individuated nature of Joyce's presentation of the internal consciousnesses of characters such as Stephen Dedalus and Leopold Bloom is somewhat deceptive, since even these highly distinctive discourses are in fact composed of a complex network of "quotations" from a variety of sources.

33. Throughout her work Woolf presents the consciousnesses of characters not in their own styles but in a consistent narrative voice, as in the free indirect discourse of *Mrs. Dalloway*, where various characters influence the content but not the style of the narration. As Maria DiBattista points out, Woolf's technique has the advantage of presenting the reader with a coherent authorial consciousness with which to engage herself: "To find the author figured forth and sublimated in the continuous style is one of the pleasures of the Woolfian text" (112).

34. This phenomenon participates in Woolf's general privileging of song as a mode of expression and can be usefully glossed in terms of Julia Kristeva's

notion of the semiotic aspect of poetic language. See Makiko Minow-Pinkney for a useful discussion of Woolf in the light of Kristeva.

35. Lucio Ruotolo suggests that all of the characters aspire "to merge with Percival's godlike being" (153). Further, he notes that Percival provides an ideal that none of the others can hope to emulate, suggesting that Woolf may have gotten the notion for this motif from Freud's discussion of Christ in *Civilization and Its Discontents* (248 n. 29). But note that the expectations of patriarchal society provide an ideal image of the hero that Percival himself cannot hope to emulate fully.

36. There is, of course, a special irony in Woolf's use of this motif, since the "primitive" Indians in fact represent a culture with a far longer and richer heritage than that of their British rulers.

37. In *Room* Woolf argues that "we think back through our mothers if we are women" (79). Unfortunately, for social and political reasons that Woolf describes, the literary tradition has been dominated almost entirely by *fathers*, placing women writers at a distinct disadvantage that is then exacerbated by domestic and economic factors that make it difficult for women to attain the physical conditions in which to read and write comfortably.

38. Actually, Rhoda is still partially determined by fixed stereotypical fantasies—of the mad or hysterical female.

39. For example, one might compare Rhoda's predicament to Fredric Jameson's discussions of "schizophrenia" as a common symptom of postmodernist society ("Postmodernism").

40. Note that Louis, too, takes a series of lovers, including Rhoda and the vulgar actress, but seems similarly unable to establish a lasting relationship with any of them. Of course, the highly normative Louis is heterosexual, whereas the "renegade" Neville seeks the company of some "lovely boy" (161).

41. Both Stephen and Neville might be compared to Greenblatt's description of the rebels in Marlowe who "imagine themselves set in diametrical opposition to their society where in fact they have unwittingly accepted its crucial structural elements" (209).

42. One might compare here Woolf's own attitude in *Moments of Being*, where she notes that "the whole world is a work of art; that we are parts of the work of art. *Hamlet* or a Beethoven quartet is the truth about this vast mass that we call the world. But there is no Shakespeare, there is no Beethoven, certainly and emphatically there is no God; we are the words; we are the music; we are the thing itself" (72).

43. Of course, in bourgeois society the two are not that easy to distinguish—the myth of the rebellious individual is a central bourgeois paradigm. See my discussion of this point in *Techniques of Subversion*.

44. On the general importance of rhythm in Woolf's work, see Ellen Rogat. Woolf's statement resonates in interesting ways with modern developments in French historiography, especially with the work of Fernand

Braudel and the Annales school. Braudel emphasizes very long time periods rather than individual events, leading to the description of "a history with gentle rhythms" as opposed to the usual narratives of events (3). Braudel's work is also reminiscent of Woolf's attacks on egotism. He downplays the importance of individual agents, calling for "an anonymous history, working in the depths, and most often in silence" (10).

45. In this final section Bernard also begins to echo quite strongly the imagery of the impersonal interludes, supporting Graham's suggestion that he has here become virtually identical to Woolf's original omniscient narrator.

46. Bernard here shows one of the many ways in which he resembles the mythical "storyteller" described by Walter Benjamin, since Benjamin emphasizes that the successful storyteller must be "rooted in the people" (101).

47. See Beth Schwartz for an extended discussion of the importance of "Anon" to Woolf's project.

48. "Anon" is also reminiscent of Benjamin's storyteller, and it is worth noting that both Woolf and Benjamin attribute the demise of communal storytelling to the rise of the printed book, which creates isolated individual writers and readers, as opposed to the communal audiences of, say, the Elizabethan drama.

49. Greenblatt notes how Edmund Spenser fashioned himself largely in accordance with existing structures of authority and in opposition to images of alien Otherness, while Christopher Marlowe seems to have fashioned himself in accordance with those images of Otherness and in opposition to structures of authority. In short, Spenser and Marlowe show very much the same strategies of envisionment as do Woolf's Louis and Neville, respectively. Interestingly, Greenblatt views Shakespeare as a sort of dialectical synthesis of the strategies of Spenser and Marlowe, just as Bernard's attitude toward authority can be seen as a synthesis of those shown by Louis and Neville.

50. Of course, literature itself can be highly conventional, a fact against which Woolf works with the intense experimentalism of works like *The Waves*.

51. Kaja Silverman notes the dual nature of such fantasies: "These contradictory views of the same image point to the profoundly ambivalent nature of the fantasy . . . an ambivalence which attests to the divided nature of subjectivity" (72). Note that these images of merger can be related, at least analogically, to the kinds of Lacanian Imaginary Order fantasies of infantile fusion of the mother that so strongly inform the work of contemporary theorists of the feminine such as Cixous and Kristeva. Note also that the contradictory nature of such fantasies participates in Woolf's dual project of deconstructing the traditional ego while maintaining some sense of subjective identity.

52. Rhoda experiences a fantasy of a quite literal "oceanic feeling" as she

contemplates her suicide, in which she and her flowers will leap into the sea: "We may sink and settle on the waves. The sea will drum in my ears. . . . Rolling me over the waves will shoulder me under. Everything falls in a tremendous shower, dissolving me" (206).

53. Of course, Bernard's sense of self is reinforced by the solidity of his social position, a solidity that Rhoda's does not share.

54. Bernard's momentary loss of selfhood clearly anticipates the almost religious transcendence associated with such loss in the work of a variety of thinkers of the 1960s, most specifically Norman O. Brown. Brown echoes Woolf's depiction of Bernard in a number of ways, as when he argues that "psychic individuals" are "an illusion" (82) and that "[t]he inner voice, the personal salvation, the private experience are all based on an illusory distinction" (87). However, Bernard's return to reality serves as a counter to the romanticism inherent in models of the dissolution of the self like Brown's. If there is transcendence in Woolf, it is extremely fleeting. Moreover, a complete surrender of selfhood leads not to ecstasy but to death as the case of Rhoda reminds us.

55. Beth Schwartz notes that Bernard here echoes a number of dying Shakespeare heroes, including Richard II, Macbeth, and Lear in addition to Hamlet. These echoes are entirely appropriate, of course—Bernard's consciousness remains creatively literary to the end. Note, too, Benjamin's suggestion that "[d]eath is the sanction of everything that the storyteller can tell. He has borrowed his authority from death" (94). For Benjamin it is only at death that the storyteller's "knowledge and wisdom, but above all his real life" assumes a form the completeness of which makes it transmissible to others in coherent form.

Chapter 3

56. See also the interesting discussion by Kovács, which explores parallels between Flaubert and Marx.

57. See Perry Anderson for a discussion of the importance of literature in Western Marxist thought.

58. In *Bend Sinister*, for example, Nabokov presents two distorted interpretations of *Hamlet* produced to achieve specific effects. One attempts to make the play a positive political statement in support of *Bend Sinister's* Stalinesque Ekwilist regime; the other is an imagined American film adaptation designed to appeal (i.e., pander) to a popular audience.

59. Lolita is not only a commodity but also a clear example of the commodity as fetish. That Humbert's fascination with Lolita partakes of fetishism is shown by, among other things, his literal treatment of her possessions as fetishes. In one scene he amorously sniffs Lolita's panties, enjoying the "faintly acrid odor in the seam" (69). And after marrying Charlotte he com-

mits a fetishistic adultery that also partakes of incest: "I deceived her with one of Lolita's anklets" (83).

60. In his marriage to Charlotte Haze, whom he finds largely repugnant, Humbert takes some solace in her being a "touching, helpless creature" who is impressed by "the magic of my manliness" (78–79). Later, he speaks of his "dream of controlling her" (85). And his final adult female companion in the book is the remarkable Rita, distinguished by a stupidity so profound that domination of her is quite easy.

61. Humbert gets his revenge on Valeria and her lover for their animalistic behavior by later depicting them as participants in an anthropological experiment in which they are reduced to walking on all fours and eating like animals (32).

62. The "uncleanness of birth" is directly associated with physicality and death in *Lolita*—both Valeria and Lolita die in childbirth.

63. Of course, Lacan and Althusser are informed by similar structuralist inclinations, so this parallel may not be entirely accidental. Note that the theme of loss in *Lolita* also recalls Adorno's critique of the nostalgic strain in the thought of Walter Benjamin. See Richard Wolin for a good summary of the close and complex relationship between Adorno and Benjamin (163–212).

64. On the other hand, Wilde reverses this motif in *The Picture of Dorian Gray*, where a painting ages with time while the mortal Dorian remains the same.

65. This point about bourgeois society is made especially well by Peter Bürger, whose *Theory of the Avant-Garde* argues that the main goal of the avant-garde was to destroy the separation between art and life effected by bourgeois society.

66. In moments of duress, Humbert sometimes reveals his true attitude toward advertising. Thus when Charlotte, inspired by travel ads, plans without his knowledge for the two of them to go to Europe, he reacts vehemently to this threat to his husbandly sovereignty. He tells Charlotte that the two of them would no doubt "make a pretty ad for the Traveling Agency," but that he has no intention of going to Europe, whose reality is nothing like that portrayed in ads: "I have nothing but very sad associations with the Old and rotting World. No colored ads in your magazines will change the situation" (92–93).

67. Of course, even the most coercive societies often employ more subtle methods of domination as well. Nabokov's critique of fictional discourses that seek to pass themselves off as reality also inevitably recall his Russian background and point toward the manipulations of reality that so strongly characterized the Soviet regime throughout Nabokov's adult life, especially during the reign of Stalin. Indeed, Hannah Arendt concludes that "[t]he ideal subject of totalitarian rule is not the convinced Nazi or the convinced Com-

munist, but people for whom the distinction between fact and fiction . . . and the distinction between true and false . . . no longer exist" (474).

68. Eagleton suggests that the "nervous tic" of placing such terms as "truth" and "fact" in scare quotes can lead to collusion with the existing order, a claim that provides an interesting dialogue with Nabokov, whose suggestion that "reality" must always be in quotes to have any meaning was a forerunner of the contemporary trend Eagleton indicates.

69. A similar process is at work in the phenomenon of Disneyland, and the extreme conformity of visitors to the park—complete with T-shirts and mouse ears—is eloquent testimony to the power of such processes of interpellation to govern behavior.

70. In a similar way, the Soviet people did not necessarily believe the various rewritings of history that characterized the Stalinist years—but they were often influenced by them nevertheless.

Chapter 4

71. There are many scenes of rape or near-rape in *V.*, all of which contribute to the depiction of sexuality as a locus of power relations. For example, Roony Winsome exerts his dominance over his wife Mafia (for once) by engaging in violent intercourse without the use of contraception, despite her fears of pregnancy (222). And Paola Maijstral is narrowly saved from being raped by Pig Bodine thanks to the intervention of Benny Profane (371–72).

72. Of these narrators, most are native workers, one (Waldetar) is a Portuguese Jew working in Egypt, and another (Maxwell Rowely-Bugge) is a disgraced English pedophile—all highly marginal figures in relation to polite European society, all "individuals strange to Karl Baedeker's way of life" (89). Note, however, that all of the narratives are apparently filtered through the consciousness of Herbert Stencil, who received the information indirectly via his father's journals, his father's contacts, and even the contacts and descendants of his father's contacts. Thus, even these attempts to show marginal points of view are highly mediated.

73. Pynchon also emphasizes the failure of Europeans to recognize the humanity of the Third World peoples they colonize by noting the suffering of the native inhabitants when the English flooded a low-lying area to form Lake Mareotis in 1801 (79). As Robert Holton points out, E. M. Forster discusses this same flooding in a book on Alexandria but mentions only the changes in the landscape, remaining totally oblivious to the fact that people were involved (Holton 338–39). In his essay "A Journey into the Mind of Watts," Pynchon suggests that a similar ideology is at work in the attitudes of contemporary whites toward the black Los Angeles ghetto, again pulling his treatment of colonialism into a contemporary context. See William Plater for

a discussion of this article in relation to Pynchon's critique of colonialism (105–9).

74. Note that the contemporary plot line of the book ends with British troops again preparing to invade northern Africa in the Suez crisis of 1956, another of the many ways Pynchon emphasizes the historical continuity of the quest for imperial mastery.

75. One might also point to V.'s comb, which features five crucified Englishmen. There is a clearly sadomasochistic implication in V.'s wearing of this comb, as in her apparent fascination with violence in general. These Englishmen were crucified for political reasons, but the link to Christ is inevitable, perhaps suggesting that a similar sadomasochistic fascination is endemic to Christianity, especially Catholicism, with its emphasis on the tortured body of Christ.

76. Profane participates in other trends as well. See Ruth Wisse for a discussion of the tradition of schlemihl "heroes" in Jewish literature. While Wisse does not mention Pynchon (and barely mentions Joyce), it is worthwhile to note that Benny Profane (like Leopold Bloom) is half-Jewish.

77. One might compare the sexual successes of Tyrone Slothrop, a fellow schlemihl who works his way across Europe moving from one woman to another in *Gravity's Rainbow*. However, Profane's mastery is still not secure. His couplings with both Paola (20) and Lucille (144) are interrupted by intrusions from the outside world just before consummation.

78. Holton notes how the Ivy League cities of Princeton and Ithaca "function here as ideological boundaries as much as geographical locations, and the epistemological limits arise here through gender as well as class" (329).

79. Compare Pappy Hod, whose usual approach to women is to effect an imitation of a movie-style gangster. Presumably they will recognize the imitation because "American movies had given them stereotypes all" (14).

80. The link between her helplessness during surgery and her perception of the woman's passive role during sex is reinforced during the operation by the salacious remarks of Trench, Schoenmaker's assistant (105).

81. Compare Rachel's diagnosis of the economic basis of sexual relations to Profane's earlier diagnosis of the sexual basis of economic relations (214).

82. Also compare the parallel story of Ralph MacBurgess (a.k.a. Maxwell Rowley-Bugge), who is disgraced after forming a sexual liaison with a ten-year-old girl. "But they know, Max told himself: no matter how young, they know what it is, what they're doing. . . . She'd wanted it" (70).

83. Richter does at least admit that he may have misread V., that Pynchon may have "merely succeeded in confusing one careful reader" (131).

84. Pynchon's sympathy for the preterite echoes Walter Benjamin's sympathy for the "masses." Indeed, Pynchon's work parallels that of Benjamin in numerous ways. William Dawers describes some of these parallels, though

unfortunately without emphasis on the political implications of the work of either author.

85. For a typical epistemological reading of *V.*, see Richard Patteson, who notes that one of the major themes of *V.* is "the form, function, and ultimate limitations of knowledge" (30).

Chapter 5

86. Such texts have much in common with Barthes's notion of the "writerly." Note Joyce's address to the reader of the *Wake* as "gentlewriter," in an anticipation of Barthes (63.10).

87. Note, too, that Virgil is forced to seek help from a heavenly messenger in circumventing this obstacle. The implication seems to be that Virgil's writing (unlike that of Dante, Joyce, or Calvino) does not lend itself adequately to the kind of reading here proposed.

88. This suggested link between reading and seduction has already been specifically made in Dante's poem in the story of Paolo and Francesca in canto V of the *Inferno*.

89. The pages in this highly experimental text are unnumbered. This citation is taken from the seventeenth and eighteenth pages of actual prose.

90. Calvino's book consists of ten fragments that describe or present portions of the novels being pursued by the Reader, interspersed with numbered chapters that describe the Reader's own adventures.

91. The many suggestions in *If on a winter's night* that the reading of a common text by two separate individuals provides a means of intersubjective contact between them echoes the Kantian notion of the aesthetic as a privileged realm of intersubjective exchange, though the difficulties that the Reader and Ludmilla have in establishing such contact perhaps turn out to illustrate better the Benjaminian argument that printed books lead to a loss of collectivity, since they tend to be read by isolated individuals.

92. This "undressing" of the text is mirrored in the later undressing of Lotaria, who wears multiple layers of uniforms and who claims, in fact, that even her naked body, with all clothing removed, is still a signifying uniform (218–19). There is, in short, no Truth beyond the mediation of signs.

93. This same difficulty inheres in the fact that "the Reader" is male, as are the readers of Gass and Pavić. See Judith Fetterley for an extended discussion of the difficulty of locating a stable feminine position from which to approach texts and for an indication of strategies by which women might read against the grain of texts that seek to force them into masculine positions.

94. De Lauretis herself notes that one could read Lotaria as an exemplar of the postmodernist author, though de Lauretis chooses not to pursue such a reading (80).

95. See my extensive discussion in *Techniques of Subversion* of alter-

native readings of the castration motif in the work of Calvino and other authors. Within the context of the current discussion, note that castration is by no means the exclusive province of feminists. It is, in fact, a traditional symbol of political domination and terror, as witnessed by the fascist-inspired castration and murder of Dupiro in *V.*, not to mention a whole litany of horrendous episodes in the history of the American South.

96. This treatment is in turn related to the dynamic shifting of objects of textual desire in the book. As Michel Butor has pointed out, the exigencies of a consumer economy require that readers continually move from one book to another, so that additional books can be manufactured and sold (42).

97. Benjamin does not seem to have foreseen fully the development of the contemporary "information society," though that society follows from his historical meditations in an interesting way. The publishing industry provides an intersection of the industrial society (with which classical Marxism is designed to deal) and the more contemporary information society (which has necessitated a great deal of retheorizing of Marxist concepts). For example, see Mark Poster for a reading of Foucault as a reaccentuation of Marxism in light of the growing importance of information as the primary "good" produced in modern society.

98. Note that Barthes points to Flaubert's copyists Bouvard and Pecuchet as exemplars of the modern decentered author ("Death" 146). Further, note that the medieval conception of the authorial role was very much that of the copyist, a fact that greatly informs the modern writing practice of Joyce, among others.

Chapter 6

99. John Pilling notes that *"The Lost Ones* is in many ways the simplest of Beckett's post–*How It Is* prose, the most easily approachable, the least fraught with potholes for the unwary." He notes that the text still has its subtleties, however (Knowlson and Pilling 157).

100. Elsewhere, Beckett notes that allegory "must always fail in the hands of a poet" (*Proust* 60).

101. The importance of Dante to Beckett is well known; see, for example, Wallace Fowlie. For a discussion of Bunyan as a structural model for *Molloy,* see John Fletcher (132–33).

102. Interestingly, when these figures are repeated on page 16 of the latest English edition, the cylinder height is erroneously given as eighteen meters, though the wall area is there given as eight hundred square meters, which corresponds to the original sixteen-meter figure. In the original French text of *Le Dépeupleur* the height is given as sixteen meters both times, while in the first English translation the height is given as eighteen both times. An additional miscalculation of surface area on page 7 has been corrected in the later English version relative to the first one. These inconsistencies appar-

ently arose in the editing and publication process—Enoch Brater reports that Beckett seems to have been "horrified" at the errors in the first English version (100). But whether these errors horrified Beckett or not, they tend to enrich the text by undercutting the narrator's pretensions to command of his material.

103. Sylvie Debevec Henning (not a naive reader by any means) shows a lingering desire to arrange things for the sake of harmony by suggesting that the five "vanquished" are not counted in the 205 total, thus making the numbers match exactly. She then proceeds to produce an allegorical interpretation of this situation, suggesting that the "vanquished" may not "exist as anything except a kind of fiction" (178). But of course nothing in *The Lost Ones* exists except as a kind of fiction. Henning's slip here illustrates the ease with which even those who know better can be seduced into making naive proclamations about Beckett.

104. See Brater for a discussion of mathematical errors in *The Lost Ones*, based on the first English version, which contains some errors that the later one does not.

105. Thus Vivian Mercier: "Beckett has long been familiar with the concept of entropy: one might say that if the Second Law of Thermodynamics did not exist, he would have found it necessary to invent it" (17).

106. Pynchon, employing a literalization of the metaphorical relationship between thermodynamic entropy and entropy in information theory, presents a box in which "sensitive" humans can employ the organizing abilities of pure thought to rearrange the molecules within the box into hot and cold segments, thus producing a thermal gradient that can be used to drive a piston, apparently producing energy without putting any energy in, thus violating the first law of thermodynamics. Such a sorting activity is precisely that performed by Maxwell's hypothetical Demon (*Lot 49* 86–87, 105–7). The concept of entropy looms large in critical discussions of Pynchon's work. Relative to *Lot 49*, see the discussions of Abernethy and of Leland.

107. On Dante's allegory within this context, see also Robert Hollander.

108. Peter Murphy emphasizes the way *The Lost Ones* comments on such literary conventions. He rejects the notion that the book provides an allegorical representation of anything beyond itself, suggesting instead that its allegory turns inward. To him, though *The Lost Ones* "tells us next to nothing about the world external to the fiction, it does tell us a great deal about fiction, especially the question of authority" (88).

109. This image of Christianity as a dead end appears elsewhere in Beckett as well. Thus, in the French version of *Murphy*, he describes the protagonist as living "dans l'impasse de l'Enfant-Jésus" (7). The English version merely suggests that he lives in West Brompton, but the resonances of that area with Catholicism (it is dominated by a prominent oratory) are clear. See Brian Fitch for a discussion of the way Beckett is here "slyly suggesting that Catholicism is a dead end" (42).

110. For example, Robert Sandarg notes the intensely political nature of *Catastrophe* and suggests that the play "marks an undeniable political engagement on Beckett's part and may lead us to reevaluate his entire canon from the perspective of social consciousness" (137).

111. Of course, these quincunxes offer many possible interpretations. The term is traditionally used to describe a pattern commonly used in the planting of trees in orchards, thus making the quincunx a symbol of a sort of dialogic interaction between culture and nature. Indeed, Murphy suggests that "[t]he crux of the problem posed by *The Lost Ones* concerns a reconciliation of the natural and the artificial" (76).

112. Conditions in the cylinder thus resonate with Foucault's description in *Discipline and Punish* of the ways modern carceral systems have been designed to involve prisoners in their own supervision and control.

113. The situation also resonates with Foucault's description of the way the Benthamite Panopticon tended to separate and individualize prisoners (*Discipline* 250–51).

114. There are, however, a number of extremely covert allusions to other authors, including Lamartine, Burton, and Beckett himself. As Pilling points out, "perhaps nowhere else has he [Beckett] embedded his allusions so deeply and subtly as in *The Lost Ones*" (Knowlson and Pilling 162).

115. Brienza notes the palinodic effect of this repeated phrase, but Murphy disagrees, declaring, "One is surely bound to balk at this" (74). I would suggest, however, that one is surely bound to balk at the suggestion that one is surely bound to any given interpretation of Beckett (including the one that one is surely bound to balk at the suggestion that one is surely bound, etc.).

116. The original French title, *Le Dépeupleur*, can be roughly translated "the depopulator" but might be better rendered "the dehumanizer," thus emphasizing the dehumanizing conditions in the cylinder.

117. Those who believe that the system of tunnels can lead to an escape from the cylinder are described as thinking that there is a passage among the tunnels "leading in the words of the poet to nature's sanctuaries" (18).

118. This phrase is from a note Beckett appended to the manuscript when he abandoned it.

119. The phrase is from Beckett's description of the contemplated death of Proust's Marcel (*Proust* 50).

WORKS CITED

Abernethy, Peter L. "Entropy in Pynchon's *The Crying of Lot 49.*" *Critique* 14 (1972): 18–33.

Adorno, Theodor W. *Aesthetic Theory.* Trans. C. Lenhardt; ed. Gretel Adorno and Rolf Tiedemann. London: Routledge and Kegan Paul, 1984.

———. *Minima Moralia: Reflections from a Damaged Life.* Trans. E. F. N. Jephcott. London: NLB, 1974.

Althusser, Louis. *Lenin and Philosophy and Other Essays.* Trans. Ben Brewster, 170–83. New York and London: Monthly Review Press, 1971.

Anderson, Perry. *Considerations on Western Marxism.* London: Routledge Chapman and Hall, 1976.

Appel, Alfred, Jr. Introduction to *The Annotated Lolita,* by Vladimir Nabokov. Ed. Alfred Appel, Jr. New York and Toronto: McGraw-Hill, 1970.

Arendt, Hannah. *The Origins of Totalitarianism.* 2d ed. Cleveland: World Publishing, 1958.

Bakhtin, Mikhail. *Problems of Dostoevsky's Poetics.* Trans. and ed. Caryl Emerson. Minneapolis: University of Minnesota Press, 1984.

———. *Rabelais and His World.* Trans. Helene Iswolsky. Bloomington: Indiana University Press, 1984.

Bakhtin, M. M./P. N. Medvedev. *The Formal Method in Literary Scholarship: A Critical Introduction to Sociological Poetics.* Trans. Albert J. Wehrle. Cambridge: Harvard University Press, 1985.

Balliett, Whitney. "Wha." *New Yorker* 15 June 1963, 113–14, 117.

Barthes, Roland. *Critical Essays*. Trans. Richard Howard. Evanston, Ill.: Northwestern University Press, 1972.

———. "The Death of the Author." In *Image—Music—Text.*, trans. Stephen Heath, 142–48. London: Collins, 1977.

———. *S/Z*. New York: Hill and Wang, 1974.

Baudrillard, Jean. *Selected Writings*. Ed. Mark Poster. Stanford, Calif: Stanford University Press, 1988.

Beamon, Darlene. "Like as the Waves Make toward the Pebbled Shore . . .": Shakespeare's Influence in *The Waves*." *Conference of College Teachers of English Proceedings* 48 (1983): 79–88.

Beckett, Samuel. "Act Without Words I." *In Collected Shorter Plays*, by Samuel Beckett, 41–46. New York: Grove Press, 1984.

———. *Disjecta*. Ed. Ruby Cohn. New York: Grove Press, 1984.

———. *How It Is*. New York: Grove Press, 1964.

———. *The Lost Ones*. New York: Grove Press, 1972.

———. *Mercier and Camier*. New York: Grove Press, 1974.

———. *More Pricks Than Kicks*. New York: Grove Press, 1972.

———. *Murphy*. New York: Grove Press, 1957.

———. *Proust*. New York: Grove Press, 1957.

———. *Three Novels:* Molloy, Malone Dies, *and* The Unnameable. New York: Grove Press, 1965.

———. *Waiting for Godot*. New York: Grove Press, 1954.

———. *Watt*. New York: Grove Press, 1953.

Benjamin, Walter. *Illuminations*. Trans. Harry Zohn; ed. Hannah Arendt. New York: Harcourt, Brace, and World, 1955.

Benstock, Shari. "At the Margin of Discourse: Footnotes in the Fictional Text." *PMLA* 98 (1983): 204–25.

Bergson, Henri. *Creative Evolution*. Trans. Arthur Mitchell. New York: Modern Library, 1944.

Booker, M. Keith. "The Baby in the Bathwater: Joyce, Gilbert, and Feminist Criticism." *Texas Studies in Literature and Language* 32 (1990): 446–67.

———. "*Finnegans Wake* and *The Satanic Verses*: Two Modern Myths of the Fall." *Critique* 32 (Spring 1991): 190–207.

———. *Techniques of Subversion in Modern Literature: Transgression, Abjection, and the Carnivalesque*. Gainesville: University of Florida Press, 1991.

Borges, Jorge Luis. *Labyrinths*. Ed. Donald A. Yates and James E. Irby. New York: New Directions, 1964.

Brand, Dana. "The Interaction of Aestheticism and American Consumer Culture in Nabokov's *Lolita*." *Modern Language Studies* 17 (Spring 1987): 14–21.

Brater, Enoch. *Modern Fiction Studies* 29 (Spring 1983): 93–109.

Braudel, Fernand. *On History*. Trans. Sarah Matthews. Chicago: University of Chicago Press, 1980.

Breazeale, Daniel, ed. *Philosophy and Truth: Selections from Nietzsche's Notebooks of the Early 1870s*. Trans. Daniel Breazeale. Atlantic Highlands, N.J.: Humanities Press, 1979.

Brienza, Susan D. *Samuel Beckett's New Worlds: Style in Metafiction*. Norman: University of Oklahoma Press, 1987.

Brown, Norman O. *Love's Body*. New York: Vintage, 1966.

Bürger, Peter. *Theory of the Avant-Garde*. Trans. Michael Shaw. Minneapolis: University of Minnesota Press, 1984.

Butor, Michel. "The Book as Object." Trans. Patricia Dreyfus. In his *Inventory*, ed. Richard Howard, 39–56. New York: Simon and Schuster, 1968.

Calvino, Italo. *If on a winter's night a traveler*. Trans. William Weaver. San Diego: Harcourt Brace Jovanovich, 1981.

Campbell, Joseph, and Henry Morton Robinson. *A Skeleton Key to Finnegans Wake*. New York: Penguin Books, 1977. (Originally published 1944.)

Carter, Angela. *The Sadeian Woman and the Ideology of Pornography*. New York: Pantheon, 1978.

Castle, Terry. *Clarissa's Ciphers: Meaning and Disruption in Richardson's "Clarissa"*. Ithaca, N.Y.: Cornell University Press, 1982.

Chamberlin, J. Edward, and Sander L. Gilman, eds. *Degeneration: The Dark Side of Progress*. New York: Columbia University Press, 1985.

Coates, Paul. "Unfinished Business: Thomas Pynchon and the Quest for Revolution." *New Left Review* 160 (1986): 122–28.

Conrad, Joseph. *Heart of Darkness*. In *"Heart of Darkness" and "The Secret Sharer."* New York: New American Library, 1950.

Cowart, David. *Thomas Pynchon: The Art of Allusion*. Carbondale and Edwardsville: Southern Illinois University Press, 1980.

Culik, Hugh. "The Place of *Watt* in Beckett's Development." *Modern Fiction Studies* 29 (Spring 1983): 57–71.

Culler, Jonathan. *Structuralist Poetics*. Ithaca, N.Y.: Cornell University Press, 1975.

Daiches, David. *Virginia Woolf*. Norfolk, Conn.: New Directions, 1942.

Dante Alighieri. *Inferno*. Trans. Allen Mandelbaum. Berkeley, Los Angeles, and London: University of California Press, 1980.

———. *Paradiso*. Trans. Allen Mandelbaum. Berkeley, Los Angeles, and London: University of California Press, 1984.

———. *Purgatorio*. Trans. Allen Mandelbaum. Berkeley, Los Angeles, and London: University of California Press, 1982.

Davie, Donald. *The Language of Science and the Language of Literature, 1700–1740*. London and New York: Sheed and Ward, 1963.

Dawers, William. "That Other Sentimental Surrealist: Walter Benjamin." *Pynchon Notes* 20–21 (1987): 39–60.

de Beauvoir, Simone. *The Second Sex*. Trans. and ed. H. M. Parshley. New York: Bantam, 1961. (Originally published in French, 1949.)

de Lauretis, Teresa. *Technologies of Gender: Essays on Theory, Film, and Fiction*. Bloomington and Indianapolis: Indiana University Press, 1987.

de Man, Paul. *Blindness and Insight: Essays in the Rhetoric of Contemporary Criticism*. 2d ed. Minneapolis: University of Minnesota Press, 1983.

DiBattista, Maria. "Joyce, Woolf, and the Modern Mind." In *Virginia Woolf: New Critical Essays*, ed. Patricia Clements and Isobel Grundy, 96–114. London: Vision Press, 1983.

Dinshaw, Carolyn. "Eunuch Hermeneutics." *ELH* 55 (1988): 27–51.

Eagleton, Terry. *The Ideology of the Aesthetic*. Oxford: Basil Blackwell, 1990.

Eco, Umberto. *The Role of the Reader: Explorations in the Semiotics of Texts*. Bloomington: Indiana University Press, 1979.

Ermarth, Elizabeth Deeds. "Conspicuous Construction; or, Kristeva, Nabokov, and the Anti-Realist Critique." *Novel* 21 (1988): 330–39.

Faulkner, William. *Mosquitos*. New York: Pocket Books, 1985.

Federman, Raymond. *Journey to Chaos: Samuel Beckett's Early Fiction*. Berkeley, Los Angeles, and London: University of California Press, 1965.

Ferguson, Frances. "Rape and the Rise of the Novel." In *Misogyny, Misandry, and Misanthropy*, ed. R. Howard Bloch and Frances Ferguson, 88–133. Berkeley, Los Angeles, and London: University of California Press, 1989.

Fetterley, Judith. *The Resisting Reader: A Feminist Approach to American Fiction*. Bloomington: Indiana University Press, 1981.

Finney, Brian. "*Assumption* to *Lessness*: Beckett's Shorter Fiction." In *Beckett the Shape Changer*, ed. Katharine Worth, 61–83. London and Boston: Routledge and Kegan Paul, 1975.

Fitch, Brian T. *Beckett and Babel: An Investigation into the Status of the Bilingual Work*. Toronto: University of Toronto Press, 1988.

Fletcher, John. *The Novels of Samuel Beckett*. 2d ed. New York: Barnes and Noble, 1970.

Foster, John Wilson. "Natural Science and Irish Culture." *Éire-Ireland* 26.2 (1991): 92–103.

Foucault, Michel. *The Care of the Self*. Trans. Robert Hurley. New York: Vintage, 1988.

———. *Discipline and Punish: The Birth of the Prison*. Trans. Alan Sheridan. New York: Vintage, 1979.

———. *The History of Sexuality, Volume I: An Introduction*. Trans. Robert Hurley. New York: Vintage, 1980.

———. *The Use of Pleasure*. Trans. Robert Hurley. New York: Vintage, 1986.

Fowler, Douglas. *A Reader's Guide to* Gravity's Rainbow. Ann Arbor, Mich.: Ardis, 1980.

Fowlie, Wallace. "Dante and Beckett." In *Dante among the Moderns*, ed.

Stuart Y. McDougal, 128–52. Chapel Hill and London: University of North Carolina Press, 1985.

Freccero, John. "Medusa: The Letter and the Spirit." In his *Dante: The Poetics of Conversion*, 119–35. Ed. Rachel Jacoff. Cambridge, Massachusetts, and London: Harvard University Press, 1986.

Gass, William. *Willie Masters' Lonesome Wife*. New York: Alfred A. Knopf, 1968.

Gilbert, Sandra M. "Woman's Sentence, Man's Sentencing: Linguistic Fantasies in Woolf and Joyce." In *Virginia Woolf and Bloomsbury: A Centenary Celebration*, ed. Jane Marcus, 208–24. Bloomington: Indiana University Press, 1987.

Graff, Gerald. *Literature against Itself: Literary Ideas in Modern Society*. Chicago and London: University of Chicago Press, 1979.

Graham, J. W. "Point of View in *The Waves:* Some Services of the Style." *University of Toronto Quarterly* 39 (1970): 193–211.

Green, Geoffrey. "Ghosts and Shadows: Reading and Writing in Italo Calvino's *If on a winter's night a traveler*." *Review of Contemporary Fiction* 6 (1986): 101–5.

Greenberg, Caren. "Reading Reading: Echo's Abduction of Language." In *Women and Language in Literature and Society*, ed. Sally McConnell-Ginet, Ruth Borker, and Nelly Furman. New York: Praeger, 1980.

Greenblatt, Stephen. *Renaissance Self-fashioning: From More to Shakespeare*. Chicago and London: University of Chicago Press, 1980.

Habermas, Jürgen. "The Entwinement of Myth and Enlightenment: Re-Reading *Dialectic of Enlightenment*." *New German Critique* 26 (1982): 13–30.

Hart, Clive. *Structure and Motif in* Finnegans Wake. Evanston, Ill.: Northwestern University Press, 1962.

Hawthorn, Jeremy. *Joseph Conrad: Language and Fictional Self-Consciousness*. Lincoln: University of Nebraska Press, 1979.

Hayman, David. *Re-Forming the Narrative: Toward a Mechanics of Modernist Fiction*. Ithaca, N.Y., and London: Cornell University Press, 1987.

Henke, Suzette. "Stephen Dedalus and Women: A Portrait of the Artist as a Young Misogynist." In *Women in Joyce*, ed. Suzette Henke and Elaine Unkeless, 82–107. Urbana, Chicago, and London: University of Illinois Press, 1982.

Henning, Sylvie Debevec. *Beckett's Critical Complicity: Carnival, Contestation, and Tradition*. Lexington: University Press of Kentucky, 1988.

Herr, Cheryl. *Joyce's Anatomy of Culture*. Urbana and Chicago: University of Illinois Press, 1986.

Herrmann, Anne. *The Dialogic and Difference: "An/Other Woman" in Virginia Woolf and Christa Wolf*. New York: Columbia University Press, 1989.

Hite, Molly. *Ideas of Order in the Novels of Thomas Pynchon*. Columbus: Ohio State University Press, 1983.

Hoeffer, Jacqueline. "*Watt*." *Perspective* 11 (Autumn 1959): 166–82.

Hollander, Robert. *Allegory in Dante's* Commedia. Princeton, N.J.: Princeton University Press, 1969.

Holton, Robert. "In the Rathouse of History with Thomas Pynchon: Rereading *V*." *Textual Practice* 2 (Winter 1988): 324–44.

Horkheimer, Max, and Theodor W. Adorno. *Dialectic of Enlightenment*. Trans. John Cumming. New York: Seabury Press, 1972.

Howell, A. C. "*Res et Verba*: Words and Things." *ELH* 13 (1946): 131–42.

Hutcheon, Linda. *A Poetics of Postmodernism: History, Theory, Fiction*. New York and London: Routledge, 1988.

———. *The Politics of Postmodernism*. London and New York: Routledge, 1989.

Iser, Wolfgang. *The Implied Reader: Patterns of Communication in Prose Fiction from Bunyan to Beckett*. Baltimore and London: Johns Hopkins University Press, 1974.

Jameson, Fredric. "Marxism and Postmodernism." In *Postmodernism/Jameson/Critique*, ed. Douglas Kellner, 369–87. Washington, D.C.: Maisonneuve Press, 1989.

———. *The Political Unconscious: Narrative as a Socially Symbolic Act*. Ithaca, N.Y.: Cornell University Press, 1981.

———. "Postmodernism and Consumer Society." In *The Anti-Aesthetic: Essays on Postmodern Culture*, ed. Hal Foster, 111–26. Port Townsend, Wash.: Bay Press, 1983.

Jones, Richard F. "Science and English Prose Style in the Third Quarter of the Seventeenth Century." In *The Seventeenth Century: Studies in the History of English Thought and Literature from Bacon to Pope*, 75–110. Stanford, Calif.: Stanford University Press, 1951.

———. "Science and Language in England of the Mid-Seventeenth Century." In *The Seventeenth Century: Studies in the History of English Thought and Literature from Bacon to Pope*, 143–60. Stanford, Calif.: Stanford University Press, 1951.

Joyce, James. *"Dubliners": Text, Criticism, and Notes*. Ed. Robert Scholes and A. Walton Litz. New York: Viking Press, 1969.

———. *Finnegans Wake*. New York: Viking Press, 1939.

———. *"A Portrait of the Artist as a Young Man": Text, Criticism, and Notes*. Ed. Chester G. Anderson. New York: Viking Press, 1968.

———. *"Ulysses": The Corrected Text*. Ed. Hans Walter Gabler with Wolfhard Steppe and Claus Melchior. New York: Random House, 1986.

Kamuf, Peggy. "Penelope at Work: Interruptions in *A Room of One's Own*. In *Feminism and Foucault: Reflections on Resistance*, ed. Irene Diamond and Lee Quinby, 149–64. Boston: Northeastern University Press, 1988.

Kaufman, Marjorie. "Brünnhilde and the Chemists: Women in *Gravity's*

Rainbow." In *Mindful Pleasures: Essays on Thomas Pynchon,* ed. George
Levine and David Leverenz, 197-227. Boston and Toronto: Little, Brown,
and Company, 1976.

Kelly, Ann Cline. "After Eden: Gulliver's (Linguistic) Travels." *ELH* 45
(1978): 33–54.

Kenner, Hugh. *Samuel Beckett: A Critical Study.* 2d ed. Berkeley, Los
Angeles and London: University of California Press, 1968.

———. *The Stoic Comedians: Flaubert, Joyce, and Beckett.* Berkeley, Los
Angeles, and London: University of California Press, 1974.

Kershner, R. B. *Joyce, Bakhtin, and Popular Literature: Chronicles of
Disorder.* Chapel Hill: University of North Carolina Press, 1989.

Klein, Karen. "The Feminine Predicament in Conrad's *Nostromo.*" In *Brandeis Essays in Literature,* ed. John Hazel Smith, 101–16. Waltham, Mass.:
Brandeis English and American Literature Department, 1983.

Knowlson, James, and John Pilling. *Frescoes of the Skull: The Later Prose
and Drama of Samuel Beckett.* New York: Grove Press, 1980.

Kovács, Katherine S. "The Bureaucraticization of Knowledge and Sex in
Flaubert and Vargas Llosa." *Comparative Literature Studies* 21 (Spring
1984): 30-51.

Kuberski, Philip. "Gravity's Angel: The Ideology of Pynchon's Fiction."
Boundary 2 15 (1987): 135–51.

Leland, John P. "Pynchon's Linguistic Demon: *The Crying of Lot 49.*"
Critique 16 (1974): 45–53.

Lund, Roger. "*Res et Verba:* Scriblerian Satire and the Fate of Language."
Bucknell Review 27 (1983): 63–80.

Macherey, Pierre. *A Theory of Textual Production.* Trans. Geoffrey Wall.
London and New York: Routledge and Kegan Paul, 1978.

Mailer, Norman. *The Presidential Papers.* London: André Deutsch, 1964.

Malmgren, Carl D. "Romancing the Reader: Calvino's *If on a winter's night
a traveler.*" *Review of Contemporary Fiction* 6 (1986): 106–16.

Martin, Rux, Huck Gutman, and Patrick H. Hutton. *Technologies of the
Self: A Seminar with Michel Foucalt.* Amherst: University of Massachusetts Press, 1988.

Martin, Stephen-Paul. *Open Form and the Feminine Imagination: The Politics of Reading in Twentieth-Century Innovative Writing.* Washington,
D.C.: Maisonneuve Press, 1988.

Mears, Russell. "Beckett, Sarraute, and the Perceptual Experience of
Schizophrenia." *Psychiatry* 36 (1973): 61–69.

Mercier, Vivian. *Beckett/Beckett.* New York: Oxford University Press,
1977.

Miller, J. Hillis. *Fiction and Repetition: Seven English Novels.* Cambridge:
Harvard University Press, 1982.

———. "Narrative and History." *ELH* 41 (1974): 455–73.

Minow-Pinkney, Makiko. "Virginia Woolf 'Seen from a Foreign Land.'" In

Abjection, Melancholia, and Love: The Work of Julia Kristeva, ed. John
Fletcher and Andrew Benjamin, 157–77. London: Routledge, 1990.

Modleski, Tania. "Feminism and the Power of Interpretation: Some Critical
Readings." In *Feminist Studies/Critical Studies*, ed. Teresa de Lauretis,
121–38. Bloomington: Indiana University Press, 1986.

Murphy, Peter. "The Nature of Allegory in 'The Lost Ones', or the Quincunx
Realistically Considered." *Journal of Beckett Studies* 7 (1982): 71–88.

Nabokov, Vladimir. *The Annotated Lolita*. Ed. Alfred Appel, Jr. New York
and Toronto: McGraw-Hill, 1970.

———. *Bend Sinister*. New York: Henry Holt, 1947.

———. *Invitation to a Beheading*. Trans. Dmitri Nabokov in collaboration
with the author. New York: Putnam, 1959.

———. *Lectures on Literature*. Ed. Fredson Bowers. San Diego: Harcourt
Brace Jovanovich, 1980.

———. *Strong Opinions*. New York: McGraw-Hill, 1981.

Naremore, James. *The World without a Self: Virginia Woolf and the Novel*.
New Haven and London: Yale University Press, 1973.

Nietzsche, Friedrich. *On the Genealogy of Morals*. In *Basic Writings of
Nietzsche*, 439–599. Trans. and ed. Walter Kaufmann. New York: Modern
Library, 1968.

———. "On Truth and Lies in a Nonmoral Sense." In *Philosophy and Truth:
Selections from Nietzsche's Notebooks of the Early 1870's*, 79–97. Trans.
and ed. Daniel Breazeale. Atlantic Highlands, New Jersey: Humanities
Press, 1979.

Olderman, Raymond M. *Beyond the Waste Land: A Study of the American
Novel in the Nineteen-Sixties*. New Haven and London: Yale University
Press, 1972.

Patteson, Richard. "What Stencil Knew: Structure and Certitude in Pynchon's *V.*" *Critique* 16 (1974): 30–44.

Pavić, Milorad. *Landscape Painted with Tea*. Trans. Christina Pribićević-
Zorić. New York: Alfred A. Knopf, 1990.

Pifer, Ellen. *Nabokov and the Novel*. Cambridge: Harvard University Press,
1980.

Plater, William. *The Grim Phoenix: Reconstructing Thomas Pynchon*.
Bloomington and London: Indiana University Press, 1978.

Poster, Mark. *Foucault, Marxism, and History: Mode of Production versus
Mode of Information*. Cambridge: Polity Press, 1984.

Prince, Gerald. "Notes on the Text as Reader." In *The Reader in the Text:
Essays on Audience and Interpretation*, 225–40. Ed. Susan Suleiman and
Inge Crosman. Princeton, New Jersey: Princeton University Press, 1980.

Pynchon, Thomas. *The Crying of Lot 49*. New York: Harper and Row, 1986.

———. *Gravity's Rainbow*. New York: Viking Press, 1973.

———. "A Journey into the Mind of Watts." *New York Times Magazine* 12
(June 1966), 34+.

————. *Slow Learner*. New York: Bantam Books, 1985.

————. *V*. New York: Harper and Row, 1986.

Rabinovitz, Rubin. *The Development of Samuel Beckett's Fiction*. Urbana and Chicago: University of Illinois Press, 1984.

Rampton, David. *Vladimir Nabokov: A Critical Study of the Novels*. Cambridge: Cambridge University Press, 1984.

Rankin, Ian. "The Role of the Reader in Italo Calvino's *If on a winter's night a traveler*." *Review of Contemporary Fiction* 6 (1986): 124–29.

Richter, David H. "The Failure of Completeness: Pynchon's *V*." In *Fable's End: Completeness and Closure in Rhetorical Fiction*, 101–35. Chicago: University of Chicago Press, 1974.

Riffaterre, Michael. "Syllepsis." *Critical Inquiry* 6 (1980): 625–38.

Rogat, Ellen Hawkes. "A Form of One's Own." *Mosaic* 8 (1974): 77–90.

Rousseau, Jean-Jacques. *The Confessions*. Trans. J. M. Cohen. Harmondsworth, England: Penguin, 1987.

Ruotolo, Lucio P. *The Interrupted Moment: A View of Virginia Woolf's Novels*. Stanford, Calif.: Stanford University Press, 1986.

Sacher-Masoch, Leopold von. *Venus in Furs*. Trans. Uwe Moeller and Laura Lindgren. New York: Blast, 1989.

Sandarg, Robert. "A Political Perspective on *Catastrophe*." In *" Make Sense Who May": Essays on Samuel Beckett's Later Works*, ed. Robin J. Davis and Lance St. J. Butler, 137–44. Totowa, N.J.: Barnes and Noble, 1988.

Schaub, Thomas H. *Pynchon: The Voice of Ambiguity*. Urbana, Chicago, and London: University of Illinois Press, 1981.

Schlack, Beverly Ann. *Continuing Presences: Virginia Woolf's Use of Literary Allusion*. University Park and London: Pennsylvania State University Press, 1979.

Schwartz, Beth C. *Virginia Woolf and Shakespeare: The Politics of a Feminist Re-reading*. Manuscript in preparation.

Schwartz, Sanford. *The Matrix of Modernism: Pound, Eliot, and Twentieth-Century Thought*. Princeton, N.J.: Princeton University Press, 1985.

Shakespeare, William. *The Complete Works of William Shakespeare*. 3d ed. Ed. David Bevington. London: Scott, Foresman and Company, 1980.

Siegle, Robert. *The Politics of Reflexivity: Narrative and Constitutive Poetics of Culture*. Baltimore and London: Johns Hopkins University Press, 1986.

Silverman, Kaja. *The Acoustic Mirror: The Female Voice in Psychoanalysis and Cinema*. Bloomington and Indianapolis: Indiana University Press, 1988.

Singleton, Charles S. "'In Exitu Israel de Aegypto.'" In *Dante: A Collection of Critical Essays*, ed. John Freccero, 102–21. Englewood Cliffs, N.J.: Prentice-Hall, 1965.

Sorapure, Madeleine. "Being in the Midst: Italo Calvino's *If on a winter's night a traveler*." *Modern Fiction Studies* 31 (1985): 702–10.

Sprat, Thomas. *The History of the Royal Society*. Ed. Jackson I. Cope and

Harold W. Jones. St. Louis: Washington University Press, 1958. (Originally published 1667).

Stoppard, Tom. *The Real Thing*. Boston and London: Faber and Faber, 1984.

Swift, Jonathan. *The Writings of Jonathan Swift*. Ed. Robert A. Greenberg and William B. Piper. New York: W. W. Norton and Company, 1973.

Swigger, Ronald T. "Fictional Encyclopedism and the Cognitive Value of Literature." *Comparative Literature Studies* 12 (1975): 351–66.

Tanner, Tony. *Thomas Pynchon*. London and New York: Methuen, 1982.

Watson, G. J. "The Politics of *Ulysses*." In *Joyce's "Ulysses": The Larger Perspective*, ed. Robert D. Newman and Weldon Thornton, 39–58. Newark: University of Delaware Press, 1987.

Waugh, Patricia. *Feminine Fictions: Revisiting the Postmodern*. London and New York: Routledge, 1989.

White, Allon. "Pigs and Pierrots: The Politics of Transgression in Modern Fiction." *Raritan* 11 (1982): 51–70.

Wilde, Oscar. "The Critic as Artist." In *The Portable Oscar Wilde*, ed. Richard Aldington and Stanley Weintraub. 51–137 London: Penguin Books, 1946.

———. *The Picture of Dorian Gray*. In *The Portable Oscar Wilde*, ed. Richard Aldington and Stanley Weintraub, 138–391 London: Penguin Books, 1946.

Winston, Mathew. "*Watt*'s First Footnote." *Journal of Modern Literature* 6 (1977): 69–82.

Wisse, Ruth R. *The Schlemihl as Modern Hero*. Chicago and London: University of Chicago Press, 1971.

Wolin, Richard. *Walter Benjamin: An Aesthetic of Redemption*. New York: Columbia University Press, 1982.

Woolf, Virginia. "'Anon' and 'The Reader': Virginia Woolf's Last Essays." Ed. Brenda R. Silver. *Twentieth-Century Literature* 25 (1979): 356–441.

———. *The Diary of Virginia Woolf*. Five volumes, 1915–1941. Ed. Anne Olivier Bell. New York: Harcourt Brace Jovanovich, 1977-1984.

———. *Moments of Being*. Ed. Jeanne Schulkind. Sussex: University Press, 1976.

———. *Mrs. Dalloway*. New York: Harcourt, Brace, 1925.

———. *A Room of One's Own*. New York: Harcourt Brace Jovanovich, 1929.

———. *Three Guineas*. New York: Harcourt Brace Jovanovich, 1938.

———. *To the Lighthouse*. New York: Harcourt Brace Jovanovich, 1955.

———. *The Waves*. New York: Harcourt Brace Jovanovich, 1931.

———. *A Writer's Diary*. New York: Harcourt, Brace, 1954.

Wyatt, Jean. "Avoiding Self-Definition: In Defense of Women's Right to Merge Julia Kristeva and *Mrs. Dalloway*." *Women's Studies* 13 (1986): 115–26.

$\mathcal{I}$NDEX

Bürger, Peter, 9, 10, 168n.65
Butor, Michel, 172n.96

Calvino, Italo, 18, 117–41, 171nn.87, 90, 91, 95
Carter, Angela, 105
Castle, Terry, 113, 135
Chodorow, Nancy, 163n.28
Cixous, Hélène, 53, 166n.51
Coates, Paul, 114
Completeness, 26, 27, 32, 62, 63, 119, 127, 141, 158, 160
Conrad, Joseph, 7, 50, 92, 98, 99, 103, 112, 113
Cowart, David, 111
Culik, Hugh, 23, 37, 38
Culler, Jonathan, 157

Daiches, David, 46
Dante Alighieri, 79, 80, 119, 120, 144, 148, 149, 153, 171nn.87, 88, 172n.101, 173n.107
Davie, Donald, 162n.14
Dawers, William, 170n.84
De Beauvoir, Simone, 77
De Lauretis, Teresa, 128, 129, 131–34, 136, 171n.94
De Man, Paul, 11, 156
DiBattista, Maria, 164n.33
Dinshaw, Carolyn, 120, 121

Eagleton, Terry, 3, 4, 12, 13, 72, 87, 88, 113, 169n.68
Eco, Umberto, 155
Eliot, T. S., 2, 3, 54
Enlightenment, 5, 14, 17, 21–23, 27, 28, 33, 34, 40, 73, 76, 77, 81, 82, 89, 114, 125, 127, 132, 146, 161n.2, 162n.12
Ermarth, Elizabeth Deeds, 71

Fascism, 4, 15, 17, 18, 71, 92, 152
Federman, Raymond, 26
Ferguson, Frances, 113
Fetterley, Judith, 171n.93
Finney, Brian, 154
Fitch, Brian, 173n.109
Flaubert, Gustave, 8, 22, 72, 79, 83, 162n.9, 167n.56, 172n.98

Fletcher, John, 162n.11
Forster, E. M., 169n.73
Foster, John Wilson, 4, 28
Foucault, Michel, 4, 14, 45, 80, 81, 129, 132, 134, 141, 161n.1, 164n.29, 172n.97, 174n.112
Freccero, John, 119, 120
Freud, Sigmund, 67, 163n.28, 165n.35

Gass, William, 120, 121, 171n.93
Gender, 15, 16, 42–44, 50–54, 56, 59, 64, 65, 77, 78, 90, 101–8, 118, 120, 121, 125, 128, 131, 165n.37, 171n.93
Gilbert, Sandra, 64, 79
Graff, Gerald, 8, 9, 11, 12
Greenberg, Caren, 15, 161n.5
Greenblatt, Stephen, 45, 66, 165n.41, 166n.49

Habermas, Jürgen, 161n.2
Hawthorn, Jeremy, 97
Hayman, David, 119
Henning, Sylvie Debec, 145, 154, 157, 158, 173n.103
Herr, Cheryl, 162n.9
Herrmann, Anne, 44
History, 10, 22, 26, 27, 40, 60, 61, 77, 79, 87, 94, 111, 115, 116, 151, 152, 165n.44
Hite, Molly, 97, 112, 116
Hoeffer, Jacqueline, 162n.13
Hollander, Robert, 173n.107
Holton, Robert, 114, 169n.73
Horkheimer, Max, 6, 14, 15, 17, 21, 22, 27, 44, 73, 77, 81, 82, 89, 114, 127, 161n.2
Howell, A. C., 162n.14
Hutcheon, Linda, 13

Imperialism, 12, 17, 18, 28, 49, 50, 90, 92–100, 101, 115, 157, 165n.36, 169n.73, 170n.74
Incest, 35, 107, 108
Iser, Wolfgang, 4

Jameson, Fredric, 4, 7–9, 12, 13, 137, 165n.39
Jones, Richard F., 29, 32, 162n.14